Preface

Even when it is not an ass, the law tends to be a rather slow moving animal. This intrinsic resistance to change is an ambivalent characteristic. In its favour, it must be said that the resultant continuity and certainty can be highly beneficial. Indeed, it is probably for these qualities more than any other that the law is invoked on a daily basis as a source of stability in social and economic relationships. Yet too much permanence in a highly impermanent world can be a recipe for friction and ultimately irrelevance. As Lord Denning has warned, "If we never do anything which has not been done before, we shall never get anywhere. The law will stand still whilst the rest of the world goes on: and that will be bad for both." (*Packer v. Packer,* [1984] P. 15 at 22 (C.A.)).

This book is about the law and computers. In particular, it is about the adequacy of the response of legislators, judges and lawyers in North America and the United Kingdom to the challenge of balancing the competing interests of creators, compilers, controllers and consumers of software and data. The world of the computer and data processing industries certainly goes on at a remarkable pace. Even if not standing still, in some jurisdictions some parts of the common law have lagged far behind. Given that digital information is no respector of national boundaries, and in view of the patchiness of the legal response on an international level, there seems much to be gained from a comparative approach to these issues. Accordingly I have looked at the availability of legal protection for computer programs and data in the United States, the United Kingdom and Canada. I have also, to a lesser extent, considered significant developments in other common law jurisdictions, notably Australia. The amount of detail in which each topic is discussed in relation to each jurisdiction is intended to reflect the relative importance or innovativeness of particular developments in each locality. Thus, for example, particular emphasis is given to American copyright law, the scope of criminal sanctions in Canada, and the Data Protection Act in the United Kingdom. Not all aspects of legal protection are covered. I have passed over areas, such as trademark law, in which the technology does not seem to present any issues of legal principle. Nor is the book intended to be a practical guide for those engaged in the drafting of software licences or technology transfer documentation. There is no substitute for specialist legal advice in those areas. For the benefit of both lawyers and non-lawyers, I have tried to avoid (or at least explain) the worst excesses of the jargon used by members of both the legal profession and the computer industry.

While responsibility for the book's shortcomings is, of course, mine alone, I am indebted to a number of people who have taken the time to read and comment upon various chapters while they were in draft form. In particular, I would like to thank Professors Friedland, Graham and Janisch of the Faculty of Law, University of Toronto; William Hayhurst Q.C. and Brian Gray of Ridout and Maybee, Toronto: Daniel Cooper of McCarthy & McCarthy, Toronto; Graham Smith, Vanessa Marsland and David Griffiths of Clifford-Turner, London; Alan Wilkinson of the Manchester Business School; my brother Jonathan Millard who is a barrister practising in Manchester; David Lewis of CLIRS Australis Pty. Ltd., Sydney; also Judge Hector Gilliand, and Derek Johnston of Russell, McVeagh, McKenzie, Bartleet & Co., Auckland. I am grateful for financial and practical assistance received from the Faculty of Law, the Centre of Criminology and Massey College, University of Toronto, and from the partners of Clifford-Turner. The assistance of the library staff of the Faculty of Law, University of Toronto; the Library of Congress, Washington D.C.; Clifford-Turner and the Institute of Advanced Legal Studies, London has also been much appreciated. Finally I would like to thank friends and family, and especially my parents, for their patience and encouragement during the book's somewhat protracted gestation.

C.J.M.
London
January, 1985

LEGAL PROTECTION

MS

CANADIAN CATALOGUING IN PUBLICATION DATA

Millard, Christopher J., 1959-
    Legal protection of computer programs and data

Includes index.
ISBN 0-459-37230-0

1. Copyright – Computer programs.   2. Copyright –
Information storage and retrieval systems.
I. Title.

K1443.C6M54 1985   346.04'82   C85-098592-7

Sweet & Maxwell, London   ISBN 0 421 33480 0

Contents

Table of Cases

Table of Statutes

CANADA

BRITISH COLUMBIA

MANITOBA

NOVA SCOTIA

ONTARIO

SASKATCHEWAN

UNITED KINGDOM

Police and Criminal Evidence Act, 1984, c. 60

UNITED STATES

ARIZONA

CALIFORNIA

FLORIDA

OTHER

Chapter 1

Introduction

1.1 The Legal Context

1.1.1 Computers and the Law

The law and the computer are not recent bedfellows. In 1649, for example, Louis XIV granted a patent to Blaise Pascal for a mechanical computer he had invented.[1] It is, however, only with the rapid development of electronic digital computing in the last two decades that the law and the computer have become significantly intertwined. Courts have increasingly been asked to adapt established legal concepts, sometimes tortuously, to the regulation of computer technology. Moreover, governments have begun to resort to specific legislative responses to those computer-related issues which are already proving to be beyond the effective scope of conventional legal regulation.

On one level such developments can be understood simply in terms of the demands of an emergent industry for a technologically relevant framework of law in which to operate. On a deeper level, however, the rapid development of "computer law" seems to be a side-effect of an extremely far-reaching "information revolution" in which the computer is the key catalyst for change. Thus, present uncertainties as to the appropriateness and practicality of using the law to protect computer programs and data are symptomatic of a far broader upheaval. For all its apparent sophistication, the law in most jurisdictions is proving to be a rather blunt regulatory tool in the face of the full social, economic and political significance of *information* in a post-industrial society.

In the developed world, computers have already permeated numerous areas of daily human activity. Apart from such prominent applications as electronic banking, weather forecasting, airline reservation systems, electronic timekeeping and, of course, videogames, the ubi-

---

1   Discussed in chapter 5, below.

quitous micro-processor is also gradually taking over such mundane operations as the control of traffic lights, the switching of telephone systems, the timing of washing machine cycles and the regulation of engine exhaust emissions. With the development of micro ("personal") computers, the technology has also become highly accessible.[2]

For the generations born before the information revolution began, "computer illiteracy" is becoming a significant concern. For those engaged in the practice of law, for example, computers are assuming a growing significance in two distinct areas. Firstly, computers are becoming an apparently indispensable aid to efficient legal practice. They are already being used quite extensively for document preparation, billing and accounting, and on-line legal research. Even in the most traditional areas of law, such as conveyancing and trusts, computers are increasingly being relied on to facilitate the drafting and engrossing of documents, the conduct of title searches, and the like. Other significant applications include litigation support, in-house information retrieval and, in larger firms, conflict of interest searches.

Secondly, lawyers and courts are being forced to address the task of developing appropriate and workable responses to the many challenges which computers present to established legal concepts. Many areas of law are being affected, but the strain is especially apparent in those fields which offer hope of protection for proprietary interests in programs and data and these matters will form a major focus of this book.[3]

1.1.2   Property: Real and Unreal

The difficulties of applying traditional intellectual property and criminal law concepts to computer technology are in some jurisdictions already forcing legislators and courts to rethink the theoretical foundations of some long-established legal doctrines. Does it, for example, make sense to extend copyright protection to a computer program which is in a

---

2   While it is undoubtedly bringing many benefits, the proliferation of computers is not of course a story of unmitigated good cheer. The spectres of steadily rising unemployment which haunt so many are not entirely the product of a global recession. To a certain extent they simply represent the economies which can be achieved where human labour is replaced by machines. Moreover, probably the most heavily funded area of research and development in computing is for applications which are far from benign. Nevertheless, the technology is clearly here to stay and we must learn to live with it.

3   Other legal areas where significant issues are arising due to computer technology include tort, taxation, banking and communications. See Soma, *Computer Technology and the Law* (New York: McGraw Hill, 1983).

form unintelligible to the human mind and designed only for "communication" with a machine? Can patent protection be granted for a computer program without giving the patent holder a monopoly on the use of the abstract mathematical formulae on which the program is based? Should information be treated as "property" for legal purposes and thus be susceptible to being stolen? Moreover, if information does qualify as property, how is it to be valued and what remedies should be granted or sanctions imposed for its misappropriation?

At the best of times, a lay person could be excused for finding the concept of incorporeal property to be one of the law's more improbable fictions. It is one thing to speak of "personal" and "movable" as distinct from "real" and "immovable" property, but to extend property rights to such intangibles as trade secrets or particular expressions of ideas must seem odd indeed. From time to time jurists too have seriously questioned the appropriateness of the law of intellectual property, and as long ago as 1841 one American court made the following telling observation:

> Patents and copyrights approach, nearer than any other class of cases belonging to discussions, to what may be called the metaphysics of the law, where the distinctions are, or at least may be, very subtile [sic] and refined, and sometimes, almost evanescent.[4]

Over the years, with the accommodation of each wave of new technology into existing legal categories, some of the "distinctions" have become extremely tenuous.

Computer software and data are placing further stresses on the already strained constructs of intellectual property law. For example, regarding the applicability of patent and copyright principles to software, Lawrence Perry has observed:

> A computer program is *sui generis*. It is a written expression of the mind of its author, and is also the means which causes a highly complex machine to work. As such, many think it too pure to merit protection under patent law and others think it too applied to be covered by copyright.[5]

Alternatively, it is argued that this dual nature of software as simultaneously "symbolic" and "mechanical" means that protection may be available for a given program under both copyright and patent law.[6]

---

4   *Folsom v. Marsh,* 9 F. Cas. 342 at 344 (C.C.D. Mass., 1841), cited by Gemignani, "Legal Protection for Computer Software: the view from '79" (1980), 7 Rutgers J. of Computers, Technology and Law 269-312.

5   "The World Intellectual Property Organization Model Provisions" in Brett and Perry, eds., *The Legal Protection of Computer Software* (Oxford: ESC Publishing, 1981), at 174.

6   Davidson, ed., "Protecting Computer Software: A Comprehensive Analysis" (1983), 4 Ariz. St. L.J. 611-784.

Leaving aside such jurisprudential difficulties for a moment, a further preliminary issue demands attention. Whether or not the established legal mechanisms can cope, does it make social and economic sense for software to be protected? Intellectual property rights, like virtually all legal constructs, are essentially a means to an end, a useful device for facilitating the attainment of some perceived moral, social, political, or economic objective. Thus, on the question of whether, for example, copyright as we now know it can be stretched to accommodate messages in object code addressed to machines, the economic realities of the software industry will be a highly significant consideration for legislators and, to a lesser extent, may also influence courts.

1.1.3 Is there a Need for Legal Protection of Programs?

"Intellectual property" has its roots in the Enlightenment.[7] Everyone is deemed to be entitled to the fruits of his or her labour or, as one American court put it,[8] "[s]acrificial days devoted to ... creative activities deserve rewards commensurate with the services rendered."[9] This "moral" argument goes hand in hand with an economic justification, an early version of which was set out by Sir Louis Mallet in a minority report to the British Royal Commission on Copyright in 1876:

> Property exists in order to provide against the evils of natural scarcity. A limitation of supply by artificial causes, creates scarcity in order to create property. . . . It is within this latter class that copyright in published works must be included.[10]

In the case of computer programs, the need for protection stems from the fact that development costs in the software industry constitute a large part of total production costs, yet, once developed, a software package can usually be produced and reproduced (*i.e.,* copied) for a nominal sum. Since piracy is so easy, the market for any particular piece of software might quickly be eroded by widespread unauthorised copying. The negative consequences of such a state of affairs are fairly obvious. As Palmer and Resendes have observed:

> Because intellectual output becomes a free good and imitative entrepreneurs will tend to copy the more valuable intellectual output, those who have the potential of generat-

---

7   See generally Patterson, *Copyright in Historical Perspective* (Nashville: Vanderbilt Univ. Press, 1968).

8   *Mazer v. Stein,* 347 U.S. 201 at 219 (1954).

9   Regarding "sacrificial days" in the present context see "Software Writing Called 5% Inspiration and 95% Perspiration by IBM Attorney," Computerworld (Aug. 6, 1969) at 7.

10   Quoted in Plant, "The Economic Aspects of Copyright in Books", *Economica* (May 1934), 167 at 193-4.

ing the output will have less incentive to do so. Fewer resources will be devoted to intellectual effort if its output carries no exclusive right of remuneration.[11]

This is, however, only half the story. While it may to some extent promote creativity, the granting of monopoly rights in any field can have a depressive effect on output. The monopolist may choose to keep production low and unit prices high.[12] The net result seems to be that creativity may be stifled both where there is too much and also where there is too little offered by way of monopolistic incentives. As Palmer has put it, "[s]ociety must choose which form of inefficiency, or more precisely, how much of each form of inefficiency to put up with."[13]

For various reasons, traditional marketing techniques are of limited use in pre-empting the widespread misappropriation of software.[14] Nor have technical protection strategies, such as special coding methods (encryption), proved generally effective. Moreover, the cost of implementing extra-legal measures to protect programs is itself a source of inefficiency. This situation highlights a basic economic rationale for the legal protection of property rights generally. As Posner has argued in his *Economic Analysis of Law*:[15]

> Observe the consequences if theft were freely permitted. Property owners would spend a great deal of money on devices for the protection of property and would substitute otherwise less valuable goods that happened to be less easy to steal.

Yet as was noted earlier, "intellectual property" is in many ways quite unlike other more conventional forms of property. The function of legal ownership of a piece of tangible property is essentially to give the owner a right of exclusive ownership, that is the power to exclude others from access to or enjoyment of the property in question. Whatever the economic merits may be of exclusive ownership in the case of tangible property, such exclusivity is certainly not appropriate in the case of intellectual property. On the contrary, it can strongly be argued that a primary objective of any intellectual property law should be to safeguard

---

11   *Copyright and the Computer* (Ottawa: Consumer and Corporate Affairs Canada, 1982).

12   See Lipsey, Sparks and Steiner, *Economics*, 3rd ed. (New York: Harper and Row, 1979), chapter 18.

13   "Patents, Licensing and Restrictions on Competition" (1984), University of Toronto, Law & Economics Workshop Series No. WS VI - 9.

14   For example, in the case of software for use on micro computers, the potential market can run into millions of units and thus customised production of packages is not feasible. Similarly, rapid marketing affords little competitive advantage where the appropriation lag is very short (*i.e.*, a program can usually be decoded and copied in a matter of hours). See Palmer and Resendes, note 11 above.

15   (Boston and Toronto: Little, Brown and Co., 1972), p. 68.

rights of access to information, the exclusive ownership of which would be economically harmful to society as a whole.[16] This is surely why copyright and patents have only ever secured a limited type of monopoly and for a limited time, and why claims to protection for ideas in the abstract have been resisted by legislators and courts alike. Information *per se* should not be tied down, and as Ploman and Hamilton have observed:

> In one sense, the history of copyright is the history of regulating the flow of information and of cultural works. The history of piracy, in this context, is part of the history of anti-control and deregulation.[17]

Moreover, as Alvin Toffler has repeatedly stressed, information is quite unlike other resources in that it is not consumed when used. On the contrary, the use of information is almost always a "generative" process.[18]

With these various considerations in mind, we should ask whether regulation by means of intellectual property protection is necessary or desirable from the perspective of the software industry. Given that intellectual property rights interfere with the free flow of information, from an economic perspective they should in theory only be introduced where necessary to prevent a market failure from occurring as a result of widespread copying. At the present time, however, the market for software, especially that catering to mini and micro computers, is probably far from saturated. Does this mean that copyright protection for programs is superfluous? In answering this question, Palmer and Resendes have drawn a useful analogy with the apparent absence of a need for protection in the rapidly expanding sound recording industry as it was seventy years ago. Though initially the industry grew rapidly, a market failure did occur and copyright was brought in to correct that failure.[19]

A remaining ground on which the extension of intellectual property rights to computer software might be resisted is that such protection would be liable to be abused for monopolistic purposes. In his dissent to the majority report of the American National Commission on New Technological Uses of Copyrighted Works,[20] Commissioner Hersey expressed concern that most of the pressure for an extension of copyright

---

16   Sieghart, "Information Technology and Intellectual Property," [1982] 7 European Intellectual Property Review (E.I.P.R.) 187-8.

17   Ploman and Hamilton, *Copyright: Intellectual Property in the Information Age* (London: Routledge and Keegan Paul), p. 202.

18   Toffler, *The Third Wave* (London: Pan Books, 1981), p. 22.

19   Palmer and Resendes, note 11 above, p. 139.

20   *Final Report of the National Commission on New Technological Uses of Copyright Works* (Washington: Library of Congress, 1979).

came from large corporations rather than from independent software houses:

> Is it not evident ... that the big companies want, by availing themselves of every possible form of protection, to lock their software into their own hardware, while the independents want to be able to sell their programs for use in all the major lines of hardware?[21]

He concluded that copyright protection would tend "to reinforce the oligopoly of those dominant companies, and to inhibit competition from and among small independents."[22]

Hersey was, however, asking too much of copyright. Whatever contribution it may make to the task of regulating flows of information, no branch of intellectual property law can be expected to function as a general anti-trust device. Monopolies legislation already exists in both the U.S., the U.K. and Canada to deal with oligopolies which abuse a dominant market position. As the majority in the CONTU Final Report argued, a direct approach to monopolistic abuses using anti-trust legislation is much more appropriate "than the invention of a class of works which are generally copyrightable but not when their authors are disfavoured, for whatever well intentioned reasons."[23] Moreover, the software industry seems by nature to be highly competitive and "[t]he absence of any significant barriers to entering the program market is striking."[24]

Thus, a convincing case has not been made out for withholding intellectual property protection from software on economic grounds. In general, laws relating to copyright, patents, trade secrets and related rights are sufficiently sophisticated and flexible to allow courts to accommodate the competing needs of authors, inventors and consumers. Where specific abuses of dominant market positions occur, these can more appropriately be dealt with by means of other existing regulatory mechanisms.

---

21   *Ibid.,* p. 36.
22   *Ibid.*
23   *Ibid.,* p. 25. As the Commissioners pointed out, the need for a judicial balancing of conflicting protection and anti-trust priorities is not a new one. See *Alfred Bell & Co. v. Catalda Fine Arts Inc.,* 191 F. 2d 99 at 106 (2nd Cir., 1951). For a case in which an action was brought under the Sherman Anti-Trust Act to challenge a tying arrangement for hardware and operating software, see *In re Data Gen. Corp. Antitrust Litigation,* 490 F. Supp. 1089 (N.D. Calif., 1980).
24   Note 20 above, p. 23.

1.1.4   Legal Frameworks for Protection of Programs and Data

Assuming that protection is to be made available, what form should such protection take? In the case of software, as was noted above,[25] it can be argued that a computer program does not fall within the scope of either copyright or patent protection, or alternatively that it qualifies for both. Such dilemmas have led some commentators to conclude that appropriate and effective regulation for computer software will only be achieved by abandoning the traditional corpus of intellectual property law and instead establishing some tailor-made protective scheme. Various proposals have been mooted,[26] but none has yet come to fruition nor does one seem likely to do so in the foreseeable future. A brief examination of these so-called "alternatives" perhaps indicates why this is so. On the whole they are not particularly radical. Most merely tinker with established copyright principles by introducing registration or deposit requirements, or by reducing the term of exclusive rights in recognition of the relatively short lifespan of much software. Such changes would either be largely cosmetic, or worse still would make the process of securing protection for software more, rather than less, cumbersome.[27] In the high-technology areas, the boundaries between patent and copyright are already becoming blurred. At first sight, bespoke protection schemes hold out the promise of preempting such demarcation disputes by creating a new space for software products. Technological advance will no doubt continue, however, and a protection scheme which is tailor-made for the technology of today may merely add another level of confusion when applied to the technology of tomorrow. Certainly none of the schemes proposed so far represents a striking improvement on existing intellectual property options.

Accordingly, a major part of this book will be devoted to the problems associated with bringing computer programs and data, and in broader terms "information" *per se,* under the aegis of the existing principles and rules of copyright, patent, trade secret, contract and

---

25   See Text accompanying notes 5 and 6, above.

26   Kinderman outlines six of these in "A Review of Suggested Systems for the Protection of Computer Software" in Brett and Perry, eds., *The Legal Protection of Computer Software* (Oxford: ESC Publishing, 1981).

27   If, for example, a program is obsolete after fifty months rather than fifty years, does it matter that copyright still subsists in it? On the other hand, there may be software packages with a fairly long lifespan. For example, there are some wordprocessing and accounting packages which are still growing in popularity after being on the market unchanged for several years. Why should these not attract a full term of protection?

criminal laws. Since on a global scale the common law is evolving unevenly, in chapters two to seven these matters will be dealt with in the comparative context of American, English and Canadian Law. Where especially significant developments have occurred in other common law jurisdictions, notably Australia, these too are discussed.

As in the software protection debate, the competing goals of "free-flow" of or restricted access to information are at the heart of the controversy surrounding privacy and data protection. Over the past two decades increasing attention has been given to the advantages and disadvantages of imposing legislative controls on the collection, processing, storage and communication of personal data. Once again there have been divergent responses in different common law jurisdictions. Historically, in the United States, and to a somewhat lesser extent in Canada also, the primary emphasis has been on providing safeguards against governmental invasions of personal privacy. In the United Kingdom, on the other hand, the Data Protection Act 1984 is applicable, admittedly with certain significant exceptions, across the board to public and private data users alike. Chapter eight will be devoted to a discussion of both the general issues in the privacy debate, and the specific legislative measures which have been introduced in the United States, Canada and England.

Finally, in chapter nine, attention will be given to some of the legal problems arising from the increasingly international nature of the data processing industry. The ease with which computer programs and data can be transmitted from one country to another greatly compounds problems of ownership, compensation for use, and privacy protection for individuals. The situation is complicated still further by the fact that some nations perceive unregulated data flows as a serious threat to their economic interests and even to their national sovereignty. While there has been considerable discussion on an international level as to the proper scope of data flow restrictions, many countries have already introduced their own regulatory schemes on an *ad hoc* basis. Without a degree of harmonization, there is a danger that data traffic of all kinds may gradually become choked by complex and contradictory regulations.

1.2 The Technical Context

1.2.1 The Mysteries of "Compuspeak"

Lawyers have often been accused of leading the field in creating smokescreens of professional jargon. It seems that in the computer industry, however, they have finally met their match. As one seemingly baffled American judge observed in *Honeywell v. Lithonia Lighting*:[28]

> After hearing the evidence in this case the first finding the court is constrained to make is that, in the computer age, lawyers and courts need no longer feel ashamed or even sensitive about the charge, often made, that they confused the issue by resort to legal jargon, law Latin or Norman French. By comparison, the misnomers and industrial shorthand of the computer world make the most esoteric legal writing as clear and lucid as the Ten Commandments or the Gettysburg Address; and to add to this Babel, the experts in the computer field, while using exactly the same words uniformly disagree as to precisely what they mean.

Many people find their initial encounter with a computer system to be a baffling and even intimidating business, and the language of the trade certainly does not help matters. For example, to be informed that one's first "hands-on interface" with what one thought was a "user-friendly" machine has in fact resulted in "graceful degradation"[29] or, worse still, "garbage,"[30] can be disconcerting to say the least. Persistence is generally rewarded, however, and, with the help of a good instruction manual or patient human guide, progress will usually be quite rapid. Moreover, for lawyers involved in computer litigation, a limited degree of expertise will often be quite adequate.[31] Here then are a few of the basic technical terms and concepts which are relevant to the legal analysis which follows. It should be stressed that no attempt will be made to give a comprehensive overview of the technology.[32]

1.2.2   Types of Computer

In the Oxford Dictionary of Computing a computer is defined as a "device or system that is capable of carrying out a sequence of operations

---

28   317 F. Supp. 496 at 408 (N.D. Ga., 1970) *per* Edenfield J.
29   "Graceful degredation" (also known as "fail-soft" or "operating in crippled mode") means that when part of a computer system fails limited operation can continue.
30   "Garbage" is simply meaningless or redundant data in any storage device.
31   As one Californian District Attorney commented in the Foreword to a Resource Manual on Computer Crime: "you will discover that you can handle a computer-related crime without a masters in math, even as an engineering degree is no prerequisite to nailing an auto theft, nor a pathology minor to despatching a murderer. Computers are not *that* difficult. Indeed . . . the biggest hurdle to prosecution is being ensnared by the jargon: the electronic red herring gambit is easily thwarted with a little confidence." U.S. Dept. of Justice, *Computer Crime: Criminal Justice Resource Manual* (Washington: Dept. of Justice, 1979), p. xxxvii.
32   For more detailed accounts see Curran and Curnow, *The Penguin Computing Book* (Harmondsworth: Penguin Books, 1983); Bender, *Computer Law: Evidence and Procedure* (New York: Matthew Bender, 1983), chapter 2 and Bigelow, ed., *Computers and the Law* (Chicago: American Bar Assoc., 1981), chapter 1.

in a distinctly and explicitly defined manner."[33] Computers can be classified in various ways. One fundamental distinction is between analog and digital machines. Analog computers use changes in mechanical, electrical, or other physical properties to represent changes in input data. Different numbers may be represented, for example, by different voltages and those voltage levels (and thus the corresponding numbers) may be continuously variable. A digital computer, however, operates in discrete steps and stores data as simply the presence or absence of a signal of some kind. Bender explains the essential difference of approach thus: "Whereas analog computers function in terms of 'how much', digital computers function in terms of 'how many'; analog computers measure, while digital computers count."[34] Some machines, known as "hybrid computers," use a combination of the two approaches. While certain specialist scientific applications are best served by analog computers, digital computers are far more common and will be the basis of discussion here.

In a digital computer, data are stored in a "two-state" form. In other words, a circuit is either on or off: there either is an electrical signal or there is no electrical signal. These two states are represented by the binary digits zero and one which are generally known as "bits." A combination of eight such bits makes up one "byte."[35] Each bit or byte is coded to represent a piece of information. Thus, in the widely used ASCII Code,[36] one byte (eight bits) represents a single letter, number or code character. A common way of classifying computers is in terms of the number of bits, or "word length," which can be processed as a unit. Hence the designations "8-bit", "16-bit" and "32-bit."

A further broad classification which is often applied to computers defines them in terms of "generations." While a number of important differences can be identified between the various generations, the critical distinction is probably that between the types of circuitry used. Thus

---

33   (Oxford: Oxford University Press, 1983). In popular parlance, the word "computer" often conveys a broader meaning than this and may include the input and output elements of a computer system. Thus *The Penguin Dictionary of Computers* (Harmondsworth: Penguin Books, 1977) defines a computer as "a machine which can accept *data* in a prescribed form, process the data and supply the results of the processing in a specified format as information or as signals to control automatically some further machine or process."

34   "An Introduction to Computer Technology" in Bigelow, note 32 above, at 10.

35   A "kilobyte" (or "Kbyte") is 1024 bytes (*i.e.*, 2 to the power of 10) and a "megabyte" (or "Mbyte") is 1,048,576 bytes (*i.e.*, 2 to the power of 20).

36   The acronym ASCII stands for "American Standard Code for Information Interchange."

the First generation contained valves (vacuum tubes); the Second, transistors; the Third, integrated circuits (chips) and the Fourth, very large scale integrated circuits (VLSIs). In 1982 the Japanese Ministry of International Trade and Industry (MITI) established an Institute for New Generation Computer Technology (ICOT) charged with the task of developing a Fifth generation of "artificially intelligent" computers.[37] Classified in these terms, which incidentally are by no means universally agreed upon, most computers in current use are Third or Fourth generation machines.

1.2.3   Hardware and Software

In a computer system "hardware" and "software" work together to effect desired changes in data. Hardware comprises the physical components of the system which provide the framework for the input, storage, processing and output of data. Hardware can take many forms depending on the size of the computer system and the purpose for which it is designed. Computers range in size from very large "mainframe" systems such as those used by NASA and the Pentagon, down to less than briefcase size "micros."[38] The hardware in a micro computer system typically includes a keyboard, various electrical and electronic components, disk drives or other storage devices, a display unit of some kind, a printer and one or more cabinets.[39] At the heart of every computer is a special piece of a hardware called the "central processing unit" (CPU) which "coordinates and controls the activities of all the other units and performs all the arithmetic and logical processes to be applied to data."[40] A CPU comprises at least two components: a control unit and an arithmetic and logic unit. Internal memory may also be included.

Hardware is usually contrasted with "software," which generally means all programs designed for use with a particular computer system. The broader term "software package" (sometimes simply "software") also covers any ancillary hardware and documentation supplied with a program.[41] The term "program" is broad in the extreme and has been a

---

37   See Feigenbaum and McCorduck, *The Fifth Generation: Artificial Intelligence and Japan's Challenge to the World* (London: Pan Books, 1984).

38   Depending on the definition of computer used, some pocket calculators may also be included.

39   A printer falls within a sub-class of "peripheral" devices but may be incorporated in the same cabinet as the main hardware components.

40   *The Penguin Dictionary of Computers*, note 33 above.

41   The words "program" and "software" are in practice often used interchangeably, however, and in this book "software" is not meant to include documentation unless specified.

source of some confusion in the courts.[42] In essence, however, a program is any set of instructions to a computer to perform a specified activity. A computer needs programs not only for making calculations or rearrangements of data, but also for controlling the operation of the various pieces of hardware which make up the system. Hence the distinction (which has, perhaps misguidedly, been found to be significant for legal purposes) between "operating systems"[43] and "applications programs." The function of the former is the organization of the various hardware components of the computer system, while the latter "perform" specific tasks.

Programs and data can be stored in various locations and forms, both within the computer itself and in external media such as cards, tapes, disks and drums. The distinction drawn earlier between hardware (the machine) and software (the programs which are run on it) is in fact complicated by the existence of firmware. Also known as "hardwired programs," firmware can perhaps best be understood as software in a "hard" form. Thus, instead of being loaded from external sources such as punched cards or floppy discs, a program may be stored in a chip contained within the computer itself.

Various types of firmware exist. The "read-only memory" (ROM) is, as the name suggests, a memory store which can not be written onto or altered.[44] Slightly more flexible than the ROM is the "write-once ROM" or PROM ("programmable read-only memory"). This can be programmed once after manufacture, but thereafter can not be changed. PROMs have now been developed, however, which can be reused. These are known by the acronyms EPROM ("erasable programmable read-only memory"),[45] and EEROM ("electrically erasable read-only memory").[46]

---

42   *E.g.,* in *Apple Computer Inc. v. Franklin Computer Corp.,* 545 F. Supp. 812 at 813 (1982), Judge Newcomer commented that "Of signal difficulty in this case is the elasticity of the word 'program'." A further point of confusion, in the United Kingdom at least, has been the spelling of the word "program" as "programme." This is perhaps a little surprising since the Concise Oxford Dictionary gives "program" as the spelling for "U.S. and computers" and both the Oxford Dictionary of Computing and the Penguin Dictionary of Computers give "program" as the only spelling.

43   Also known as "software tools."

44   The acronym ROM should not be confused with RAM ("random access memory") which refers to a read-write memory store.

45   The contents of an EPROM are erased by exposure to ultra-violet light.

46   The EEROM is also known as the EAROM ("electrically alterable read-only memory"). For obvious reasons, the various types of firmware are sometimes described collectively as ROMWARE.

1.2.4 Computer Languages and Programming

There are often various stages to the writing of a computer program. Once a particular problem or desired operation has been identified, the steps to its solution or execution may be set out in the form of a "flowchart." Next, a set of instructions for the various steps will be prepared and fed into the computer in some form which it can "understand," formerly often on punched cards (which the computer "reads") but more likely these days directly via a keyboard. Finally, the program must be tested and "debugged" until it performs as desired. Debugging is essentially the process of identifying and correcting errors in a program.

A program is usually entered into a computer in the form of a series of "statements" written in a "high level" language such as FORTRAN, ALGOL, COBOL, BASIC, etc. Each of these languages is designed to facilitate the solution of a particular type of problem, and programs in source code are thus said to be "problem oriented" rather than "machine oriented." As such, they are far too complex for a computer to process directly and must be converted into "machine" or "object" code[47] before they can be executed by the CPU (*i.e.*, "run"). The job of translating the program from source to object code is done by one or more special programs known as "compilers" and "assemblers."[48]

1.2.5 Computer Output and Communications

Data which have been loaded into a computer and processed can then be dealt with in a number of ways. They may be stored in memory or unloaded from the machine as "output." Output can take a number of forms, including direct control of equipment, a printout on paper, storage on, for example, disks or tapes, or visual display on a cathode ray tube, liquid crystal display (LCD) or some other form of "screen" (also known as a visual display unit or VDU). The form of output may be important for determining whether a copyright work has been copied or

---

47   For present purposes the terms "object code" and "machine code" will be treated as synonymous. This is a slight simplification as "object language is usually but not necessarily a machine language directly understandable by a computer; some high level languages are translated initially into a lower level object language which then requires further translation before it is converted into machine language" (*The Penguin Dictionary of Computers*, note 33 above at 291). In computer literature, however, the terms "object code" (or "object language") and "machine code" (or "machine language") are frequently used interchangeably, and for the purposes of legal analysis the distinction seems irrelevant.

48   A line of code may also be executed directly (*i.e.*, without a machine code translation) by means of an "interpreter."

reproduced in some material form. Output may also constitute part of a larger machine process and this may be significant for patent purposes.

"Communication" is often possible between quite separate computer systems, and is essential where various terminals or "screens" are connected to a central CPU. Types of communication systems include "local area networks" (LANs) at a local level, and satellite data links on an international level. A very common medium of communication between computers is the public switched telephone network (PSTN).[49]

---

49   To transmit digital data over an analog communication channel a "modem" (modulator and demodulator) must be used at each end of the link to convert outgoing digital bit streams into analog signals and incoming analog signals back into a digital form.

Chapter 2

General Copyright Issues

2.1 The Boundaries of Copyright as a Legal Concept

In view of the diverse and often conflicting demands placed upon it, the somewhat erratic development of the legal construct of copyright is not really surprising.[1] True, the purpose and scope of protection may have seemed fairly clear and manageable to those who drafted the first statute to deal with copyright in 1709.[2] But theirs was a relatively easy task. They were only concerned with balancing the interests of authors *vis-à-vis* publishers, and had only to think in terms of books. By contrast, modern copyright statutes must deal with the complex interests of such additional groups as composers, sculptors, translators, editors, public performers, film makers and distributors, cable and satellite television operators, compilers of databases and, indeed, members of the public generally as consumers in an information age. Moreover, diverse methods of creating, publishing and copying literary works now exist, many of which were confined to the realms of science-fiction only a few years ago.

So far, copyright has always risen to meet the challenge of accommodating new forms of expression. Some commentators argue that it should continue to do so. As Le Stanc[3] has observed, "copyright law is by definition an elastic, comprehensive and pragmatic legal system. Creative imagination has many forms, and copyright must take them all into account." Not all writers, however, have such confidence in the resilience and adaptability of the copyright model. Some have urged

---

1 See Sieghart, "Information Technology and Intellectual Property," [1982] 7 European Intellectual Property Review (E.I.P.R.) 187-88.

2 8 Anne, c. 21.

3 "Copyright Protection of Computer Software in Civil Law Countries" in Brett and Perry, eds., *The Legal Protection of Computer Software* (Oxford: ESC Publishing, 1981), at 113.

caution in pushing copyright to any further levels of abstraction,[4] while others feel that the construct has already been stretched beyond reason.[5]

What, then, are to be the limits of copyright? As with most questions regarding the boundaries of legal concepts, at least two types of answer can be given. A functional analysis will evaluate copyright as a device of economic regulation. As such it should be used for balancing the conflicting priorities of limited monopoly incentives against a general goal of free competition. Considerations of efficiency alone will dictate where copyright must stop. A more formal legal analysis, however, might find in the law as it has so far developed an internal coherence. The violation of this coherence might undermine the rationale and structure of copyright completely. It would be unrealistic to believe that legislators or courts would permit the constraints of the latter approach to impede the dictates of the former for long. Yet objections on grounds of principle to unlimited copyright protection of computer programs and data should not be dismissed lightly.

There have been two major points of contention in most jurisdictions. Firstly, whether copyright protection should be available for programs in object or machine code form. Secondly, whether protection should extend not only to applications programs which produce copyrightable output, but also to operating programs and other system software. A number of arguments have been advanced for limiting the scope of protection. The first is that to afford copyright protection to object code is tantamount to recognizing copyright in ideas, contrary to all existing law and practice.[6] Secondly, it has been suggested that operating systems and perhaps all programs in object code are effectively machine parts which should thus be dealt with under the aegis of patent, not copyright law.[7] A third argument is that object code programs, and especially operating systems in object code, merely perform mechanical or utilitarian functions and cannot therefore be regarded as appropriate subject matter for copyright.[8] Finally, concern is expressed that an

---

4   Breyer, "The Uneasy Case for Copyright: A Study of Copyright in Books, Photocopies and Computer Programs" (1970), 84 Harvard L.R. 281-351; Ploman and Hamilton, *Copyright: Intellectual Property in the Information Age* (London: Routledge and Keegan Paul), chapter 7.

5   *E.g.*, Sieghart, note 1 above.

6   *Final Report of the National Commission on New Technological Uses of Copyrighted Works* (Washington: Library of Congress, 1979), p. 33 (dissent of Commissioner Hersey). Hereafter cited as CONTU. For a discussion of this report see section 3.2, below.

7   *Ibid.*, pp. 28, 32.

8   Stern, "Another Look at Copyright Protection of Software: Did the 1980 Act Do Anything For Object Code?" (1981), III Computer/Law Journal 1-17 at 15.

extension of protection to object code "would mark the first time copyright had ever covered a means of communication, not with the human mind and senses, but with machines."[9] Again, this fourth concern is exacerbated in the case of operating programs. Each of these objections will be considered in turn.

2.2 The Merger of Idea and Expression

It has long been established that copyright cannot protect ideas *per se* but only expressions of ideas.[10] As one writer has put it, "copyright does not protect the heart of the work but only the tissue that surrounds it."[11] The logical necessity of this rule was well illustrated by the Supreme Court of Canada in *Cuisenaire v. South West Imports Ltd.*[12] The case concerned a book which outlined a method of teaching arithmetic using coloured rods. In rejecting an argument that, by making the rods as described in the book, the defendant had infringed the plaintiff's copyright, the court commented that " 'were the law otherwise, . . . everybody who made a rabbit pie in accordance with the recipe of *Mrs. Beeton's Cookery Book* would infringe the literary copyright in that book.' "[13]

Obvious though it may seem, on many occasions courts have had to struggle hard to implement this principle of protecting expressions of ideas without tying down the ideas themselves. As Judge Learned Hand observed in *Nichols v. Universal Pictures Corp.*:[14]

> Upon any work, and especially upon a play, a great number of patterns of increasing generality will fit equally well as more and more of the incident is left out. The last may perhaps be no more than the most general statement of what the play is about, and at times might consist only of its title; but there is a point in this series of abstractions where they are no longer protected, since otherwise the playwright could prevent the

---

9   CONTU, note 6 above, at p. 28 (*per* Hersey).

10   *Baker v. Selden*, 101 US 99 (1879); *Donoghue v. Allied Newspapers Ltd.*, [1938] 1 Ch. 106, [1937] 3 All E.R. 503. For a suggestion that copyright should in fact be extended to cover ideas see Hopkins, "Ideas, Their Time Has Come: An Argument and a Proposal for Copyrighting Ideas" (1982), 46 Albany L.R. 443-73.

11   Le Stanc, note 3 above, at 111.

12   [1969] S.C.R. 208, 40 Fox Pat. C. 81, 57 C.P.R. 76.

13   *Ibid.*, at 212, citing Pape J. in *Cuisenaire v. Reed*, [1963] V.R. 719 (Australia). Note, however, that in the United Kingdom a product built from a blueprint may constitute an infringing copy of that blueprint: *L.B. (Plastics) v. Swish Products*, [1979] F.S.R. 145 (H.L.). See also comments of Stern, note 8 above.

14   45 F. 2d 119 at 121 (1930).

use of his "ideas," to which, apart from their expression, his property is never extended. Nobody has ever been able to fix that boundary, and nobody ever can.

In the case of software, the "ideas" might be the algorithm on which a program is based, or the methods or processes which the program implements.[15] Yet these kinds of "ideas" present even greater problems than, for example, the plot of a play, due to the limited number of ways in which any particular algorithm may be expressed or method or process can be performed.[16]

It is partly for this reason that, in his dissent to the CONTU *Final Report,* Commissioner Hersey urged that copyright should not be extended to "a computer program in the form in which it is capable of being used to control computer operations."[17] In particular, Hersey took issue with the majority's recommendation that copyright protection should be extended to adaptations of programs.[18] He cited expert testimony given to CONTU to the effect that, when a program is taken from a lower to a higher language and then back again, "all that survives from one version to the other is 'the essential underlying idea, not the mode, not the form of expression'."[19] Hersey concluded that, in classifying such versions as "adaptations," the Commission had "bypassed a fundamental distinction of copyright from other forms of protection and may well have opened the way for covert protection in the name of copyright of the underlying mechanical idea or ideas of a program, rather than of its original means of expression."[20] While commentators disagree as to whether "expressions" and ideas merge at the machine code level, ultimately the issue must be resolved as a question of fact in each case. It may be that, given sufficient time and resources, a skilled programmer would be able to write a new program to emulate the functioning of virtually any existing program.[21] If, however, it could be demonstrated that a particular outcome or process could only be achieved by means of

---

15   See U.S. Congress discussions of Copyright Law Revision: U.S. Congress, Senate, Judiciary Committee, 94th Congress, 1975, S. Rept. 473 at 54; U.S. Congress, House, Judiciary Committee, 94th Congress, 2d Session., 1976 H. Rept. 1476 at 57.

16   Miller, "Copyright and Computers" in Holmes and Norville, eds., *The Law of Computers* (Ann Arbor, Michigan: Institute of Continuing Legal Education, 1971), at 113-14.

17   Note 6 above, p. 37.

18   *Ibid.,* at 33.

19   *Ibid.,* citing testimony of Prof. J.C.R. Licklider of Massachusetts Institute of Technology.

20   *Ibid.,* at 34.

21   In the case of some programs, such as multi-tasking operating systems, the cost of emulation may be very considerable.

one program, then presumably idea and expression would have merged.[22] The likelihood of such mergers occurring may have increased recently with the growing popularity of microcode and programmed logic arrays as media for storing program instructions.[23]

So far, however, the issue has tended to arise in the context of computer "cloning" where, to provide purchasers with ready access to an existing pool of software, a manufacturer produces a machine which is closely compatible with some well established computer system.[24] In order to achieve a high degree of compatibility, the manufacturer furnishes the clone with an operating system which is virtually identical to that used in the established machine. Yet provided such compatibility is achieved by independent effort and not by copying, no infringement of copyright will occur.[25] Indeed, copyright never guards against such independent creation, or recreation, of the essence of a work, but is only meant to prevent others from "free-riding" on an author's investment of time and skill.

The second and third major objections to software copyright both concern the status of programs as "writings" under American law,[26] and as "literary" or "artistic works" in England and Canada.[27] The argument, at its strongest, is that programs, in object code at least, are merely machine parts and thus not proper subjects for copyright. An alternative approach is to concede that programs may be "writings" or "literary works" of some kind, but maintain that as they merely perform mechanical or utilitarian functions they should not be protected.

---

22   See discussion of *Apple v. Formula* in section 3.1.5, below, where a defence was based in part on this argument.

23   See Harris, "Apple Computer Inc. v. Franklin Computer Corp. - does a ROM a Computer Program Make?" [1984] Jurimetrics J. 248-53.

24   The most popular subjects for cloning have been the IBM PC and the Apple II computers.

25   Thus, Brooks has argued that it would be quite legitimate for engineers to "write their own code and through a process of elimination assure that application programs yield the same results on the original and cloned machines." "Object Code in ROM: Is It Really a Problem?" in *Computer Law Institute* (New York: Practising Law Institute, 1983), 335-71 at 371. Direct copying would, of course, still be prohibited. Moreover, where the physical appearance or "get-up" of a machine is copied, a quite separate action may lie for passing-off, unfair competition, or unfair trade practices.

26   *Per* U.S. Constitution (1790), Art. 1, s. 8, cl. 8.

27   *Per* UK Copyright Act (1956), 4 & 5 Eliz. 2, c. 74, s. 48(1); Canadian Copyright Act, R.S.C. 1970, c. C-30, s. 4(1).

2.3 Programs as Machine Parts

Commissioner Hersey argued in his dissent to the CONTU Report that a program in its "mature" form is essentially "a machine control element, a mechanical device, having no purpose beyond being engaged in a computer to perform mechanical work."[28] Indeed, he went further and drew an analogy between programs in their machine-control form and "that relatively primitive mechanical device, the cam."[29] The majority in CONTU attempted to sidestep this objection by drawing a counter analogy between computers and other multiple-use machines such as video projectors and record players.[30] Moreover, looking at the matter from a starting point of the hardware rather than the software, another commentator has observed that "the question whether a computer without its program is still a computer is analogous to the question whether a piano without someone playing it is still a piano."[31]

Yet these analogies are not entirely apposite for two reasons. Firstly, unlike videotapes and phonorecords, applications software is frequently designed to function interactively with the hardware it programs. As Gemignani[32] has observed:

> The purpose of the computer . . . is generally not to play back the data, but to transform it. People rate a record player according to the quality at which it reproduces the sound of the recording. But a computer which merely plays back the data fed into it is of little use to anyone.

Secondly, in the case of operating systems it could be argued that, without such programs, a so-called computer is not really a computer at all. Hardware without an operating system is perhaps more like a projector without a bulb, a record player without a stylus or a piano without hammers.

Nevertheless, despite the fact that programs interact with hardware and some are essential to the functioning of the machines on which they are run, it is still possible to classify all programs as simply expressions of ideas which have been "fixed" in a tangible form. The embodiment of the

---

28   CONTU, note 6 above, p. 28.
29   *Ibid.*, p. 29.
30   "Programs should no more be considered machine parts than videotapes should be considered parts of projectors or phonorecords parts of sound reproduction equipment." *Ibid.*, p. 21.
31   Saltman, *Computer Science and Technology: Copyright in Computer-Readable Works. Policy Impacts of Technological Change.* (Washington: National Bureau of Standards, 1977), p. 60.
32   "Legal Protection for Computer Software: the View from '79" (1980), 7 Rutgers J. of Comp. Tech. & L. 269-312 at 280.

"writing" or "literary work" in a piece of physical apparatus need not affect the applicability of copyright law. Copyright applies to a work rather than its storage medium. Thus, for copyright purposes, computer-readable object code is no more "mechanical" than a sound recording.[33]

2.4 Functionality and Utility

What of the related concern that if operating systems, or object code programs generally, can be copyrighted, then protection is being extended to works of a purely functional or utilitarian nature? The short answer is that this objection comes much too late. Copyright has for a long time extended to mundane compilations of data.[34] As for utilitarian objects, it is now three decades since, in the case of *Mazer v. Stein,* an American Supreme Court Justice bemoaned the extension of copyright registration to such articles as "statuettes, book ends, clocks, lamps, door knockers, candlesticks, inkstands, chandeliers, piggy banks, sundials, salt and pepper shakers, fish bowls, casseroles, and ash trays."[35] Despite this complaint, a majority in the Supreme Court declared that they found "nothing in the copyright statute to support the argument that the intended use or use in industry of an article eligible for copyright bars or invalidates its registration."[36] Moreover, as the CONTU Report noted,[37] in the United States at least, "courts have assiduously avoided adopting the critic's role in evaluating the merits of works of authorship. To attempt to deny copyrightability to a writing because it is capable of use in conjunction with a computer would contravene this sound policy." English courts have displayed a similar reluctance to become involved in questions of quality control or literary criticism. Indeed, they have stressed the irrelevance of artistic merit as a criterion for protection. As Lord Halsbury put it in *Walter v. Lane,*[38] the first producer of a book gets

---

33   Note, "Copyright Protection of Computer Program Object Code" (1983), 96 Harvard L.R. 1723-44 at 1735.

34   *E.g.,* railway timetables: *H. Blacklock and Co. v. C. Arthur Pearson Ltd.,* [1915] 2 Ch. 376.

35   Douglas J. dissenting in *Mazer v. Stein,* 347 U.S. 201 at 221 (1954).

36   *Ibid.,* at 218.

37   CONTU, note 6 above, p. 25.

38   [1900] A.C. 539 at 549 (H.L.). Note, however, that to secure copyright protection a work must still be original in the sense that "labour, skill, and capital should be expended sufficiently to impart to the product some quality or character which the raw material did not possess, and which differentiates the product from the raw

copyright "whether that book be wise or foolish, accurate or inaccurate, of literary merit or of no merit whatever."

Yet if copyright were to be granted to software on an indiscriminate basis, would there not be a danger that protection might be extended far beyond the present domain of copyright law, and indeed even beyond the boundaries of intellectual property generally? Commissioner Nimmer, while concurring with the Majority's recommendations in the CONTU Report, expressed concern at this possibility:

> What is most troubling about the Commission's recommendation of open-ended protection for all computer software is its failure to articulate any rationale which would not equally justify copyright protection for the tangible expression of any and all original ideas (whether or not computer technology, business, or otherwise). If *literary works* are to be so broadly construed, the Copyright Act becomes a general misappropriation law, applicable as well in what has traditionally been regarded as the patent arena, and indeed, also in other areas to which neither copyright nor patent law has previously extended.[39]

As a check on such creeping distension, Nimmer proposed "a possible line of demarcation which would distinguish between protectible and unprotectible software in a manner consistent with limiting such protection to the conventional copyright arena."[40] The line might, he suggested, most logically be drawn between programs which produce copyrightable works, such as data bases or video games, and those which merely regulate processes, such as traffic signals or heating.[41] This argument is superficially attractive, especially since the latter category of programs may end up qualifying, in the United States at least, for patent protection as part of such processes.[42] Yet, together with the "communication" issue which will now be discussed, the "functionality" objection is fatally flawed in making the "purpose" of a work, rather than simply its form or content, a critical factor in determining the scope of protection under copyright law.

---

material." *Macmillan & Co. v. Cooper* (1923), 40 T.L.R. 186 at 188, *per* Lord Atkinson (P.C.).

39   CONTU, p. 26.
40   *Ibid.*, at 27.
41   *Ibid.* Nimmer added as a caveat that, if a process program also provided for a printout of instructions, protection might be available for that part of the program only.
42   *E.g., Diamond v. Diehr*, 450 U.S. 175 (1981). See discussion in section 5.2.3, below.

2.5 The Communication Issue

Copyright frequently subsists in material which is not directly intelligible by humans. Music recordings on magnetic tape or phonorecords are obvious examples of protected works stored in machine code form. Why should computer programs expressed in object code form be treated any differently? The alleged distinction has really nothing to do with the issue of intelligibility at all. Rather, it is the difference in the intended recipients of the coded messages which is crucial. Commissioner Hersey contrasts the two thus:

> The aim of all writing, be it for art or use, is communication. Up to this time . . . copyright has always protected the means of expression of various forms of "writing" which were perceived, in every case, by the human sense for which they were intended: written words by the human eye, music by the ear, paintings by the eye, and so on. Here, for the first time, the protection of coyright would be offered to a "communication" with a machine.[43]

This same argument can be used to refute the suggestion that the transformation of source into object code is analogous to translations of conventional messages, either into foreign languages or into codes such as braille and shorthand. As Lucas has pointed out, to argue thus "is to ignore [the fact] that braille is addressed to the blind and shorthand to stenographers while program languages are addressed to the computer."[44]

The merits of drawing a firm line between human and machine communication were argued forcefully before a Pennsylvania district court in the case of *Apple v. Franklin.*[45] Judge Newcomer was clearly impressed by the proposed demarcation and commented:

> If the concept of "language" means anything, it means an ability to create human interaction. It is the fixed expression of this that the copyright law protects, and only this. To go beyond the bounds of this protection would be ultimately to provide copyright protection to the programs created by a computer to run other computers. With that, we step into the world of Gulliver where horses are "human" because they speak a language that sounds remarkably like the one humans use.[46]

---

43   CONTU, note 6 above, p. 36.

44   "La Protection des Creations Industrielles Abstraites" (1975), LITEC, Coll. CEIPI No. 304 at 193. (cited by Le Stanc in "Copyright Protection of Computer Software in Civil Law Countries" in Brett and Parry, eds., *The Legal Protection of Computer Software* (Oxford: ESC Publishing, 1981).

45   *Apple Computer Inc. v. Franklin Computer Corp.,* 545 F. Supp. 812 (E.D. Penn., 1982), reversed 714 F. 2d 1240 (3rd Cir., 1983). English courts have also from time to time suggested that a literary work must be intended to communicate with a human audience: *Hollinrake v. Truswell,* [1894] 3 Ch. 420 (C.A.); *Exxon Corp. v. Exxon Ins. Consultants Int.,* [1982] Ch. 119, [1981] 3 All E.R. 241 (C.A.).

46   545 F. Supp. 812 at 825.

Accordingly, the district court reached the conclusion that because they were not directed at a human audience, Apple's operating systems could not be copyrighted.

Yet both this communication test and the functionality argument seem to be derived from a false premise. As one commentator has put it, "[t]he fallacy in the 'communication' argument is that it presumes that the copyrightable work in question is the *functioning* of the program and not the *writing* of it."[47] Reference has already been made to the irrelevance of literary or artistic merit in determining the scope of copyright. The function of a work of authorship and its intended audience must be equally irrelevant. Where direct protection for a program is sought, the potential output of that program is not in issue. Rather, the test for copyrightability is whether a particular program is in itself an original work of authorship. As will be seen, this was the approach which the Third Circuit adopted in deciding to allow Apple's appeal from Judge Newcomer's ruling.[48]

The controversy surrounding machine "communication" may, however, soon be resurrected in a rather different context. As "artificially intelligent" computers come to display more and more of the characteristics of authors, legislators and courts may be forced to address the converse question of whether a machine can itself communicate with humans and be granted protection for apparently original works of authorship.

2.6 Questions of Authorship and Ownership

The scope of copyright protection for programs and data depends not only on the form in which a particular work subsists. In determining questions of authorship and ownership the manner in which a work is "created" may also be crucial. For some computer scientists a long term research goal is the production of computer systems which can mimic and eventually surpass the capabilities of the human brain. While "Artificial Intelligence" (AI) may still be far from this objective, computers already exist which are sufficiently "smart" as to give at least an appearance of independent creativity. Consequently, a reappraisal of the

---

47   Davidson, "Protecting Computer Software: A Comprehensive Analysis" (1983), 23 Jurimetrics 339-425 at 373.
48   714 F. 2d 1240 (3rd Cir., 1983). See discussion in section 3.5., below.

traditional criteria for establishing who is the author and/or owner of a work seems important.

Composers have been using computers as aids to musical composition for almost three decades, and applications of computers in graphic design and other visual arts are also well known.[49] Computers have even been known to write fiction.[50] Who, then, should be deemed the author of an original work produced by or with the assistance of a computer? Could a work produced by a computer with minimal or no human intervention still be a work of "authorship" attracting copyright protection?

In the CONTU Report the Commissioners gave some consideration to this problem but concluded that, in the present state of the art, computers only extend human powers. As such, they are merely creative tools the use of which can have no more effect on copyright than the use of cameras, tape recorders or typewriters.[51] However, like the Commissioners' earlier comparison between programs and videotapes or phonorecords, this analogy is not particularly helpful. Cameras, tape recorders and typewriters are designed to reproduce accurately the data fed into them. In marked contrast, computers not only rearrange inputted data but they may also produce output which is quite unpredictable. Thus, to some extent computers can emulate the vagaries and spontaneity of the human brain. Writing in 1956, the British logician Alan Turing suggested that, if a person asked a computer questions and could not tell from the answers whether a machine was being addressed, it would be reasonable to say that the computer could think.[52]

---

49   See Risset, "Copyright Problems Arising From the Use of Computers for Creation of Works," [1979] WIPO: Copyright 232-242.

50   Racter, "Soft Ions" in Omni (April 1981), 96. For a discussion of other applications of AI, both actual and potential, see Butler, "Can a Computer be an Author? Copyright Aspects of Artificial Intelligence" (1982), 4 Comm/Ent 707-47.

51   CONTU, p. 45. The Commission did note, however, that "the dynamics of computer science promise changes in the creation and use of authors' writing that cannot be predicted with any certainty" and recommended that Congress "continuously monitor the impact of computer applications on the creation of works of authorship" (p. 46). In the UK, the Whitford Committee similarly regarded the computer as "a mere tool in much the same way as a slide rule or even, in a simple sense, a paint brush. A very sophisticated tool it may be, with considerable powers to extend man's capabilities to create new works, but a tool nevertheless." *Report of the Committee to consider the Law on Copyright and Designs* (London: HMSO, Cmnd. 6732, 1977), para. 514.

52   Turing, "Can a Machine Think?" 4 World of Mathematics (New York: Simon & Schuster, 1956), 2099-123 quoted by Milde, "Can a Computer be an 'Author' or an 'Inventor'?" (1969), 51 J.P.O.S. 378 at 382.

Machines which can fool humans in this manner now exist.[53] Perhaps, however, a more rigorous test is necessary. For example, the exercise of "free will" might be deemed an essential prerequisite for creativity. Yet even then it could be argued that, negatively at least, computers can in some areas avoid predictability and determinism in a way no human can.[54] This line of analysis need not be pursued further for it to be clear that a case could be made out for treating some automatic computer output as being sufficiently creative and original as to merit copyright protection.

There is, however, a major stumbling block in the way of protection for computer-created output. Most copyright statutes impose at least an implicit stipulation that an "author" must be human. The American, British and Canadian copyright statutes all contain nationality or citizenship requirements[55] and, despite the fact that copyright may be *owned* by bodies corporate, human *authorship* seems always to be presumed. If, then, a machine rather than a person seems to have "-authored" or "co-authored" a work, should copyright protection be available? Timothy Butler[56] has suggested four possible responses:

> (1) disallow copyright completely; (2) give authorship and copyright to the computer and its software or find authorship "shared" between the AI software and a human; (3) settle copyright upon the owner of the underlying AI software or the machine owner; or (4) create a fictional human author and assign its copyright to the AI software owner, the problem-specifier or the computer owner either individually, jointly or in part.

In Britain, the Whitford Committee favoured a fifth option. In cases where data is provided by a human, copyright should be granted to that person alone or jointly with the owner of the AI software.[57] Yet another candidate was proposed in a 1981 Green Paper put out in response to the Whitford Report.[58] The British Government felt that the creative tool in question was not a computer alone but rather a programmed computer. This premise led to the conclusion that the author of the new work is "neither of the two parties proposed by Whitford, but

---

53   See Hofstadter, *Godel, Escher, Bach: An Eternal Braid* (Toronto: Vintage Books, 1983).

54   *E.g.*, a computer can select random numbers *ad infinitum* and use those numbers for such applications as musical composition. See Rissett, note 49, above.

55   17 U.S.C., s. 104; U.K. Copyright Act (1956), 4 & 5 Eliz. 2, c. 74, s. 1(5); Canadian Copyright Act, R.S.C. 1970, c. C-30, s. 4(1).

56   Butler, note 50 above, at 734.

57   *Report of the Committee to Consider the Law of Copyright and Designs,* note 51 above, para. 515.

58   *Reform of the Law Relating to Copyright, Designs and Performers Protection* (London: HMSO Cmnd. 8302, 1981).

is instead a third person, namely the one responsible for running the data through the programmed computer in order to create the new work."[59]

None of these six options provides a straightforward solution to the authorship dilemma. The first (no copyright at all) leaves the work completely unprotected, while the second (machine or shared human and machine ownership) would necessitate absurd legal gymnastics to accommodate established copyright principles. For example, how long should a computer be deemed to live for the purpose of fixing the term of protection for a work? Moreover, how could a computer assign or otherwise administer its rights and how should it be rewarded for its "creative" effort?[60]

The third option is also highly problematic. Awarding copyright to the owner of the software or hardware might be effectively to grant a monopoly over a process for producing a vast number of different works. In the case of computer music, for example, this approach might mean that:

> The author of a program providing for a random selection of a sufficiently large number of musical symbols could then claim artistic property in all musical composition written in conventional notation (just as there is a slight but greater than zero possibility that an army of monkeys typing at random might reproduce the British Museum Library).[61]

Moreover, this third approach, like the fifth and sixth, may fail to establish protection for want of a sufficient creative link between the finished work and the person or persons who own the software or hardware, provide the data or run the program.[62]

While not without its difficulties, the fourth approach, that of creating a fictional author and assigning his or her copyright to other

---

59   *Ibid.,* at 35, para. 7.
60   For these and other related reasons Butler (note 56 above) considers option two both theoretically unsatisfactory and practically unworkable.
61   Rissett, note 49 above, at 234.
62   The importance of requiring some creative contribution was also stressed by the World Intellectual Property Organization Committee of Governmental Experts on Copyright Problems Arising From the Use of Computers for Access to or the Creation of Works (2nd Report, *Copyright,* (1982), 239-47 at 244). In this regard the option contained in the British Green Paper does not seem particularly appropriate: it is quite unlikely that the person who runs the data would have a better claim to copyright on creative grounds than the person(s) who authored the software and provided the raw data. However, this approach might still have some merit since the person who runs the data through the computer will generally be the person or an employee of the person who has invested financially in the hardware and software. See Hewitt, "Protection of Works Created by the Use of Computers" (1983), 133 New L.J. 235-7.

parties, seems to be the most reasonable solution. Butler favours this option as it both ensures protection without violating the concept of creativity as a distinctively human endeavour, and awards copyright protection to human beneficiaries.[63] Such a system would, however, prove quite unworkable if every instance of computer "authorship" had to be adjudicated by the courts. In practice, the benefits of copyright would in most cases presumably have to be allocated between the various potential claimants by contractual agreement. Moreover, the longevity of the fictional author would remain to be determined in some manner.[64]

A different authorship problem has already reached the courts. What happens when a copyright work stored in a computer program can be manipulated in such a way that it is virtually recreated by the person accessing the data? In the United States this issue has arisen in some of the disputes over videogame piracy. On occasion, defendants have alleged that a player influences the course of a game to the extent of creating a new audiovisual work each time the game is played. In the United States the fact that this work is not registered means that copyright cannot be enforced. In *Stern v. Kaufman*,[65] the Second Circuit concluded that, although each game was different, protection was nevertheless available because "a sufficiently substantial portion of the sights and sounds of the game" was always repeated.[66]

A further assessment of the effect of the creative input of video game players was made in *Midway v. Artic*.[67] The Seventh Circuit felt that playing a videogame is "a little like arranging words in a dictionary into sentences or paints on a palette into a painting."[68] If the role of a player in a game were sufficiently inventive then he or she, rather than the game's creator, would be the author of that particular audiovisual work.[69] The court concluded, however, that, in view of the limited choices available to a player, "[p]laying a videogame is more like changing channels on a television than it is like writing a novel or painting a picture."[70]

Yet how much flexibility in a game would be necessary for this analogy to break down? In *Stern v. Kaufman* the court emphasized the

---

63   Note 50, above. Butler does point out that copyright statutes might need minor amendments to permit a presumption of authorship where there is no apparent human author.

64   Given the current speed with which hardware reaches obsolescence, a relatively short "lifespan" might be appropriate.

65   533 F. Supp. 635 (N.Y., 1981); affirmed 669 F. 2d 852 (2nd Cir., 1982).

66   669 F. 2d at 856.

67   547 F. Supp. 999 (N.D., Ill., 1982); affirmed 704 F. 2d 1009 (7th Cir., 1983).

68   704 F. 2d at 1011.

69   *Ibid.*

70   *Ibid.*, at 1012.

fact that the player had no control over the appearance of the spaceships and other visual images,[71] while in *Midway v. Artic* the player's lack of control over the sequencing of images was stressed.[72] Even with present technology, however, a game could be devised which permitted each player to set up customised images and sounds by drawing on a screen and recording via a microphone. Moreover, a game could include a very considerable number of sequencing permutations thus giving a player extensive control over the course of a game. Would these changes be sufficient to make a player at least co-author of a game?

Given the complexity and speed of development of computer technology, it seems likely that the application of copyright principles to programs and data will continue to be problematic for some time. Even when courts have come to terms with object code and operating systems, as indeed they now largely have done in the United States, there will probably still be stumbling blocks in the path of program and data copyright. The current availability of protection under American, English and Canadian law will now be assessed.

---

71   669 F. 2d at 856.
72   704 F. 2d at 1012.

Chapter 3

Copyright Protection of Programs and Data in the United States

3.1 The 1976 Copyright Act

Under the United States Constitution, Congress is empowered to:

promote the Progress of Science and Useful Arts, by securing for limited times to Authors and Inventors the exclusive Right to their respective Writings and Discoveries.[1]

As the CONTU Report noted,[2] the history of copyright law in the United States since 1790 has been one of steady and frequent expansion. As new forms of expression have been developed, the definition of "writings" has been gradually broadened to include them. The current definition of copyrightable subject matter under the 1976 Copyright Act reflects this pragmatic flexibility:

Copyright protection subsists, in accordance with this title, in original works of authorship fixed in any tangible medium of expression, now known or later developed, from which they can be perceived, reproduced, or otherwise communicated, either directly or with the aid of a machine or device.[3]

Following a non-exclusive list of seven categories of protected works,[4]

---

1   Article 1, s. 8., c. 1.8.
2   *Final Report of the National Commission on New Technological Uses of Copyrighted Works* (Washington: Library of Congress, 1979) at 14-15. Hereafter cited as CONTU.
3   17 U.S.C., s. 102(a).
4   These are: (1) literary works; (2) musical works, including any accompanying words; (3) dramatic works, including any accompanying music; (4) pantomimes and choreographic works; (5) pictorial, graphic, and sculptural works; (6) motion pictures and other audiovisual works; and (7) sound recordings. The first of these categories is the most obviously applicable to software and data. "Literary Works" are defined in the Act as "works, other than audiovisual works, expressed in words, numbers, or other

the Act goes on to reiterate the well established caveat that:

> In no case does copyright protection . . . extend to any idea, procedure, process, system, method of operation, concept, principle, or discovery, regardless of the form in which it is described, explained, illustrated, or embodied in such work.[5]

Provided copyright can be shown to subsist in a work, however, the benefits to the owner can be considerable. Subject to certain limitations, the owner of copyright in a work has the exclusive right to reproduce the work, prepare derivative works, distribute copies of the work and perform or display the work publicly.[6] Remedies for infringement of copyright include injunctions,[7] impounding and disposition of infringing articles,[8] and either an account of profits made by the infringer or statutory damages.[9] Willful infringement of copyright "for purposes of commercial advantage or private financial gain" constitutes a criminal offence.[10] The Act also provides for the seizure, forfeiture and destruction of certain infringing articles,[11] and for orders to be made prohibiting the importation of infringing articles.[12]

The appropriateness of extending these benefits for copyright owners, and the corresponding restrictions on users, to cover new types of copyright material was quite widely debated in the United States in the 1970s. The National Commission on New Technological Uses of Copyrighted Works was set up part way through the copyright revision program which led to the new Act, to assess the impact of new technology on copyright law.[13] In particular, its mandate was to prepare recommendations regarding the regulation of photocopying and computers.[14] Pending the outcome of the CONTU study, section 117 of the new Copyright Act purported to freeze the law relating to program copyrights as of 31 December 1977 (the new legislation came into force on 1 January 1978).[15]

---

verbal or numerical symbols or indicia, regardless of the nature of the material objects such as books, periodicals, manuscripts, phonorecords, films, tapes, disks, or cards, in which they are embodied." *Ibid.*, s. 101.

5   *Ibid.*, s. 102(b).
6   *Ibid.*, s. 106. For "fair use" and other limitations on these exclusive rights see ss. 107-12.
7   *Ibid.*, s. 502.
8   *Ibid.*, s. 503.
9   *Ibid.*, s. 504. A court may also award a copyright owner costs and attorney's fees: s. 505.
10   *Ibid.*, s. 506. See discussion of criminal sanctions in section 7.2.1, below.
11   *Ibid.*, ss. 506, 509.
12   *Ibid.*, s. 603.
13   CONTU, p. 1.
14   *Ibid.*
15   Section 117 provided: "Notwithstanding the provisions of sections 106 through 116

Despite section 117, however, the new Act had already paved the way for wholesale protection of computer programs. In particular, the fact that a work might only be perceived, reproduced, or otherwise communicated "with the aid of a machine or device" was in itself to be no bar to protection. Previously, a Supreme Court decision of 1908[16] had established that copyright could only subsist in subject matter which was perceptible to the human eye. Machine-readability is now, for copyright purposes, just as good.

Another significant change brought about by the new Act was the effective abolition of the old distinction between common law and statutory copyright. The latter used only to take effect on registration, but section 302 now provides that statutory copyright subsists in a new work automatically from the date of creation. Nevertheless, registration will usually still be highly desirable as it constitutes *prima facie* evidence of originality,[17] and is, in any event, a prerequisite to an infringement suit.[18]

Since 1964 the Copyright Office had been accepting computer programs for registration under a "rule of doubt."[19] Certain conditions had to be satisfied, including the deposit of "copies" in human-readable form for the purposes of publication.[20] While the general tone of the circular which announced these arrangements was cautious, and, in particular, doubt was expressed as to the copyrightability of programs in machine-readable form, this extension of registration to cover programs was an early sign that the Copyright Office was sympathetic to the idea of protection for software. The 1964 ruling was never challenged,[21] and, when Congress came to review the position prior to the enactment of the new copyright law, the Judiciary Committees of both the Senate and the House concluded, without reservation, that programs were copyrightable works.[22]

---

and 118, this title does not afford to the owner of copyright in a work any greater or lesser rights with respect to the use of the work in conjunction with automatic systems capable of storing, processing, retrieving, or transferring information, or in conjunction with any similar device, machine, or process, than those afforded to works under the law, whether title 17 or the common law, or statutes of a State, in effect on December 31, 1977, as held applicable and construed by a court in an action brought under this title."

16   *White-Smith Music Publishing Co. v. Apollo Co.,* 209 U.S. 1 (1908).
17   17 U.S.C., s. 410(c). See *Flick-Reedy v. Hydro Line,* 351 F. 2d 546 (7th Cir., 1965); cert. den. 103 U.S. 958 (1966).
18   17 U.S.C., s. 411.
19   Copyright Office Circular 31 D (Jan. 1965).
20   To satisfy the *White-Smith* requirement.
21   CONTU, p. 16.
22   U.S. Congress, Senate, Judiciary Committee, 94th Congress, 1975, S. Rept. 473 at 50;

3.2 The CONTU Report and the Computer Software Copyright Act 1980

The National Commission on New Technological Uses of Copyrighted Works published its Final Report on 31 July 1978. It too stated a "unanimous . . . belief that computer programs are entitled to legal protection,"[23] and, moreover, that "it was clearly the intent of Congress to include computer programs within the scope of copyrightable subject matter in the Act of 1976."[24] Where the Commission was not unanimous was on the question of "the precise form that protection should take."[25] As we have already noted, the most contentious issue was that of copyright protection for programs in their object code form.[26] It is perhaps unfortunate then that the majority's report not only sidestepped this question in its discussion of software copyrights, but also failed to make any express reference to object code in its "Recommendations for Statutory Change."

While they conceded that there must come a point in the actual operation of software in a computer system where "copyright has no control,"[27] the Commissioners retreated from drawing any line of demarcation:

> To attempt to establish such a line in this report written in 1978 would be futile. . . . Should a line need to be drawn to exclude certain manifestations of programs from copyright, that line should be drawn on a case by case basis by the institution designed to make fine distinctions – the federal judiciary.[28]

Thus, in its "Recommendations for Statutory Change," the Commission limited itself to the following proposals. First, that the existing section 117 be repealed, thus unfreezing program copyright.[29] Second, that section 101 of the Act be amended to add a definition of a "computer program" as being "a set of statements or instructions to be used directly

---

U.S. Congress, House, Judiciary Committee, 94th Congress, 2nd sess., 1976, H. Rept. 1476 at 51.

23   CONTU, p. 12.
24   *Ibid.,* p. 16.
25   *Ibid.,* p. 12.
26   See chapter 2, above.
27   CONTU, p. 22.
28   *Ibid.,* pp. 22-3. More specifically, the CONTU Report made it clear that the issue of the copyrightability of integrated circuit chips remained unresolved: "The question of copyright protection for the topography of microcircuit chips was raised by a manufacturer of these devices too late to be dealt with adequately by the Commission" (p. 79).
29   *Ibid.,* p. 22.

or indirectly in a computer in order to bring about a certain result."[30] Third, that a new section 117 be enacted to authorize the making of a copy or adaptation of a program where necessary for use of the program with a particular machine, or for archival purposes only.[31]

At the end of 1980 Congress passed the Computer Software Copyright Act,[32] implementing the CONTU recommendations virtually verbatim. Section 101 of the Copyright Act was amended to include a definition of "computer program" as being "a set of statements or instructions to be used directly or indirectly in a computer in order to bring about a certain result."[33] The Act also amended section 117 to read:

> Notwithstanding the provisions of section 106, it is not an infringement for the owner of a copy of a computer program to make or authorize the making of another copy or adaptation of that computer program provided:
>
> (1) that such a new copy or adaptation is created as an essential step in the utilization of the computer program in conjunction with a machine and that it is used in no other manner, or
>
> (2) that such new copy or adaptation is for archival purposes only and that all archival copies are destroyed in the event that continued possession of the computer program should cease to be rightful.
>
> Any exact copies prepared in accordance with the provisions of this section may be leased, sold, or otherwise transferred, along with the copy from which such copies were prepared, only as part of the lease, sale, or other transfer of all rights in the program. Adaptations so prepared may be transferred only with the authorization of the copyright owner.

While this section represents an attempt to anticipate statutorily the difficulties of applying the "fair use" doctrine to copyrighted programs, problems may still arise. For one thing, a significant change from the CONTU proposals on this point was the use in section 117 of the term "owner," rather than "rightful possessor" of a copy of a program. This greatly limits the scope of the exemption, as a lawful possessor will quite often not technically "own" a piece of software. Moreover, the Supreme Court's recent ruling in *Sony Corp. of Amer. v. Universal City Studios*[34]

---

30   *Ibid.*
31   *Ibid.*
32   Public Law 96-517, 94 Stat. 3028-29 (Dec. 12, 1980).
33   Some commentators felt that the use of the phrase "directly or indirectly" in the statutory definition of "computer program" amounted to a clear indication that protection was to extend to object code. For example, Christopher Kern, a lawyer writing in the computer enthusiasts' magazine *Byte*, confidently asserted that "[t]he word 'directly' refers, of course, to the object code." ("Washington Tackles the Software Problem," Byte (May 1981), 128 at 130). Others were, however, more cautious, *e.g.*, Root, "Protecting Computer Software in the 80s: Practical Guidelines for Evolving Needs." (1981), Rutgers Computers and Technology L.J. 205.
34   52 L.W. 4090 (Jan. 17, 1984), reversing 659 F. 2d 963 (9th Cir., 1981), 480 F. Supp. 429 (C.D. Cal., 1976).

is an indicator of the generally uncertain scope of the "fair use" doctrine as applied to new technologies.[35]

3.3 Cases Arising under the 1909 Copyright Act: A Legacy of Confusion

Probably the two most important software copyright actions to arise prior to the coming into force the new legislation were *Synercom Technology Inc. v. Univ. Computing Co.,*[36] and *Data Cash Systems Inc. v. JS & A Group Inc.*[37] Both pointed to a narrow delimitation of copyright protection for programs, and *Data Cash* in particular cast a thick cloud of confusion over the issue of object code copyrightability.

Synercom concerned a claim of infringement of copyright in certain instruction manuals and input formats used with a computer program for structural analysis in engineering design.[38] The allegedly infringed software package, though not entirely original, represented a great improvement on earlier manuals and input formats and was held to be sufficiently original to warrant copyright protection.[39] The trial court found that the plaintiffs had invested substantial sums in marketing their package and had carefully trained customers in its use.[40] There was clear evidence that the defendants, though they vigorously denied doing so before the trial,[41] had deliberately set out to "pluck the fruit of Synercom's labors and risks" by marketing a package entirely compatible with Synercom's input formats.[42]

Synercom succeeded in its suit for copyright infringement of the manuals, but failed to establish any good cause of action with regard to

---

35   By a bare majority of five to four the Supreme Court found home videotaping to be fair use of the copyright in the respondent's films. For general discussions of the problems of applying the fair use doctrine to new technology see Timberg, "A Modernized Fair Use Code for the Electronic as well as the Guttenberg Age" (1980), 75 Northwestern Univ. L.R. 193-244; Walker, "Fair Use: The Adjustable Tool for Maintaining Copyright Equilibrium" (1983), 43 Louisiana L.R. 735-57.

36   462 F. Supp. 1000 (N.D. Tex., 1978).

37   480 F. Supp. 1063 (N.D. Ill., 1979); affirmed on other grounds 628 F. 2d. 1038 (7th Cir., 1980).

38   462 F. Supp. 1000 at 1004.

39   *Ibid.,* at 1006.

40   "[I]ncurred costs approached $500,000." *Ibid.,* at 1008.

41   *Ibid.,* at 1015.

42   *Ibid.,* at 1008.

the input formats. The court gave alternative grounds for rejecting the latter claim. Either the formats in question lacked sufficient originality of expression and were merely "expressed ideas," or, alternatively, input formats were *per se* uncopyrightable.[43] The court went further than this, however, and offered an opinion as to the scope of copyright protection for programs generally. While satisfied that it would be an infringing act to take a program from one high level language to another,[44] and that it would probably also be a violation of copyright to prepare a source code program from a detailed flow chart,[45] Judge Higginbotham felt that a firm line should be drawn at that point:

> [H]ere the similarity to literary translation ends. The preparation of a computer program in *any* language from a general description of the problem to be solved . . . is very dissimilar to the translation of a literary work, or to the translation of a program from one language to another. In most cases, the formulation of the problem in sufficient detail and with sufficient precision to enable it to be converted into an unambiguous set of computer instructions requires substantial imagination, creativity, independent thought, and exercise of discretion, and the resulting program can in no way be said to be merely a copy or version of the program statement. The program and the statement are so different, both in physical characteristics and in intended purpose, that they are really two different expressions of the same idea, rather than two different versions of the same expression.[46]

While purely *obiter,* this statement had substantial, and probably unintended, repercussions. In the *Data Cash* case, it was quoted in support of the proposition that "In its object phase . . . the computer program is a mechanical tool or machine part but it is not a 'copy' of the source program."[47] As will be seen, this seems to have been a gross misconstruction of the *dicta* in *Synercom.*

Briefly, the facts of *Data Cash* were as follows. The plaintiff company had commissioned the design of a program for a computerized hand-held chess game. It called the game "Compuchess" and began marketing it in 1977.[48] The essential program was encoded on a "read only memory" chip (a ROM).[49] In 1978, the defendants began marketing

---

43   *Ibid.,* at 1014.
44   "[I]t is as clear an infringement to translate a computer program from, for example, FORTRAN to ALGOL, as it is to translate a novel or play from English to French. In each case the substance of the expression (if one may speak in such contradictory language) is the same between original and copy, with only the external manifestation of the expression changing." *Ibid.,* at 1013 note 5.
45   *Ibid.*
46   *Ibid.*
47   480 F. Supp. 1063 at 1069.
48   *Ibid.,* at 1066.
49   *Ibid.,* at 1067.

a "Chess Computer" which contained a ROM identical to the plaintiff's. The plaintiff brought an action for copyright infringement and unfair competition. District Court Judge Flaum was satisfied that direct copying had occurred. He nevertheless granted summary judgment in favour of the defendants on the copyright infringement issue, on the ground that object code could not be protected and nothing else had been taken. Thus he concluded that the defendants had "a complete defence as a matter of law."[50]

In so ruling, Judge Flaum took a retrograde step in jurisprudential terms. He probably also caused considerable consternation in the software industry by speculating that he would have reached the same conclusion even if the 1976 Act had applied.[51] He argued that, by analogy with a building constructed from architectural plans, object code constituted the physical embodiment of a computer program. Just as, under American law, a building is not a "copy" of its plans, so too a ROM is not a "copy" of a source program.[52] Judge Flaum claimed support for this conclusion from two sources. First, he resurrected the old *White-Smith* "visible similarity" test. As we have seen, section 102 of the 1976 Act had once and for all laid this doctrine to rest in respect of works created from 1 January 1978.[53] Earlier works may still fall foul of *White-Smith,* however, and as one commentator has dryly observed, "the case stubbornly retains its legal force as well as its indisputable power to fascinate and confound attorneys and textwriters."[54] Indeed, *Data Cash* may represent "its last gasp."[55] The ruling in *White-Smith* was simply that a pianola roll could not infringe copyright in the sheet music from which it was copied, on the ground that it did not constitute "a copy which appeals to the eye."[56] This reasoning, which started the whole controversy over copyright in machine-readable works, was probably spurious even when it was decided in 1908.[57] Nevertheless, Judge Flaum had no

50   *Ibid.*
51   "[T]he court believes that the 1976 Act applies to computer programs in their flowchart, source and assembly phases but not in their object phase, *ie* the ROM" *Ibid.,* note 4.
52   *Ibid.,* at 1069.
53   See section 3.1, above.
54   Schmidt, "Legal Proprietory Interests in Computer Programs: The American Experience" (1981), 21 Jurimetrics J. 345 at 367.
55   *Ibid.,* at 368.
56   209 U.S. 1 at 17 (1908).
57   "It is true that most people cannot read pianola rolls. It is also true that 98% of the American public cannot read sheet music, but the Court found sheet music copyrightable." Miller, "Copyright and Computers" in Holmes and Norville, eds., *The Law of Computers* (Ann Arbor: Institute of Continuing Legal Education, 1971), at 110.

reservations in concluding that "since the ROM is not in a form which one can 'see and read' with the naked eye, it is not a 'copy' within the meaning of the 1909 Act."[58]

In attempting to draw support from the *Synercom dicta,* Judge Flaum was on even shakier ground. It will be recalled that the court in *Synercom* had suggested that a computer program in any language prepared from a general description of a problem "can in no way be said to be merely a copy or version of the problem statement."[59] This argument clearly concerned the preparation of a program from a set of instructions set out in even more general terms than a detailed flow chart. It has absolutely nothing to do with a translation from source to object code.

Not surprisingly, Data Cash appealed. Unfortunately, the Seventh Circuit expressly avoided the issue of object code copyrightability.[60] Instead, it affirmed the district court's decision on the different ground that, as a publication of the Chess program, Data Cash's ROM was not protected as it lacked the requisite copyright notice.[61] Yet in discussing the ROM as a publication, the court surely *was,* by implication at least, treating the object code as a protectible copy of the source program. If not, it would have made no sense to take into consideration the absence of a copyright notice. The only other possible construction of the Seventh Circuit's ruling is that a copyright notice on the ROM would have protected the underlying source code, but not the object code contained in the ROM. While one court cited *Data Cash* as support for just such a proposition,[62] an increasing number of cases decided under the new law favours both indirect and direct protection for programs in object code form.

3.4 Protection of Videogames and other Applications Programs

These are still early days for predicting the full implications of the new Copyright Act. Nevertheless, a judicial consensus is gradually emer-

---

58   480 F. Supp. 1063 at 1069.
59   462 F. Supp. 1000 at 1013, note 5.
60   "The parties had neither briefed nor argued that issue and neither side on appeal defends the district court's position, so we do not consider it further." 628 F. 2d 1038 at 1041.
61   The court had no sympathy for the plaintiffs' assertion that it did not realize that it was possible to unload the ROM and thus read their program. *Ibid.*
62   *Re Data Gen. Corp. Antitrust Litigation,* 490 F. Supp. 1089 (N.D. Cal., 1980).

ging as regards the scope of copyright protection for programs and data. Much of the litigation in this area has concerned alleged piracy of video games. In such instances, the straightforward copyrighting of the output of a game program as an audiovisual work can provide a means of indirectly protecting the object code in which it is stored. Perhaps due to the uncertainty caused by the *Data Cash* ruling, for some time following that decision plaintiffs sought only such indirect protection for their game programs.

The video game cases have generally arisen where entrepreneurs have apparently "unloaded" ROMs containing a video game and have then marketed a variation of the game, usually under a different name. In *Midway Mfg. Co. v. Dirkshneider,*[63] the plaintiff, which had registered the copyrights in a number of games, including "Galaxian", "Pac-Man", and "Rally X", claimed infringement by the defendants' games "Galactic Invaders", "Mighty Mouth", and "Rally X". The plaintiff sought and obtained a preliminary injunction. In deciding the underlying issue of the games' copyrightability, Chief Judge Urbom made two inquiries. First, did the plaintiff's works fall within one of the copyrightable subject matters of the 1976 Act, and second, were they fixed in a tangible medium of expression?[64] He found the games to be copyrightable as audiovisual works under section 102(a)(6), and had no doubt that they were "fixed" in a manner which satisfied the statutory requirements:

> [I]t is clear that the plaintiff's audiovisual works are fixed in the printed circuit boards. The printed circuit boards are tangible objects from which the audio-visual works may be perceived for a period of time which is more than transitory. The fact that the audiovisual works cannot be viewed without a machine does not mean the works are not fixed.[65]

The other criteria necessary for a successful infringement action had also apparently been satisfied. On the question of notice, the court found that, although there was no copyright notice on the printed circuit boards themselves, the affixing of a notice on the game cabinets or within the visual display was sufficient.[66] Regarding proof of copying, while a plaintiff must normally show both access to his or her work and that the defendant's work is substantially similar, the need to prove

---

63   543 F. Supp. 466 (D. Neb., 1981).

64   *Ibid.,* at 479.

65   *Ibid.,* at 480.

66   *Ibid.,* at 482. The court was impressed that the plaintiff had complied with proposed regulations for the notice section (s. 401(c)) found in 37 F.C.R. ss. 201-20(g)(1) and (3).

access may be waived where similarity is striking.[67] This was so in the present case.[68] The direct issue of program copyright was avoided, however. The defendant argued that the plaintiff was in effect trying to protect the computer programs contained in the printed circuit boards of the games and, since those programs were not registered for copyright purposes, no infringement suit could be brought. The court disagreed and held that the plaintiff's action concerned audiovisual works, the copyright in which had been properly registered.[69]

A number of other district courts soon reached similar conclusions. In *Atari Inc. v. Amusement World Inc.*,[70] an application for a preliminary injunction to restrain the defendants from infringing the copyright in certain games was denied on the facts. Nevertheless, the court stated its belief that video games were copyrightable as audiovisual works, and that a printed circuit board was an adequate "medium of expression" for the purposes of section 102 of the Act.[71] The plaintiff claimed that the copyright in its video game "Asteroids" had been infringed by the defendants' game "Meteors." The case turned on the degree of similarity between the works and, more fundamentally, on whether anything more than the underlying "idea" of the plaintiff's game had been taken. Judge Young saw the idea/expression distinction to work as follows:

> Defendants are entitled to use the idea of a video game involving asteroids, so long as they adopt a different expression of the idea - *ie* a version of such a game that uses symbols, movements, and sounds that are different from those used in the plaintiff's game.[72]

On the facts, the court found that the defendants had only used the idea of the game, together with "those portions of plaintiff's expressions that were inextricably linked to that idea."[73] Thus the test of substantial similarity was not satisfied, and infringement could not be shown.[74]

---

67   *Ibid.*, at 482. On this point see also *Atari Inc. v. North Amer. Inc.*, 672 F. 2d 607 (7th Cir., 1982).

68   *Ibid.*, at 483.

69   *Ibid.*, at 481.

70   547 F. Supp. 222 (D. Md., 1981).

71   "A video game's printed circuit board is clearly such a medium of expression, since the 'work,' the audiovisual presentation, can be communicated from the printed circuit board with the aid of the game's display screen." *Ibid.*, at 226.

72   *Ibid.*, at 227.

73   *Ibid.*

74   *Ibid.* A similar conclusion was reached in *Atari Inc. v. Williams*, 217 U.S.P.Q. 746 (E.D. Cal., 1981): "[T]he unprotectable idea includes the rules, strategy of the . . . game. . . . There is no similarity between the expression of the games of Plaintiff and

Substantial similarity may occur despite the fact that the works in question are stored in different media. In *Midway v. Bandai Amer. Inc.*[75] the owner of the copyright in certain arcade video games (and a licencee) obtained an injunction against a distributor of handheld versions of a game. An injunction was also granted in *Atari Inc. v. North Amer. Inc.*[76] where the defendants had allegedly made a home video version of a coin-operated arcade game.

The first appeal court ruling in a video game copyright case, *Stern v. Kaufman*,[77] went some way towards clarifying the status of programs contained in ROMs. The Second Circuit affirmed an order enjoining the defendants from infringing the plaintiff's copyright and trade mark in a game called "Scramble." The program for "Scramble" was contained in a version of a ROM known as a "programmable read only memory" (or PROM).[78] While the plaintiff was only seeking protection for the game's display as an audiovisual work, the PROM was relevant regarding the question of fixation. Mr. Justice Newman, for the court, asserted that "the memory devices of the game satisfy the statutory requirement of a 'copy' in which the work is 'fixed' ".[79] In a footnote he went further and made the more general observation that:

> Whether located in the PROM prepared for this particular game or elsewhere in the total assembly, all portions of the program, once stored in memory devices anywhere in the game, are fixed in a tangible medium within the meaning of the Act.[80]

As the plaintiff was only claiming protection for the images and sounds of "Scramble" and not for the game's program *per se,* these latter comments are *obiter.* Nevertheless, in *Stern v. Kaufman,* the Second Circuit laid the foundations for an appeal court to address directly the issue of copyright in video game programs.

Such an opportunity arose in *Williams v. Artic.*[81] In that case the defendant company was appealing a district court's final injunction order restraining and enjoining it from infringing the plaintiff's copyrights, not only in certain audiovisual works, but also in a computer program relating to the video game "Defender." As the Third Circuit noted, this was the first time the issue of program copyright had arisen

---

Defendant because the symbols and graphics of the game are such that the ordinary observer would not notice the similarity." *Ibid.,* at 748.
75   546 F. Supp. 125 (D.N.J., 1982).
76   672 F. 2d 607 (7th Cir., 1982).
77   669 F. 2d 852 (2d Cir., 1982); affirming 523 F. Supp. 635 (N.Y., 1981).
78   See section 1.2.3., above, for a definition of a PROM.
79   669 F. 2d 852 at 855.
80   *Ibid.,* at 856, note 4.
81   685 F. 2d 870 (3rd Cir., 1982).

directly in such a case.[82] Mr. Justice Sloviter, for the court, dealt first with the copyright in the games as audiovisual works. He dismissed the defendant's argument that ROMs could not be protected as they were merely "utilitarian objects or machine parts:"[83]

> The issue in this case is not whether plaintiff, if it sought, could protect the ROM itself under the copyright laws. Rather, before us is only the plaintiff's effort to protect its artistic expression in original works which have met the statutory fixation requirement through their embodiment in the ROM devices.[84]

This conclusion was consistent with the *dicta* of *Stern v. Kaufman.*

On the program copyright issue, the defendant claimed that the copyright in a computer program is not infringed when a program is "loaded into electronic memory devices and used to control the activity of machines."[85] As a related point, the defendant asserted that a distinction should be drawn between source and object code. A program in the latter form should not be deemed a protectible "copy" as it was not "intelligible to human beings" nor "intended as a medium of communication to them."[86] The Third Circuit was evidently not impressed by these arguments. Mr. Justice Sloviter pointed out the comprehensive nature of section 101 of the 1976 Act and concluded that Congress clearly intended the provision to "encompass technological advances such as those represented by the electronic devices in this case." To follow the defendant's suggestion "would afford an unlimited loophole by which infringement of a computer program is limited to copying of the computer program text but not to duplication of a computer program fixed on a silicon chip."[87] This surely is the crux of the matter: unless copyright extends to object code, any claim to copyright in a work stored in a computer-readable form can be very easily defeated.

A few months prior to the Third Circuit's ruling in *Williams v. Artic,* an Illinois district court had reached a similar conclusion in another case involving the same defendant. In *Midway v. Artic*[88] the defence "launched a massive scattershot of arguments"[89] against Mid-

---

82   *Ibid.,* at 875.

83   *Ibid.,* at 876.

84   *Ibid.*

85   *Ibid.*

86   *Ibid.,* at 877. This was essentially the position which Commissioner Hersey had taken in his dissent to the CONTU Report. See section 2.5, above.

87   *Ibid.* The court was equally unimpressed with the defendant's reliance on the lower court's analysis in *Data Cash* and concluded that the defendant had "failed to provide any persuasive reason which would overcome the statutory presumption of the copyright registration."

88   547 F. Supp. 999 (N.D. Ill., 1982); affirmed 704 F. 2d 1009 (7th Cir., 1983).

89   547 F. Supp. at 1005.

way's claim that its copyrights in Galaxian and Pac-Man had been infringed. The defendant had been selling "speed-up" kits for the Galaxian game and also marketed a game called "Puckman" which was "apart from trivial differences . . . absolutely identical to Midway's Pacman."[90] Artic resisted the infringement claims on the following grounds, *inter alia:* first, that the only protected versions of the game were those contained in the videotapes which had been submitted to the Copyright Office for registration;[91] secondly, that the fixation requirements of the Copyright Act had not been met;[92] and thirdly, that the games could not be copyrighted because they were utilitarian objects.[93]

All these defences were rejected by the court. On the first issue the court ruled that "the videotapes were merely copies of the protected work" which was "the audiovisual display reflecting the author's creativity."[94] Regarding fixation, the court ruled that the Copyright Act did not require that a work "be written down or recorded somewhere exactly as it is perceived by the human eye."[95] Rather, it merely needs to be in a form from which it can be "reproduced . . . with the aid of a machine or device."[96]

On the question of utility, the court noted that Artic had initially argued that the ROMs containing the games could not be copyrighted. Later they alleged that it was the games themselves which were unprotectible utilitarian works. Regarding the ROMs Judge Decker commented:

> While the court agrees that utilitarian objects may not be copyrighted, it appears that Artic had misconstrued the copyrights at issue in this case. . . . Midway has sought and obtained protection for the audiovisual aspects of its games that appear on the screen. Midway no more restricts the use of ROMs than an author with a valid copyright restricts the use of books.[97]

Thus the ROMs were not themselves protected works but simply a medium of fixation. The court also agreed with Artic's contention that games *per se* could not be copyrighted, but again distinguished the plaintiff's claims. Midway's copyrights resided not in their games but only in the artistic expression of those games.[98]

---

90   *Ibid.*
91   *Ibid.*, at 1006.
92   *Ibid.*, at 1007.
93   *Ibid.*, at 1008.
94   *Ibid.*, at 1007.
95   *Ibid.*
96   *Ibid.*, at 1008 quoting 17 U.S.C., s. 102(a).
97   *Ibid.*, at 1008-9.
98   *Ibid.*, at 1009.

Accordingly, Judge Decker was satisfied that a preliminary injunction should be ordered. In affirming this ruling on appeal, the Seventh Circuit analysed further a number of the trial issues. The problem of alteration of the game each time it is played has already been discussed.[99] Regarding the fixation of the copyrighted works in ROMs, the Seventh Circuit observed that "[r]ecording images and sounds in circuit boards does not destroy their copyrightability any more than does recording them on rolls of cellulose."[100] While it had no doubt that video games could be protected as audiovisual works, the court was less certain as to the effect of speed-up kits on the copyright in such games. The defendant had argued that speeding up a video game was analogous to playing at 45 or 78 RPMs a record recorded at 33. Chief Judge Cummings, for the Seventh Circuit, disagreed and pointed out as a practical distinction the "critical difference" that "there is an enormous demand for speeded-up video games but there is little if any demand for speeded-up records."[101] As a matter of law, the speeded-up games could be regarded as "derivative works" over which the copyright owner has exclusive rights.[102] The Chief Judge conceded that such games do not fit with complete ease the definition of derivative work in section 101 of the 1976 Act.[103] Nevertheless the court concluded that "the amount by which the language of section 101 must be stretched to accommodate speeded-up video games is, we believe, within the limits within which Congress wanted the new Act to operate."[104]

It was not until June 1983 that the question of copyright protection for video game programs *per se* was tackled by a court. The plaintiff in *Midway Mfg. v. Strohon*[105] claimed that the defendant's "speed-up" or "enhancement" kits infringed the copyright in the plaintiff's video game, "Pac-Man." On the facts, Judge Will found there to be no infringement of the game's audiovisual copyright since the defendant's "Cute-

---

99   See section 2.6, above.
100   704 F. 2d at 1012.
101   *Ibid.,* at 1013. Such games are not only more challenging for the player, but are also of shorter duration, thus potentially increasing the licencee's revenue from each machine. "Video game copyright owners would undoubtedly like to lay their hands on some of that extra revenue and therefore it cannot be assumed that licencees are implicitly authorized to use speeded-up circuit boards in the machines plaintiff supplies."
102   Under 17 U.S.C., s. 106(2).
103   704 F. 2d at 1014.
104   *Ibid.*
105   564 F. Supp. 741 (N.D. Ill., 1983).

See" version of the game used quite different characters from those in "Pac-Man."[106]

The court did find, however, that, where an enhancement kit was only partly installed, the resulting "Cute-See" game was substantially similar to "Pac-Man". Such partial modification had been discouraged by the defendant and, accordingly, the court rejected Midway's allegation of contributory infringement by Artic. On this point Judge Will distinguished the Ninth Circuit's ruling in *Universal City Studios v. Sony* since there the infringing use had been found to be "intended, expected, encouraged, and ... the source of the product's consumer appeal."[107] In any event, the *Sony* judgment has since been reversed by the United States Supreme Court.[108]

Thus the infringement claims relating to the game as an audiovisual work failed. However, the court gave separate consideration to a claim of infringement of copyright in the game's underlying computer program, rejecting the defendant's contention that "the program and display are intertwined to the extent that it is impossible to consider one without the other."[109] Rather the program, for which copyright had been registered separately, was a "distinct creation."[110]

Turning to the definition of "computer program" in section 101 of the 1976 Act, Judge Will found it to be "certain as a general matter that the current copyright legislation is intended to protect object code as well as source code."[111] For there to be any realistic protection for programs, such a conclusion was a logical necessity.[112] Moreover, the physical medium in which object code is stored does not affect the availability of copyright protection:

> The fact that, as we understand it, electrical current moves through a silicon chip rather than being remotely directed in its movement by information on a tape or disc, does not in our view serve as a tenable basis for concluding that a ROM is somehow

---

106   *Ibid.*, at 747.

107   659 F. 2d at 975.

108   52 L.W. 4090 (Jan. 18, 1984).

109   564 F. Supp. at 749.

110   *Ibid.* In *Stern v. Kaufman* the Second Circuit had recognized that a video game copyright could be infringed by means of a quite different program. Here the court concluded that "[t]he converse possibility ... that a game's computer program but not its audiovisuals could be an infringement, is not foreclosed as a matter of logic and should not be as a matter of policy."

111   *Ibid.*, at 750.

112   "To allow protection of the source code version of a program would be pyrrhic indeed if the object code version, the mechanical implementation of the same program, stored and marketed on discs or tapes, for example, could be freely reproduced without constituting an infringement." *Ibid.*, at 750.

more "utilitarian" than a tape or disc. In both cases, the function of the object is to store information which directs the operation of a computer.[113]

In the light of recent decisions dealing with protection for operating systems,[114] it seems unlikely that the ratio of *Strohon* will be upset. Thus it now seems settled that in the United States video games can be protected by both audiovisual copyright in their displays and literary copyright in their underlying programs. Similar protection is presumably also available for other types of applications programs.

3.5 Protection of Operating Systems

It was relatively easy for American judges to find that copyright works are not deprived of protection simply because of their storage in computer readable form. Applications software such as that used in video game machines generally produces output in which copyright can subsist, and section 101 of the 1976 Act has made it quite clear that copyrighted material can be fixed in any form. From this point it was a logical step to conclude that Congress must have intended applications programs to be protected *per se* as literary works. What has proved more problematic for the courts is the status of operating programs in machine code form which regulate the functioning of a computer without necessarily producing copyrightable output. While it now seems clear that these programs are literary works entitled to the full protection of copyright, the various theoretical objections to object code copyright have been raised in litigation. The first reported case on the point arising under the Act was *Tandy Corp. v. Personal Micro Computers Inc.*[115]

Tandy alleged that an "input-output routine" used in one of its home computers, the Radio Shack TRS-80, had been copied by the defendants for use in their own computer designed for home use, the PMC-80.[116] The program in question was contained in a ROM. The

---

113   *Ibid.*, at 751-2.
114   See section 3.5, below.
115   524 F. Supp. 171 (N.D. Cal., 1981).
116   Input/output (I/O) routines are "Routines specifically designed to simplify the programming of standard operations involving input/output equipment, e.g. the blocking of records, use of input/output buffers." Chandour, *The Penguin Dictionary of Computers* (Harmondsworth: Penguin Books, 1977), p. 216. The contentious program in *Tandy* was a *compiler, i.e.,* a program which converts source code instructions into object code, and was thus not strictly speaking an I/O routine, though it might have made use of such routines. Such technical imprecision in judgments has not been uncommon in computer-related litigation.

defendants contended that a ROM was not a copy of the original computer program and thus the copying of a ROM could not infringe the copyright in that program. The plaintiff, however, argued that storage in a ROM was a valid form of "fixation" under the Copyright Act, and thus a program in that form was itself copyrightable. The court looked to sections 101 and 102 of the Act and declared itself convinced that:

> (1) a computer program is a "work of authorship" subject to copyright, and (2) that a silicon chip is [sic] "tangible medium of expression", within the meaning of that statute such as to make a program fixed in that form subject to the copyright laws.[117]

In reaching these conclusions, Chief Judge Peckham reviewed the legislative history of the 1976 Act and noted the all-inclusive nature of the definition of "fixed form" in section 102(a).[118] Moreover, he concluded that Congress understood computer programs to have been copyrightable even prior to the new Act.[119] The latter conclusion is *obiter,* as the Chief Judge rejected an argument by the defendants that section 117, the freezing provision, compelled the court to apply pre-1978 law in determining whether the ROM was a "copy." His reasoning is significant:

> [S]ection 117, as it existed in the 1976 Act, was aimed at the problem of copyrighted material inputted into a computer, such as books, magazines, and even computer programs. It was not intended to provide a loophole by which someone could duplicate a computer program fixed on a silicon chip. It did not refer to the unauthorized duplication of a silicon chip upon which a properly copyrighted computer program is imprinted. Such a *duplication* of a chip is not the use of a copyrighted program "in conjunction with" a computer; it is simply the copying of a chip. Moreover, any other interpretation would render the theoretical ability to copyright computer programs virtually meaningless.[120]

With the repeal of section 117, the first part of this argument became of historical interest only. The second part, however, retains at least its logical force. As with applications programs, if the contents of ROMs can not be protected, the copyright in many operating programs will rapidly evaporate.

The court in *Tandy* was fully aware that this interpretation departed from the ruling of the Illinois district court in *Data Cash.* Although in no way bound by that earlier decision, Chief Judge Peckham was careful to distance himself from it. He observed that the Seventh Circuit in *Data Cash,* while explicitly avoiding the issue of object code

---

117   524 F. Supp. at 173.
118   *Ibid.*
119   This conclusion was based on the discussion of "works of authorship" in the House Report, Judiciary Committee, 94th Congress, 2nd sess. 1976, H. Rep. 1476 at 173.
120   *Ibid.,* at 174-5.

copyrightability, had implicitly rejected the lower court's reasoning on the point. Of the district court's ruling he added, "nor are we convinced of the merits of the basis of that decision."[121]

As further support for the plaintiff's case, Chief Judge Peckham noted that the chip may have been duplicated by a two stage process which would undoubtedly have necessitated infringement of the copyright in the program:

> [T]he plaintiff has suggested that the evidence may well show that the chip was duplicated by first taking a visual display or printout of the program in question, making a copy of that display or printout, and then having that program imprinted on a silicon chip. . . . If this method of unauthorized duplication in fact is proved, there can be no doubt that the unauthorized duplication of a visually displayed copy of the program would fall within the reach of the federal copyright laws.[122]

Thus, a *prima facie* case had been made out that the program copyright had been infringed either directly, by duplication of the ROM, or indirectly, by "unloading" the ROM and copying the resulting printout or visual display.

In *GCA Corp. v. Chance*[123] a Californian district court followed the approach of the *Tandy* court to copyright in object code operating programs. The case concerned, *inter alia,* allegations of copyright infringement in certain diagnostic and operating systems owned by GCA. In granting a preliminary injunction, Judge Patel ruled that copyright protection was available for programs of all types in both source and object code form.[124] However, in *Apple Computer Inc. v. Franklin Computer Corp.,*[125] a Pennsylvania district court again raised serious doubts as to the copyrightability of operating systems.

In *Apple v. Franklin* the plaintiffs sought a preliminary injunction to restrain the defendants from "using, copying, selling, or infringing in any other way first computer company's registered copyrights on object codes expressing operating programs."[126] The motion was denied. Following a review of the relevant sections of the 1976 Act, its legislative history, the case law to date and academic commentaries on the subject,

---

121 *Ibid.,* at 175.
122 *Ibid.*
123 217 U.S.P.Q. 718 (N.D. Cal., July 12, 1982).
124 "Plaintiff's source code falls within the protection of copyright as a work of authorship fixed in any tangible medium of expression from which it can be communicated. . . . Because the object code is the encryption of the copyrighted source code, the two are to be treated as one work; therefore, copyright of the source code protects the object code as well." *Ibid.,* at 720.
125 545 F. Supp. 812 (E.D. Pa., 1982).
126 *Ibid.,* at 812.

Judge Newcomer concluded that the issues of the copyrightability of operating systems and the status of object code stored in ROMs had by no means been resolved.[127] Thus, while the plaintiff's position was "not implausible,"[128] the judge had "considerable doubts about its likelihood of success on the merits."[129]

Judge Newcomer was especially concerned at the utilitarian nature of the programs and their lack of communicative purpose. He placed considerable emphasis on the differences between "operating" and "application" programs in terms of their functions and output:

> An application program has a specific task, ordinarily chosen by the user, such as to maintain records, perform certain calculations, or display graphic images. Application programs are normally written in high level languages which are designed to be easily used by the unsophisticated. An operating program, by contrast, is generally internal to the computer and is designed only to facilitate the operating of the application program.[130]

Thus, application programs generally produce human intelligible output, whereas operating programs merely facilitate the working of the computer as a machine. Indeed, the court went further and suggested that "it may be more accurate to say that operating systems are an essential element of the machine."[131]

The operating programs at issue in the case were stored either on floppy discs or in ROMs. Judge Newcomer paid little attention to the former but discussed the ROMs in some detail. On the question of utility, three contentious points were identified. First, could a ROM be viewed as a three-dimensional, pictorial, graphic or sculptural work, or should it rather be compared to a "physical structure with an essentially useful purpose or function, like that of a bridge . . . or to an architectural work like a house"?[132] Judge Newcomer felt that the court in *Tandy,* by implicitly adopting the former construction, had "contradict[ed] somewhat the view of the CONTU Majority that a 'tapped off' ROM may not be protected from copyright infringement."[133]

This reference to CONTU is worth pursuing briefly as it illustrates how easily the fine distinctions in this area can be blurred. In fact, the CONTU Report never mentions ROMs.[134] Indeed, the passage to which

---

127   *Ibid.,* at 817.
128   *Ibid.,* at 819.
129   *Ibid.,* at 825.
130   *Ibid.,* at 814.
131   *Ibid.,* at 821.
132   *Ibid.,* at 823 (citations omitted).
133   *Ibid.*
134   Indeed, as has already been noted, the question of copyright protection for IC chips was left undiscussed. CONTU, p. 79.

Judge Newcomer was referring made it quite clear that, when a program is loaded into the memory of a computer, "it still exists in a form from which a human-readable version can be produced,"[135] and thus can still be protected. The ability to be copied is in this sense only lost when the program is actually processed so that "electrical impulses are sent through the circuitry of the processor to initiate work."[136] It was to these impulses that the Report referred when it mentioned "tapping-off" and not to a program stored in discs, ROMs or any other non-volatile memory. A human-readable copy can certainly be produced from a ROM.

The defendant's second line of attack was the assertion that "the programmed ROM is an object that merges idea and expression to the point they are indistinguishable . . . or merges its utilitarian function and expressive purpose so that they too are inseparable."[137] Such a construction clearly points to patent rather than copyright law as the appropriate device for protecting operating systems. While noting that some firmware has already been successfully patented, Judge Newcomer was careful to point out that there could obviously be no guarantee that Apple's programs would "satisfy the rather rigorous test of the patent law."[138]

Finally, the subject of communication was discussed. The court felt the critical issue to be the following: "no matter how exotic the form of expression or the medium used, the question must be: is the expression directed to a human audience?"[139] The origins of this criterion were traced to the cases of *Baker v. Selden*[140] and *Accord Taylor Instrument Co. v. Fawley-Brost Co.*[141] The ruling in *Baker* was that, while a copyright owner could protect the description of an accounting form in a book, the owner could not exercise any control over the form itself: "the object of the one is explanation; the object of the other is use."[142] In *Taylor,* the Tenth Circuit established that the distinction between explanation and use was also the appropriate demarcation line between copyright protection (for that which "teaches . . . [and] explains the use of the art"), and patent protection (for that which "is an essential element of the machine").[143] Judge Newcomer concluded that these two

---

135   *Ibid.,* at 22.
136   *Ibid.*
137   545 F. Supp. at 823 (citations omitted).
138   *Ibid.,* at 824.
139   *Ibid.*
140   101 U.S. 99 (1879).
141   139 F. 2d 98 (10th Cir., 1943).
142   101 U.S. 99 at 105.
143   139 F. 2d at 100 (quoted in *Apple*).

cases suggested a limitation of the scope of copyright "to material that can claim an underlying expressive or communicative purpose."[144] The protection granted to ROM-based video games was quite consistent with this test, as the purpose of such works was "to generate an image that could be *perceived* and its goal was to attract and engage a human audience."[145] Such protection should not however be afforded to programs with only machine "audiences."

This district court ruling and the appeal which followed are undoubtedly a watershed in the debate surrounding program copyright, and in these rulings the various theoretical objections to a broad extension of copyright protection to software have finally received thorough judicial scrutiny.[146] The principal grounds for unease are not difficult to grasp. On the one hand, the possibility of a distinction between operating and applications programs as a demarcation between the domains of copyright and patent law is certainly attractive.[147] But at the same time, "[i]t is indeed ironic that an intent to advance 'science and useful arts' should ultimately promote questionably useful video games yet deny protection to the clearly valuable operating software of the Apple personal computer."[148]

Judge Newcomer's ruling was appealed to the Court of Appeals for the Third Circuit. Meanwhile, after the *Franklin* appeal had been argued but before judgment was handed down, Apple obtained a preliminary injunction in a California action concerning some of the same programs but a different defendant. The defendant in *Apple v. Formula*[149] had marketed computer kits under the trade mark "Pineapple."[150] The external appearance of the assembled computer was "virtually indistinguishable" from the Apple II computer, and some of the programs supplied with the kits were "virtually identical copies" of five of Apple's programs.[151] Judge Irving Hill granted an injunction restraining Formula both from using the name "Pineapple" or other trade marks confusingly similar to

---

144   545 F. Supp. at 824.

145   *Ibid.*, at 825 (emphasis supplied).

146   See section 2.1, above, for the background to the debate.

147   Chisum, "Copyright, Computer Programs and the Apple Cases: A Compromise Solution," [1983] 9 E.I.P.R. 233.

148   Brody, "Copyright Protection for Video Games, Computer Programs and Other Cybernetic Works" (1983), 5 Comm/Ent 477-515 at 489.

149   562 F. Supp. 775 (C.D. Cal., 1983).

150   It did not, however, manufacture the kits but purchased them from Taiwanese and Hong Kong suppliers. *Ibid.*, at 777.

151   *Ibid.*, at 778.

the plaintiff's and from further infringing Apple's copyrights in its five programs.[152]

Formula had conceded that the programs in question satisfied the Copyright Act requirement of fixation and also that a program protected in source code would not lose protection merely by being converted into object code. What the defence had disputed, however, was the availability of copyright protection for such programs as are "integral to the operation of the machine [and] which do not directly produce visual communication with the user of the machine."[153] The programs in issue were all of this type. In support of this argument, the defendants relied mainly on the statement in section 102(b) of the Copyright Act that copyright protection would never extend to "any idea, procedure, system, method of operation, concept, principle, or discovery." However, Judge Hill felt this to be a misapplication of the section, the purpose of which was to distinguish copyrightability from patentability rather than to define categories of copyrightable subject matter.[154] The court was equally unconvinced by the defendant's reliance on the distinction between "expression" and "use" set out in *Baker v. Seldon*.[155] On the contrary, the court declared that "*all* computer programs are designed to operate a machine in such a way as to ultimately produce some useful communication to the user."[156]

This raises a significant issue. Should copyright be available in respect of any and every part of a computer system which contributes to a process of useful communication? As Chisum has observed, "[a]ll the 'hardware' in a computer – the keyboard, screen, printer, telephone system, *etc.* – work together to eventually result in communication."[157] Why should not these be protected along with operating systems? The simple answer is that, regardless of how "hard" a form they are fixed in, all programs can reasonably be viewed as "writings" of some kind, whereas hardware components can not. A line has to be drawn somewhere. Having ruled out hardware components from copyright protection, however, it makes little sense to draw a distinction between operating and application programs in terms of communication. Many operating programs are in fact used to initiate communication with a

---

152   *Ibid.*, at 779.
153   *Ibid.*, at 780.
154   *Ibid.*
155   101 U.S. 99 (1879).
156   562 F. Supp. at 780.
157   [1983] 9 E.I.P.R. at 234.

user via screen and keyboard.[158] Conversely, application programs do n
merely produce communication, but also function extensively
organisers of hardware.

The court in *Formula* examined the legislative history of the nev
Copyright Act and found there to be "no doubt" that Congress in the
1980 Software Copyright Act had implemented the "crystal clear"
CONTU recommendation of protection for *all* computer programs regardless of their method of fixation or function.[159] Judge Irving Hill also
found this construction to be consistent with public policy goals. Formula had argued that Apple was attempting to use copyright as a device
to "preserve its market position and hinder competition."[160] The court
disagreed, pointing out that Apple was not attempting to suppress the
marketing of "programs which performed the *exact same function or
purpose*" as their own, but only those which did so "in the *exact same
manner.*"[161] The court did comment, *obiter,* that "[i]f there were only
one or two ways to write a program for a particular function" then a grant
of copyright to the author of such a program "might in effect give its
author a patent on the idea itself."[162] That was not the case here.

The findings of the *Formula* court were endorsed by the Third
Circuit in its reversal of the district court's ruling in *Apple v. Franklin.*
Circuit Judge Sloviter, for the court, declared unequivocally that computer programs in both source and object code are "literary works" and
protectable as such, and that such protection extends to programs in
object code form embedded in ROMs.[163] Indeed, he found both of these
issues to have been foreclosed by the court's earlier ruling in *Williams v.
Artic.*[164] The question of the copyrightability of operating system programs was new to the court and merited a deeper analysis.[165]

Regarding Franklin's contention that the operating programs were
processes, systems or methods of operation and therefore within the
domain of patent not copyright law, the court commented: "Franklin
misapplies the distinction in this case. Apple does not seek to copyright
the method which instructs the computer to perform its operating

---

158 For example, when a formatting program is run, the user may be asked which disk is
     to be formatted and according to what configuration of tracks. The generation of such
     screen messages by operating programs is very common.
159 562 F. Supp. at 781.
160 *Ibid.,* at 782.
161 *Ibid.* (emphasis supplied).
162 *Ibid.*
163 714 F. 2d 1240 at 1249.
164 685 F. 2d 870 (3rd Cir., 1982), discussed in section 3.4, above.
165 714 F. 2d at 1249.

functions but only the functions themselves."[166] Moreover, the court
pointed to the inconsistency in Franklin's position in that it had conceded that copyright could subsist in applications programs. In fact both
operating and applications programs "instruct the computer to do something."[167] Turning to the claim that operating systems were essentially
machine parts, the court again found the defendant to be focussing
wrongly on "the physical characteristics of the instructions," whereas in
fact "the medium is not the message."[168] The court also observed that the
utilitarian use objection had been laid to rest thirty years previously by
the Supreme Court in *Mazer v. Stein*.[169] Still on the question of the
patent/copyright distinction the court found perhaps the most convincing pointer to be the absence of any distinction between application and
operating programs in the statutory definition of computer program in
section 101 of the Copyright Act.[170]

The court proceded with a little more caution in dealing with the
idea/expression dichotomy, as expressly recognized in the section 102(b)
preclusion of copyright for "any idea." In the present context, the court
felt that the line between idea and expression "must be a pragmatic one"
and that the balance between competition and protection must be taken
into consideration.[171] The central question was deemed to be whether
the functions performed by Apple's operating systems could be achieved
by means of different programs, thus indicating that merger of idea and
expression had not occurred.[172] This question of fact was one to be dealt
with, if necessary, by the trial court. Accordingly, the Third Circuit
reversed the denial of the preliminary injunction and remanded the case
for reconsideration. Franklin failed to obtain a rehearing of its appeal[173]
and has since settled its dispute with Apple out of court.[174]

---

166 *Ibid.*, at 1250.
167 *Ibid.*, at 1251.
168 *Ibid.*
169 347 U.S. 201 at 218 (1954), discussed in section 2.4, above.
170 17 USC, s. 101 defines a computer program as "a set of statements or instructions to be
     used directly or indirectly in a computer in order to bring about a certain result."
171 714 F. 2d at 1253.
172 The court found Franklin's desire to make its computers totally compatible with the
     Apple II to be "a commercial and competitive objective which does not enter into the
     somewhat metaphysical issue of whether particular ideas and expressions have
     merged." *Ibid.*
173 Rehearing and Rehearing *en banc* denied, Sept. 23, 1983. *Ibid.*
174 "Franklin Settles with Apple," Businessweek (Jan. 16, 1984) at 24. The agreement
     included the following terms: $2.5 million payment by Franklin to Apple; Apple to
     review replacement operating systems which Franklin is developing; meanwhile
     Franklin can continue to sell its computers with Apple's software. *Ibid.*

The rulings in these two Apple cases have greatly clarified the status of programs under the new American copyright legislation, but the issue of copyrightability of programs is only one of many matters which the courts must address. The problematic nature of the "authorship" concept in computer-assisted works has already been mentioned.[175] Other areas of continuing uncertainty include the application of the fair use doctrine, the rights of copyright owners whose works are stored in both on- and off-line data bases, and the extent to which copyright protection covers microcode and microprograms.[176]

One area of uncertainty which has recently been clarified is the question of copyright protection for integrated circuit chip designs.

3.6 The Semiconductor Chip Protection Act 1984

Although it remains open to the Supreme Court to take a different view, the *Apple* cases have for the time being at least established that copyright protection is available under the 1976 Act for programs fixed in any medium, including ROM. It was left to Congress, however, to determine the availability of protection for designs of semiconductor chips. A single chip might contain not merely programs in "hard-wired" form in ROM, but also elements generally considered to be "hardware" such as a central processing unit and RAM. With copyright protection available, indirectly at least, for a ROM configured in a particular way, a given chip might be partly protected by copyright and partly unprotected.

The process of designing the masks from which chips are manufactured is both lengthy and expensive. Such masks can, however, be reverse engineered with relative ease by means of photographic processes and a given chip can thus be reproduced at a fraction of the original development costs.[177] In 1979, Congressman Edwards of California introduced Bill H.R. 1007 which would have extended the Copyright Act's definition of "pictorial, graphic, and sculptured works" so as to include "the photographic masks used to imprint patterns on integrated

---

175   See section 2.6, above.
176   See Harris, "Apple Computer Inc. v. Franklin Computer Corp. – Does a ROM a Computer Program Make?" (1984), Jurimetrics J. 248-53.
177   For a detailed discussion of the practical and legal issues in the chip protection debate see Oxman, "Intellectual Property Protection and Integrated Circuit Masks" (1980), 20 Jurimetrics J. 405-59.

circuit chips and . . . the imprinted patterns themselves." The Bill was not acted on.[178]

In January 1983, Representative Edwards introduced the somewhat more tightly drafted Bill H.R. 1028 to amend the Copyright Act so as "to protect semiconductor chips and masks against unauthorized duplication." Like H.R. 1007, H.R. 1028 would have extended a conventional form of copyright protection to "mask works."[179] The Senate Judiciary Committee subsequently approved a version of Bill H.R. 1028 framed in these terms.[180] The House Subcommittee on Courts, Civil Liberties and the Administration of Justice adopted a quite different version of the Bill, however, which would have established a completely new form of protection for chip products.[181] A joint House/Senate Committee reached a compromise between the two versions of the Bill, and a revised Bill was passed by Congress in October 1984.[182]

The Semiconductor Chip Protection Act 1984 has added a new Chapter 9 to title 17 of the U.S. Code.[183] Provided certain conditions are satisfied, protection is available under the Act for "a mask work fixed in a semiconductor chip product."[184] In addition to the fixation requirement,[185] to be protected a mask work must be "original,"[186] and must not

---

178   A further chip protection Bill introduced in 1981 (H.R. 7207) also failed.
179   Protection under H.R. 1028 would, however, only have been for ten years and not the usual copyright term.
180   S. 1201.
181   H.R. 5525.
182   The Semiconductor Chip Protection Act of 1984 (Title III of H.R. 6163) was passed by the Senate on October 3, 1984 and by the House of Representatives on September 9, 1984. Signed by President Reagan on November 8, 1984, the Act resembles much more closely H.R. 5525 than S. 1201.
183   Chapters 1-8 contain the Copyright Act.
184   17 U.S.C., s. 902(a)(1). "Mask work" is defined as "a series of related images, however fixed or encoded – (A) having or representing the predetermined, three-dimensional pattern of metallic, insulating, or semiconducting material present or removed from the layers of a semiconductor chip product; and (B) in which series the relation of the images to one another is that each image has the pattern of the surface of one form of the semiconductor chip product" (s. 901(a)(2)). "Semiconductor chip product" is defined as "the final or intermediate form of any product – (A) having two or more layers of metallic, insulating, or semiconducting material, deposited or otherwise placed on, or etched away or otherwise removed from, a piece of semiconductor material in accordance with a predetermined pattern; and (B) intended to perform electronic circuitry functions" (s. 901(a)(1)).
185   The test for fixation is whether a mask work's "embodiment in the product is sufficiently permanent or stable to permit the mask work to be perceived or reproduced from the product for a period of more than transitory duration" (s. 901(a)(3)).
186   Section 901(b)(1).

be a design or an unoriginal variation of a design which is "staple, commonplace, or familiar in the semiconductor industry."[187] Moreover, protection is only available in respect of a mask work if either the owner satisfies a nationality or domicile requirement,[188] or the work is first "commercially exploited" in the United States.[189] Protection runs for ten years from the date of registration of a mask work or the date on which it is first commercially exploited, whichever is sooner.[190] Registration is not a prerequisite for protection, but protection will end if a work is not registered within two years of first commercial exploitation.[191] A "mask work notice" may be affixed to mask works and semiconductor chip products embodying them.[192] A notice must consist of the words "mask work" or the symbol "M" or the letter M in a circle, together with the name of the owner or owners of the mask work.[193]

Protection of a mask work under the Act gives the owner the exclusive rights to do or authorize any of the following:

> (1) to reproduce the mask work by optical, electronic, or any other means; (2) to import or distribute a semiconductor chip product in which the mask work is embodied; and (3) to induce or knowingly to cause another person or do any of the acts described in paragraphs (1) and (2).[194]

---

187 Section 902(b)(2). The Act expressly excludes from protection "any idea, procedure, process, system, method of operation, concept, principle, or discovery" (s. 902(c)).

188 An owner will qualify under s. 902(a)(1)(A) if, at the time of registration of the mask work or its first exploitation anywhere in the world, he or she is "(i) a national or domiciliary of the United States, (ii) a national, domiciliary, or sovereign authority of a foreign nation that is a party to a treaty affording protection to mask works to which the United States is also a party [at the time of writing no such treaty had been made], or (iii) a stateless person." An owner may also qualify if a mask work comes within the scope of a Presidential proclamation regarding a particular nation (s. 902(a)(2)). At the time of writing no such proclamations had been made. Section 914 contains "International transitional provisions" which somewhat mitigate the potentially prejudicial effect of the s. 902 requirements for foreign owners. (See PTO "Guidelines for the Submission of Applications for Interim Protection of MaskWorks under 17 U.S.C. 914": 49 Fed. Reg. 44517.) Moreover, the provisions relating to the status of foreign owners must be reviewed by the Senate and House Judiciary Committees at the end of 1986 (s. 914(f)(2)), and the Secretary of Commerce may at any time extend the Act's application to nationals, domiciliaries, and sovereign authorities of a given foreign nation (s. 914(a)).

189 Section 902(a)(1)(B). For the definition of to "commercially exploit" see s. 901(a)(5).

190 Section 904.

191 Section 908(a). A certificate of registration constitutes *prima facie* evidence both of the facts stated in the certificate and that the registration requirements have been complied with (s. 908(f)).

192 Section 909(a). Affixation of a notice is not obligatory for protection but constitutes *prima facie* evidence that notice of protection has been given.

193 Section 909(b).

194 Section 905.

These "exclusive rights" are limited in three significant respects. First, there is an expanded version of the "fair use" exception found in the Copyright Act. Section 906 not only permits reproduction for purposes of teaching, analysis or evaluation, but also authorizes unrestricted use of the results of reverse engineering.[195] Secondly, the owner of a mask work cannot restrict the use, importation, distribution or other disposal of a particular chip product after its first sale.[196] Thirdly, the Act grants immunity to innocent purchasers of infringing chip products in some instances, and limited liability in others.[197] Remedies for infringement of the exclusive rights to a mask work include injunctive relief, and either actual damages which may be supplemented by an account of profits, or statutory damages of up to a maximum of $250,000.[198]

Protection under the Act lasts for ten years from either the date when a mask work is registered or the date on which it is first commercially exploited, whichever is the earlier.[199] Although the Act will pre-empt State laws providing equivalent rights or remedies,[200] it will in no way affect any rights or remedies to which a person is entitled under the Copyright or Patent Acts.[201] Where, for example, an unauthorised copy is made of a chip containing a program, remedies may be available not only under Chapter 9 but also under Chapters 1 to 8 of Title 17.[202] Thus, it will often be advisable to effect two registrations with the Copyright Office and affix two notices in respect of the rights in a given chip.

---

195   Section 906(a).
196   Section 906(b). Direct reproduction is, however, expressly prohibited.
197   Section 907. If an innocent purchaser subsequently receives notice of the rights of the mask work owner and, after receiving such notice, imports or distributes an infringing chip product, the mask work owner will be entitled to payment of a "reasonable royalty" (s. 907(a)(2)).
198   Section 911(a), (b), (c). A court may also make other orders including for "the destruction or other disposition of any infringing semiconductor chip products, and any masks, tapes or other articles by means of which such products may be reproduced" (s. 911(e)).
199   Section 904.
200   Section 912(c). This preemption provision is effective from January 1, 1986.
201   Section 912(a).
202   Chapters 1-8 contain the Copyright Act.

Chapter 4

Copyright Protection of Programs and Data in the United Kingdom and Canada

4.1 United Kingdom Copyright Law

4.1.1 The 1956 Copyright Act

A major overhaul of U.K. copyright law is long overdue. The current statute of 1956,[1] "although drafted in the computer age, betrays no sign of the slightest realization of that fact."[2] An attempt was made to shed some light on the issues in this area by the Whitford Committee in its 1977 report on *Copyright and Designs Law*,[3] and more recently the Thatcher Government expressed its views in a Green Paper in 1981.[4] The Current statutory position is as follows.

Of the various categories of copyright subject matter recognized by the 1956 Copyright Act, two are of particular relevance to the protection of software and data. First, under section 2(1), copyright subsists in

---

1   4 & 5 Eliz. 2, c. 74.
2   Tapper, *Computer Law,* 3rd ed. (London and New York: Longman, 1983), p. 18.
3   *Report of the Committee to consider the Law on Copyright and Designs* (London: HMSO Cmnd. 6732).
4   *Reform of the Law relating to Copyright, Designs and Performers Protection* (London: HMSO Cmnd. 8302). In December 1983 the government issued a further Green Paper dealing more generally with *Intellectual Property Rights and Innovation* (London: HMSO Cmnd. 9117). The paper proposed a rationalization of the British system of industrial property rights and recommended that there be a major statement of government policy in the form of an "Intellectual Property and Innovation Bill."

"every original literary, dramatic, or musical work." Restricted acts in relation to such a work include "reproducing the work in any material form; publishing the work" and "making any adaptation of the work."[5] As a separate head of protection, section 3(2) extends copyright to "every original artistic work." In respect of this category of works, restricted acts again include "reproducing the work in any material form" and "publishing the work",[6] but there is no express restriction on the making of adaptations.

While it is unlikely that a computer program would itself qualify as an artistic work, there is no obvious reason why protection should not be available for artistic works stored in computer-readable form. Indirect protection would then be available, as in the United States, for the underlying program in which an artistic work is stored.[7] The increasing use of computers in such fields as technical drawing, graphic design and, of course, video games, suggests that such protection may be highly relevant. Similarly, indirect protection may be available for programs embodying "musical works."[8]

More directly applicable, however, is the protection afforded under section two of the Act to "literary works." Such works are defined as including "any written table or compilation,"[9] and " 'writing' includes any form of notation, whether by hand or by printing, typewriting or any similar process."[10] The applicability of these provisions to programs written as flow charts or source code seems straightforward, and there is little doubt that copyright could also subsist in a printout of a program listing.[11]

What of programs which are entered directly into a computer via a keyboard and which are then stored on magnetic tape, disks, or ROMs? Could these qualify as literary works? Section 49(4) is of relevance here:

> References in this Act to the time at which, or the period during which, a literary, dramatic or musical work was made are references to the time or period at or during which it was first reduced to writing or *some other material form.*[12]

---

5   See note 1 above, ss. 2(5)(a), (b) and (f).
6   *Ibid.*, ss. 3(5)(a) and (b).
7   See section 3.4, above. Artistic copyright may also be applicable to IC designs. See Tettenborn, "Using the Law to Protect Computer Software" (1984), Sols. J. 6 July (supp.) at 12-16.
8   Note 1 above, s. 2(1). See also s. 12 (sound recordings) and s. 13 (cinematograph films).
9   Section 48(1).
10   *Ibid.*
11   The coding of programs on punched cards or paper tape would also seem to be analogous processes to printing or typewriting.
12   Emphasis added.

As will be seen, this section has been quoted by counsel in support of a claim to copyright in a magnetic recording of a program.[13]

A further significant matter to be considered is the relationship between source and object code. In particular, would the making of an unauthorized copy of an object code program infringe the copyright in any corresponding source code? While at one time English law, like American, applied the test of visible similarity in infringement cases, recent decisions indicate that the courts now adopt a more flexible approach.[14] In *Merchant Adventurers v. M. Grew & Co.*[15] Graham J. stressed that copying is a question of fact which must be decided "having regard to all the evidence and all the surrounding circumstances."[16] Visible similarity is only one component in such a test. This more complex approach makes good sense for, as Henry Carr has noted:

> A slavish copy of a work in a different medium may appear entirely dissimilar, whereas an independent development in the same medium may display a close resemblance. But in fact the former is a copy, the latter an original work.[17]

This distinction is of considerable importance in the present context as two programs performing similar functions, for example, structuring profit and loss accounts, may be quite dissimilar to each other in either their source or object code versions, or both. Conversely, substantial parts of a program may be copied verbatim without the plagiarised work in any way resembling the original when actually run.

As was noted earlier, the 1956 Copyright Act restricts not only the reproduction of protected works, but also the making of "any adaptation."[18] In relation to a literary work, section 2(6) defines "adaptation" to include "a translation of the work." There can be little doubt that the preparation of a version of a protected source code program in a different high level language would infringe this right.[19] It is also arguable that, where a source code program is compiled into object code, even if it is not considered a reproduction, the latter will constitute an "adaptation" of the former.

---

13   *Gates v. Swift,* [1982] R.P.C. 339. See section 4.1.3, below.

14   See the case comment by Henry Carr, Case Comment "Copyright Protection for Computer Software-A UK Perspective," [1982] 3 E.I.P.R. 88-91.

15   [1972] 1 Ch. 242, [1971] 2 All E.R. 657, [1973] R.P.C. 1.

16   *Ibid.,* at 9.

17   Note 14 above, at 89.

18   Section 2(5)(f). N.B.: this restriction applies only in the case of literary, dramatic or musical works as defined in s. 2. There is no express restriction on the making of adaptations of artistic works (s. 3).

19   In the U.S., the court in the *Synercom* case certainly had no doubts on this issue: *Synercom Technology Inc. v. Univ. Computing Co.,* 462 F. Supp. 1000 at 1013, note 5. (N.D. Tex., 1978).

Where infringement of copyright can be proved, the copyright owner is entitled to "all such relief . . . as is available in any corresponding proceedings in respect of infringements of other proprietary rights."[20] The principal remedies are injunctions to prevent further or anticipated infringements, orders for delivery up of infringing copies, an account of profits, and damages for either breach of copyright or for conversion of infringing articles. Various orders may be sought at the pre-trial stage, including interlocutory injunctions and "Anton Piller" orders.[21] The latter may authorize a plaintiff to enter premises and seize evidentiary material which otherwise might disappear before trial.[22] In certain cases a copyright owner can restrain the importation of infringing copies of a work by requesting the Commissioners of Customs and Excise to treat such copies as prohibited goods.[23] Limited criminal sanctions can also be invoked against some copyright infringers.[24]

However, the extent to which any of the benefits of copyright protection is available in respect of software remains uncertain. As will be seen, the complex questions relating to program copyright which in the United States have been addressed in detail by either Congress or the courts, have only been subjected to cursory judicial consideration in the United Kingdom. A general revision of the Copyright Act has, however, been promised for some years and, in the meantime, moves have recently been made towards specific legislative intervention to confirm the availability of protection for software.

4.1.2 Proposals for Reform: Whitford, the 1981 Green Paper and the Copyright (Computer Software) Amendment Bills 1984 and 1985

In 1974, a departmental committee was set up, under the chairmanship of Mr. Justice Whitford, with a general mandate "to consider and report whether any, and if so what changes are desirable in the law

---

20   Copyright Act 1956, 4 & 5 Eliz. 2, c. 74, s. 17(1). The section refers specifically to relief by way of "damages, injunction, accounts or otherwise."

21   Named after its first use in *Anton Piller K.G. v. Manufacturing Processes,* [1976] Ch. 55, [1976] 1 All E.R. 779 (C.A.).

22   Such an order was granted in *Gates v. Swift,* note 13 above discussed in section 4.1.3, below.

23   Note 20 above, s. 22(1). This section applies only to "printed copies" which infringe literary, dramatic or musical copyright. Its application to software may, therefore, be limited to infringing copies of program documentation and not to programs *per se.* See s. 22(2).

24   *Ibid.,* s. 21. Criminal penalties are discussed in section 7.3.1, below.

relating to copyright."[25] The committee reported in 1977. In a chapter on computers,[26] the current scope of protection for programs was reviewed, and recommendations were made for a clarification and strengthening of the law.

The committee observed that, while programs are probably already protected to some degree under the 1956 Act, at the time of writing there was no case law and the position was uncertain.[27] As they were of the opinion that "clear and effective protection" was appropriate, the committee members recommended that:

> all computer programs and software which have involved a sufficient degree of skill and/or labour to be considered as works in the normal copyright sense and which have been reduced to writing or other material form should be clearly and effectively protected against copying.[28]

Evidently in agreement with this position, in 1981 the government of the day issued a Green Paper in which it indicated its intention "to make explicit in new legislation that computer programs attract protection under the same conditions as literary works."[29]

The question of object code protection was also addressed in the Whitford Report and the Green Paper, and both agreed that the physical form in which a program is fixed should be irrelevant to the question of protection.[30] Accordingly, the government proposed "that copyright protection should extend to works fixed in any form from which they can be reproduced."[31] There was also agreement that the storage or loading of a program should be a restricted act.[32] Thus the Green Paper proposed that the definition of "reproduction" be amended so as to clearly cover the loading of a program into a computer.[33] The government disagreed, however, with a proposal made by the majority of the Whitford Committee that the "use" of programs should also be regulated by statute:[34]

---

25   Whitford Committee, *Report of the Committee to Consider the Law on Copyright and Designs* (London: HMSO Cmnd. 6732), p. 1.

26   *Ibid.*, chapter 9.

27   *Ibid.*, p. 126 (para. 479).

28   *Ibid.*, p. 128 (para. 489).

29   Green Paper, *Reform of the Law relating to Copyright, Designs and Performers Protection* (London: HMSO Cmnd. 8302), p. 33, para. 2.

30   Whitford, note 25 above, p. 128 (para. 492); Green Paper, *ibid.*, at 34 (para. 4).

31   Green Paper, *ibid.* See discussion of *Copyright (Computer Software) Amendment Bill*, below.

32   Whitford, note 25 above, p. 129 (para. 498); Green Paper, note 29 above, p. 34 (para. 4).

33   Green Paper, *ibid.*

34   Whitford, note 25 above, p. 130 (para. 499).

It is the Government's view ... that it is sufficient for the copyright owner to have control of the initial loading of his program into the computer. If the creator of an original program wishes to retain control over the use of his program beyond that inherent in his control over the reproduction involved in the initial loading into the computer, or to obtain recompense for such use, he has the possibility of achieving this through appropriate licensing terms.[35]

A statutory restriction on use might be redundant in any event, as arguably the use of a program will almost inevitably require reproduction or adaptation.[36]

Unlike Congress in the United States, the United Kingdom Parliament has not yet seen fit to issue legislative guidelines as to the scope of copyright protection for programs and data. A further Green Paper published at the end of 1983, while reiterating the Government's commitment to developing a coherent and effective system of intellectual property protection did nothing to advance the discussion of computer related issues.[37]

In July 1984, however, a Copyright (Computer Software) Amendment Bill was introduced in the House of Commons under the ten-minute rule.[38] The proposed legislation, which was to have been partially retroactive in effect,[39] would have amended the statutory definition of "literary work" so as to include "any computer programme or compilation of computer programmes,"[40] "computer programme" being defined as

including an expression, in any form and on any medium, of a set of instructions intended (whether directly or after adaptation) to cause or enable a device having information processing capabilities to perform a particular function.[41]

An "adaptation" of such a program would have included "a version of the programme in a different computer language, code or notation or a

---

35 Note 29 above, p. 34. Protection through licensing terms is of course of no value against the unlicensed user.

36 See the case comment by Henry Carr, "Software Protection in the United Kingdom – Competing Policy Considerations," [1982] 6 E.I.P.R. 181. The copying of a program from a disk or ROM into volatile memory would seem to in itself constitute "reproduction." See Prescott, "Copyright and Microcomputers," in Campbell, ed., *Data Processing and the Law* (London: Sweet & Maxwell, 1984).

37 *Intellectual Property Rights and Innovation* (London: HMSO Cmnd. 9117, 1983).

38 Bill 216, 24 July 1984. The full title was: "A Bill to Amend the Copyright Act 1956 so as to provide new penalties for offences relating to infringing copies of computer programmes; to provide for the issue and execution of search warrants in relation to such offences; and to confirm that copyright subsists in computer programmes."

39 *Ibid.*, cl. 2(4).

40 *Ibid.*, cl. 1(3)(c).

41 *Ibid.*, cl. 1(3)(b). It is significant that the definition of "programme" was to be non-exclusive.

recording of the programme in a different material form."[42] The Bill also contained a new definition of "material form" as including "any form of notation, whether expressed by mechanical, electrical, magnetic, optical, chemical or other means."[43]

In addition to confirming the availability of civil remedies for infringement of copyright in programs, the Bill provided new criminal penalties for unauthorised dealing in protected programs up to a maximum of two years imprisonment and an unlimited fine.[44] Although the Bill progressed no further than its first reading, a private members' bill to amend the Copyright Act in relation to software was tabled in the next session of Parliament.[45]

In the absence of specific statutory guidance, courts which have looked at computer copyright issues have generally done so in a superficial manner, and the central issues have yet to be debated in a full trial. While there have been judicial indications that copyright can subsist in programs in both their source and object code forms, it is still impossible to state with any certainty the extent of such protection.

4.1.3   The Current Scope of Copyright Protection

In England, all of the judicial commentary so far on the scope of copyright protection for programs and data has occurred in interlocutory proceedings. Yet, despite the fact that the substantive issues have yet to be assessed in any depth, a judicial consensus that copyright will protect software in its various forms has nevertheless emerged, albeit in a rather casual and *ad hoc* manner.

For example, in October 1980, the plaintiff in *Gates v. Swift*[46] applied successfully for an "Anton Piller" order to authorize the seizure of cassette tapes allegedly containing copies of programs in object code form. When asked by Graham J. whether the works were in "writing," counsel for the plaintiff replied:

> It is submitted that they are: the printout at least must be. But even if it were the case that writing neither on paper nor to a video screen was involved (which is unlikely), they are still literary works. The Act does not require writing at all: any material form of fixation (such as a magnetic recording) suffices: Copyright Act 1956 section 49(4)

---

42   *Ibid.,* cl. 1(3)(a).

43   *Ibid.,* cl. 1(3)(d).

44   *Ibid.,* cl. 1(2). *Criminal Penalties etc. (Increase) Order 1984,* S.I. 1984, No. 447, art. 2, para. 4, and sch. 4. See discussion of criminal sanctions in section 7.3.1, below.

45   The Bill, which at the time of writing had not been printed, received its first reading on December 5, 1984.

46   [1982] R.P.C. 339.

.... Were the foregoing wrong, a man who dictated a novel into a tape recorder would get no copyright, whereas he who dictated to a stenographer would.[47]

The court was evidently satisfied with this argument, as it granted the Anton Piller order as requested.[48] Discussion of the merits of the copyright infringement claim was, however, minimal.

While no English program copyright case has yet reached trial, a number of significant issues, including the question of fixation, were tackled by the Supreme Court of South Africa in *Northern Office Microcomputers Ltd. v. Rosenstein.*[49] A central question in that case was whether a suite of computer programs had been "written down, recorded or otherwise reduced to material form" as required for copyright purposes under section 2(2) of the South African Copyright Act of 1978. Marais A.J., for the court, reached the following conclusions:

> The formulae which were evolved were written by hand on paper. The source code which was used has been recorded upon a computer printout. In my opinion, there can be no doubt that a computer printout is a reduction to material form of the information which it contains. It has long been held that, to qualify for copyright protection, it is not necessary that what is written or recorded should express a meaning in language. As for the floppy discs, once the instructions to the computer have been recorded upon them, I think one can say rightly that the instructions have been reduced to material form.[50]

Satisfied also that the programs were original works of authorship the court declared them to be entitled to copyright protection. *Obiter,* the court went on to discuss whether programs stored on discs might also qualify as "recordings" under the 1978 Act. As under the English statute, a "record" is defined in section 2(2)(b) of the South African statute as "any disc, tape, perforated roll or other device in which *sounds* are embodied."[51] Marais A.J. was not completely deterred by this reference to "sounds" and offered the following interpretation of the provision:

---

47 *Ibid.,* at 340. A similar argument was raised in Wilson, "The Protection of Computer Programs under Common Law – Procedural Aspects and UK Copyright Law and Trade Secrets" in Brett and Perry, eds., *The Legal Protection of Computer Software* (Oxford: E.S.C. Publications, 1981), at 82.

48 An Anton Piller order will only be granted where the plaintiff has shown that he or she has a clear case against the defendant (*Roamer Watch Co. S.M. v. African Textile Distributors,* [1980] R.P.C. 457 at 475 (S.A. Sup. Ct.)). Interestingly, the terms of the order were that, *inter alia,* the defendant must "cause to be displayed or printed out by a computer or computers any such documents as are in computer-readable form": [1982] R.P.C. at 341.

49 [1982] F.S.R. 124.

50 *Ibid.,* at 133-34.

51 *Ibid.,* at 134 (emphasis supplied).

> As I understand the evidence before me no sounds are stored upon the floppy discs. It may therefore be suggested that the instructions which have been encoded upon the floppy discs have not been recorded upon them. I think that the answer to this suggestion is that the definition of "record" is confined to the noun and does not necessarily restrict the meaning of the verb "recorded." Alternatively, the definition applies only where the context does not indicate the contrary.[52]

It would be open to an English court to reach a similar conclusion regarding the definition of "record" in the 1956 Copyright Act.

In May 1982, the English Court of Appeal alluded to the *Rosenstein* decision in certain interlocutory proceedings concerning alleged videogame piracy. The plaintiff in *Sega Enterprises v. Alca Electronics,*[53] a Japanese manufacturer of videogames, alleged that the defendants had infringed its copyrights in a game called "Frogger." Lawton L.J. noted that there were decisions in the United States and South Africa favouring the plaintiff's position, but he observed that "so far copyright in this kind of electronic device has never been recognized by a United Kingdom court."[54] This then was a major issue to be decided at trial.

However, a few weeks later in other interlocutory proceedings involving the same plaintiff and the same videogame, a High Court judge ventured to express a "provisional opinion" on the question of copyright protection for programs.[55] In *Sega v. Richards* the plaintiff alleged that the first defendant had infringed the literary copyright in the game's computer program *per se,* the artistic copyright in the drawings which were produced when the program was in use, and the film copyright in the visual images recorded on the circuit board containing the program. The defendants admitted that their program was based on the plaintiff's, but claimed they had modified it considerably and that, in any event, computer programs *per se* were not copyrightable in England. Before granting an interlocutory injunction, Goulding J. briefly considered the first defendant's submission that there can be no copyright in a program:

> On the evidence before me in this case I am clearly of the opinion that copyright under the provisions relating to literary works in the Copyright Act 1956 subsists in the assembly code program of the game "Frogger." The machine code program derived from it by the operation of part of the system called the assembler is to be regarded, I think, as either a reproduction or an adaptation of the assembly code program, and accordingly for the purposes of deciding this motion I find that copyright does subsist in the program.[56]

---

52   *Ibid.*
53   [1982] F.S.R. 516 (C.A.).
54   *Ibid.,* at 532.
55   *Sega Enterprises v. Richards,* [1983] F.S.R. 73.
56   *Ibid.,* at 75.

In reaching this provisional opinion Goulding J. did, however, comment that he would be "careful not to say more than necessary because it is a most important question and will have to be thoroughly ventilated at trial, if this action indeed comes to trial."[57]

This highly tentative statement of the law was later followed by Megarry V.C. in *Thrustcode Ltd. v. W.W. Computing Ltd.*[58] *Thrustcode* concerned alleged infringement of copyright in certain computer programs designed to control manufacturing processes by regulating the flow of work on production lines. On the preliminary question of whether literary copyright could subsist in programs, the Vice-Chancellor was content to follow Goulding J.'s "clear conclusion" in *Sega v. Richards* that it could.[59] Of far greater concern to the court was the general difficulty of establishing that a program had been copied. Copyright is claimed in a program *per se* rather than the results it produces, yet "[m]any different processes may produce the same answers and yet remain different processes that have not been copied one from another."[60] More particularly, the court noted the plaintiff's complete failure to demonstrate that copying had occurred in the present case. Sega had only introduced in evidence 75 lines of source code as a sample of their program yet claimed that this was "enough for the purpose of claiming copyright in the whole, like quotations from a book."[61] No part of the defendant's program was presented to the court. Not surprisingly, the Vice-Chancellor was at a loss to see "any real evidence of copying."[62]

A further important matter which the court noted was the need to distinguish carefully between ideas and their expression. The plaintiff, who knew little about computing, had effectively employed the second defendant to convert his ideas into programs or, as he put it, "to translate my designs into computer readable form."[63] As the second defendant was an independent contractor the plaintiff could not claim copyright as his employer.[64] However, counsel for the plaintiff suggested that the defendant's position might be analogous to that of a "ghost writer" who prepared a book or article from information supplied by the nominal author. The court responded thus:

---

57   *Ibid.,* at 74.
58   [1983] F.S.R. 502.
59   *Ibid.,* at 505.
60   *Ibid.* Megarry V.C. gave the following illustration: "2 and 2 make 4. But so does 2 times 2, or 6 minus 2, or 2 per cent of 200, or 6 squared divided by 9, or many other things."
61   *Ibid.,* at 507.
62   *Ibid.*
63   *Ibid.*
64   As per *Copyright Act* 1956, 4 & 5 Eliz. 2, c. 74, s. 4.

No authority on this was cited, but as at present advised, and in the absence of any agreement to the contrary (as there will be in the great majority of cases), I would have thought that the ghost writer who chose and wrote the words would have copyright in them. Though the ideas were not his, the language was. I leave on one side any direct quotations of what the nominal author said or gave to him.[65]

By implication, source code prepared by a programmer from another person's flow chart will also be an independent creation rather than an infringing copy or even a derivative work. The relationship between object code and the source code from which it is prepared will, however, be very much closer. Object code may well constitute a copy, or at least an adaptation, of any source code from which it is compiled.[66]

Yet the application of the English copyright law to programs and data remains unclear. There can be no guarantee that, in the absence of clear statutory mandates, judges outside the United States will feel able to open up copyright protection to programs in the way that their American counterparts have now done. In this respect, recent developments in Australia are most instructive.

4.1.4   The Evolution of Software Copyright in Australia

In a case decided in December 1983, an Australian Federal Court judge opted for a restrictive approach to copyright protection of software. While both the works in suit in *Apple v. Computer Edge*,[67] "Applesoft" and "Autostart," had also been at the centre of Apple's American litigation with Franklin, Beaumont J. made no apology for departing from the Third Circuit's conclusions in that case.[68]

The Australian Copyright Act 1968 covers not only original literary, dramatic, musical and artistic works,[69] but also specific "subject matter other than works."[70] In *Apple v. Computer Edge,* the plaintiff claimed that its programs were literary works and thus subject to copyright protection. Beaumont J. disagreed. Quoting Davey L.J. in the nine-

---

65   [1983] F.S.R. 502 at 507.

66   See discussion in section 3.1.1, above.

67   *Apple Computer Inc. v. Computer Edge Pty. Ltd. and Suss,* [1984] F.S.R. 246, often referred to as the "Wombat" case.

68   "Because of the 1976 and 1980 amendments to the United States copyright legislation, specifically dealing with copyright protection for computer programs, decisions of the courts of that country . . . cannot assist in the present case." *Ibid.* at 257. See section 3.5, above, for a discussion of *Apple Computer Inc. v. Franklin Computer Corp.,* 545 F. Supp. 812 (E.D. Pa., 1982).

69   Copyright Act 1968, Part III.

70   *Ibid.,* part IV. These are sound recordings, cinematograph films, television and sound broadcasts, and published editions of works.

teenth-century English case of *Hollinrake v. Truswell*,[71] he concluded that a literary work is "something which was intended to afford 'either information of instruction or pleasure in the form of literary enjoyment.'" Since the function of a computer program is to control computer operations, "a contrast may properly be drawn between something which is merely intended to assist the functioning of a mechanical device and literary work so called."[72] In support of this conclusion, Beaumont J. noted that, when Parliament extended copyright protection to the various categories of "subject matter other than works," computers had already "been developed and were well known." The omission of computer programs was, he felt, quite deliberate and was an indication that "this field was not to be afforded the significant privilege given by copyright."[73]

While commentators had predicted the inadequacy of Australian copyright protection for software,[74] this ruling nevertheless represented a major setback for program owners in that country. In response to threats by some American software houses to ban exports of their products to Australia, the Australian Federal Government prepared legislative amendments to secure protection for programs under the Copyright Act.[75] In the meantime, an appeal by Apple against Beaumont J.'s ruling was heard by a full bench of the Federal Court of Appeal. On 29 May 1984, by a two to one majority, the panel of three judges allowed the appeal and made an order restraining the defendants from further infringing Apple's copyrights.[76]

Allowing the appeal, Fox J. rejected Beaumont J.'s finding that programs had been deliberately excluded from the Act. To the contrary, he noted that there had "long been a tendency (not invariably observed) to apply the language of the statutory law governing copyright in a practical manner, consistently with the needs of the time, and the then current concepts."[77] Discussing source code, he observed that the distinction between operating and applications programs was "rather too

---

71   [1894] 3 Ch. 420 at 428.

72   Note 67 above, at 257.

73   *Ibid.* Parliament "intended rather to leave such matters to be dealt with by other legislation dealing with patents and industrial designs."

74   *E.g.*, Burnside, "The Legal Implications of Computers" (1981), Australian L.J. 79-97; Cohen, "Computer Programs – Does the Law Provide an Adequate Protective Mechanism?" 56 Australian L.J. 219-33.

75   Chapman, "Software Law Postponed," Financial Times (31 May 1984), at 6.

76   *Apple Computer Inc. v. Computer Edge Pty. Ltd. and Suss,* [1984] F.S.R. 481. The appeal on the trade practices issue was allowed unanimously.

77   *Ibid.*, at 496.

arbitrary and not very useful,"[78] and stressed that copyright is essentially concerned with "expression and not function."[79] As for literary quality and communicative intent, he found that, provided at least some skill goes into its creation, the quality of a literary work is irrelevant for protection purposes. Moreover, even applying the *Hollinrake v. Truswell* test favoured by Beaumont J., Fox J. found it "difficult to exclude the possibility that a reader may have got instruction and information from reading it."[80]

Turning to the question of copyright in Apple's object codes, Fox J. found them to be indirectly protected as adaptations of the protected source codes: "I think . . . they can fairly be described as translations. Transliterations may more precisely explain what happens, but this is plainly comprehended within 'translation' ".[81] Looking at the next stage in the chain of events, he found that the copying of the object code programs contained in Apple's ROMs was an infringing act as it constituted a reproduction of the adaptations of the protected source code.

Lockhart J. similarly found the copying of the object code programs to be an infringing act. Like Fox J., he concluded that the object codes were indirectly protected as adaptations of the original source codes.[82] Having reached this conclusion, he found it unnecessary to decide whether the object code programs were not merely adaptations but actually reproductions in a material form of the source code programs, nor whether the object code programs qualified for direct protection as literary works.

Sheppard J., dissenting, accepted that the programs, as originally written in source code, were literary works but decided that the object code versions were neither infringing copies nor adaptations.[83] In reaching these conclusions, he placed considerable weight on the communication issue. He found that, while source code is human-intelligible, "only the machine itself, that is, the microprocessor . . . can 'understand' or 'see,' and thus deal with, the object code."[84] In his view, this not only barred programs in object code from qualifying as literary works but

---

78   *Ibid.*, at 491.
79   *Ibid.*, at 495. Fox J. expressly rejected the characterization of programs as merely machine parts: *Ibid.*, at 496.
80   *Ibid.*, at 495.
81   *Ibid.*, at 496.
82   *Ibid.*, at 522-526.
83   *Ibid.*, at 537-541.
84   *Ibid.*, at 538-539.

prevented them from constituting adaptations as defined exhaustively in the Copyright Act.[85]

Even apart from the doubts raised by this dissent, the majority's view that copyright protection is available indirectly for object code programs was not an entirely satisfactory result for program owners. For example, what would have been the copyright position where, to achieve a faster execution speed, a program was written directly in machine language without any source code ever existing? The majority left this as an open question, with Lockhart J. expressing "considerable reservations" as to whether object code programs could qualify as literary works.[86]

Presumably to dispel this lingering uncertainty, the Australian Federal Government decided to proceed with its draft Copyright Amendment legislation and the Bill was speedily pushed through its remaining stages in Parliament, receiving Royal Assent on 15 June 1984. The Act,[87] which has some retroactive application to programs already in existence,[88] has extended the definition of "literary work" in the 1968 Copyright Act to include "a computer program or compilation of computer programs."[89] Protection is now available for such programs stored in any form from which they can be reproduced.[90] "Computer program" is broadly defined in the Act as:

> an expression, in any language, code or notation, of a set of instructions (whether with or without related information) intended, either directly or after either or both of the following: (a) conversion to another language, code or notation; (b) reproduction in a different material form, to cause a device having digital information processing capabilities to perform a particular function.[91]

Programs originating in object code can clearly be covered by this definition but, to ensure that nothing slips through the statutory net, the Act has also extended the definition of "adaptation" under the

---

85 *Ibid.*, at 539-541.

86 *Ibid.*, at 524.

87 Copyright Amendment Act 1984, No. 43 of 1984. The Act came into force immediately on receiving Royal Assent.

88 *Ibid.*, s. 7. Copyright will subsist in programs written prior to the Act, but it will not be possible to sue for infringements which occurred before the Act came into force. See s. 7(2).

89 *Ibid.*, s. 3(f), amending s. 10(1) of the Copyright Act 1968.

90 Section 3(g) of the Copyright Amendment Act 1984 provides that " 'material form' in relation to a work or an adaptation of a work, includes any form (whether visible or not) of storage from which the work or adaptation, or a substantial part of the work or adaptation, can be reproduced."

91 *Ibid.*, s. 3(b).

Copyright Act to cover any version of a program which is not a reproduction of it.[92]

In terms of enforcement, the Act has extended the offence of distributing infringing copies to cover the transmission of a computer program which is "received and recorded so as to result in the creation of an infringing copy."[93] Moreover, a new offence has been created of publishing an advertisement for the supply of an infringing copy of a program.[94] The penalty for a first offence is a $1,500 fine, and for a second or subsequent offence $1,500 or imprisonment for six months.[95] Unless expressly forbidden by the owner of the copyright in a program, however, the Act authorises the making of back-up copies provided they are not made from an infringing copy.[96]

What, then, can be learned from the Australian experience of protecting programs by copyright? While courts in England have so far been fairly flexible in entertaining claims to copyright in software, the issues remain to be fully canvassed at trial. It is quite possible that an English court could find either that protection is limited to source code, or alternatively that it extends only indirectly to object code. Either conclusion would undermine the effective protection of software by copyright in the United Kingdom, especially as more programs are written directly in object code. Thus, to avoid confusion and ensure the establishment of a coherent and comprehensive scheme of copyright protection for programs, a clear legislative mandate would seem the most satisfactory solution at this stage. As well as declaring the status for copyright purposes of both source and object code programs, Parliament would do well to make a clear statement as to the scope of the "fair use" doctrine in the program context. In addition to authorising the making of back-up copies, as under the Australian Copyright Amendment Act 1984, a statutory exemption covering adaptations necessary for use would also seem appropriate.[97]

---

92   *Ibid.,* s. 3(a). Unauthorised reproductions and adaptations equally constitute infringing copies: see s. 3(c).

93   *Ibid.,* s. 5.

94   *Ibid.,* s. 6. This offence covers the transmission of a program which results in the creation of an infringing copy (as per s. 5) and liability extends to a person who has reasonable grounds for believing that the copy is, or will be, an infringing copy.

95   *Ibid.*

96   *Ibid.,* s. 4. There is no limit on the number of back-up copies which may be made, but such copies must not be used for any purpose other than "being used . . . in lieu of the original copy in the event that the original copy is lost, destroyed or rendered unusable."

97   This situation is covered by the U.S. Computer Software Copyright Act 1980. See discussion in section 3.2, above. The U.K. 1984 Copyright (Computer Software)

4.2 Canadian Copyright Law

4.2.1   The 1921 Copyright Act

The current Canadian Copyright Act[98] came into force over six decades ago. A major revision of the law, promised for many years, came closer with the publication by the federal government in 1984 of a White Paper setting out in some detail proposals for legislation.[99] In the meantime, however, an attempt must be made to deal with computer programs and data in the context of the rather archaic wording of the 1921 statute.

The Copyright Act is a federal statute.[100] Section 4(1) provides that copyright subsists "in every original literary, dramatic, musical and artistic work" automatically on creation, subject only to the author satisfying a broad nationality or residence requirement.[101] The owner of the copyright in a work has "the sole right to produce or reproduce the work or any substantial part thereof in any material form whatever."[102] This includes the making of "any translation of the work"[103] and, in the case of a literary, dramatic or musical work, the making of "any record, perforated roll, cinematograph film, or other contrivance by means of which the work may be mechanically performed or delivered."[104] A copyright owner also has the exclusive right to authorize any of these restricted acts.[105] Copyright is infringed by "any person who, without the consent of the owner of the copyright, does anything that, by this Act, only the owner of the copyright has the right to do."[106]

Amendment Bill covered neither of these eventualities.

98   R.S.C. 1970, c. C-30. Originally enacted S.C. 1921, c. 24. Entered into force January 1, 1924.

99   *From Gutenberg to Telidon: A White Paper on Copyright* (Ottawa: Minister of Supply and Services Canada, 1984). See discussion in section 4.2.2, below.

100   Section 91 of the Constitution Act 1867 (formerly the British North America Acts, 1867-1975, 30 & 31 Vict., c. 3) exclusively assigns jurisdiction over "copyrights" to the federal government.

101   The author must be "at the date of the making of the work a British subject, a citizen or subject of a foreign country that has adhered to the Convention and the additional Protocol thereto set out in Schedule II, or resident within Her Majesty's Realms and Territories; [or] . . . in the case of a published work, the work was first published within Her Majesty's Realms and Territories. . . ." R.S.C. 1970, c. C-30, s. 4(1). Canada is a signatory to both the Berne and Universal Copyright Conventions.

102   *Ibid.*, s. 3(1).

103   *Ibid.*, s. 3(1)(a).

104   *Ibid.*, s. 3(1)(d).

105   *Ibid.*, s. 3(1).

106   *Ibid.*, s. 17(1). This is subject to the exceptions listed in s. 17(2) (fair dealing, etc.).

In addition to the statutory requirements for copyright protection, there is also a judicially developed principle that a work can only attract protection where the subject matter is sufficiently "fixed." Thus, in the *Canadian Admiral* case, Cameron J. stated that, "for copyright to subsist in a 'work' it must be expressed to some extent at least in some material form, capable of identification and having a more or less permanent endurance."[107] On the basis of this statement, commentators have doubted whether works recorded on videotape[108] or in computer memory[109] would satisfy the fixation requirement.

However, with regard to works contained in computer programs, both the Copyright Office and the courts seem willing to give works stored in computer memory the benefit of the doubt as regard the question of fixation. As in the United States, it seems that many of the issues regarding program copyright in Canada will initially arise in litigation regarding video games. The Registrar of Copyrights has granted registrations for a number of such games,[110] and this registration constitutes *prima facie* evidence of copyright ownership.[111] Where infringement of copyright has been proved, a court can award a broad range of civil remedies,[112] and in certain cases criminal penalties may also be imposed.[113]

4.2.2 Proposals for Reform

In its 1971 "Report on Intellectual and Industrial Property," the Economic Council of Canada concluded that there was no pressing need for an extension of either copyright or patent protection to cover computer software.[114]

A few years later, however, in a report published by Consumer and Corporate Affairs Canada, Keyes and Brunet observed that "the growing interest in software protection indicates a growing need for such protec-

---

107   *Can. Admiral Corp. v. Rediffusion Inc.*, [1954] Ex C.R. 382, 14 Fox Pat. C. 114 at 125, 20 C.P.R. 75.

108   Perry, "Copyright in Motion Pictures and other Mechanical Contrivances" (1972), 5 C.P.R. (2d) 256.

109   Campbell, "Copyright Protection for Video Games in Canada" (1982), 15 Pat. & T.M. Inst. of Can. Bull. 948-956.

110   See *Nintendo of Amer. Inc. v. Coinex Video Games Inc.*, [1983] 2 F.C. 189, 69 C.P.R. (2d) 122, 34 C.P.C. 108, 46 N.R. 311 (Fed. C.A.).

111   Copyright Act, S.C. 1970, c. C-30, s. 36(2).

112   These include an injunction, damages, an account of profits and delivery up of infringing copies. *Ibid.*, ss. 20-24.

113   *Ibid.*, ss. 25-26. See discussion in section 7.3.1, below.

114   (Ottawa: Information Canada, 1971), pp. 101, 144.

tion, and the urgency of the need might become more apparent in the near future."[115] Nevertheless, the authors were not convinced that an extension of copyright would be the best means of protecting software. They saw a danger of "copyright principles being twisted beyond recognition,"[116] and argued instead for the adoption of some special scheme of software protection.

The most recent report in this area is the 1982 study by Palmer and Resendes entitled "Copyright and the Computer," also published by Consumer and Corporate Affairs.[117] As has already been noted,[118] these authors argued on economic grounds in favour of copyright protection for software and concluded that it was "time for Parliament to consider seriously once again the extension of copyright protection to cover new media for the expression of ideas to correct new market failures."[119]

In its 1984 White Paper, the federal government finally declared its intention to revise the Copyright Act generally and, at the same time, to create "an entirely new regime" of protection for computer programs in machine-readable form.[120] This proposed special scheme would not, however, be intended to affect computer programs in human-readable form, which would continue to be "protected under copyright law in the same way as any other form of literary or scientific work."[121] The authors of the White Paper noted the present uncertainty as to the scope of protection available for programs, but felt that any judicial decision on the matter based on general copyright principles would result in either no protection at all or inappropriately broad rights and remedies being granted to program owners.[122] However, the alternative approach which they have outlined may be far from a straightforward solution.

Under the proposed scheme of special protection for programs the definition of "computer program" would be something like "a set of instructions intended to operate a machine having information processing capabilities."[123] As a subset of this definition, "computer program in

---

115 (Ottawa: Consumer and Corporate Affairs Canada, 1977)
116 *Ibid.,* p. 110.
117 (Ottawa: Consumer and Corporate Affairs Canada, 1982).
118 See Chapter 1, above.
119 Note 117 above, p. 139.
120 *From Gutenberg to Telidon: A White Paper on Copyright* (Ottawa: Ministry of Supply and Services Canada, 1984), p. 80. See section XII of the Paper generally.
121 *Ibid.,* p. 79.
122 *Ibid.* The specialized scheme would thus be intended to "foster the creation and dissemination of such programs while attempting to minimize possible abuses of monopoly power or unnecessary litigation." *Ibid.,* p. 80.
123 *Idid.,* p. 81, para. 1.1. This definition is intended to cover both machine and human-readable programs. *Ibid.,* p. 80.

machine-readable form" would be defined in terms such as "a computer program that is not intended for human comprehension."[124] There is already a fallacy inherent in this intended demarcation between human and machine-readable programs which could substantially undermine the rationale of the proposed scheme.

Put simply, the quandary is that humans can, if they so wish, both read and write object code, and machines can, with the assistance of a compiler program, "read" source code. Indeed, to achieve greater execution efficiency, it is not uncommon for programmers to write programs in machine code in preference to higher level languages. At the same time, every computer program, regardless of the language in which it is written or the medium in which it is stored, is ultimately intended for machine rather than human "comprehension." Will the classification of a program as human- or machine-readable thus depend on the programming capabilities of the humans who are likely to look at it, and the compiling capabilities of the computers on which it is likely to be run?

Even if this threshold definitional problem can be overcome, it is difficult to see how, given the rights of the respective copyright holders, the proposed distinction between machine- and human-readable programs would be preserved in practice. It is intended that, for five years from the date of its creation, the owner of the copyright in a human-readable program will have the exclusive right to authorize the making of machine-readable versions of that program.[125] Such machine-readable versions will qualify for "computer program copyright" which, *inter alia,* will include the right "to make a human-readable program that is based upon and identical or substantially similar to the machine-readable program."[126] It is also stated that "[n]o act done with respect to a machine-readable program will be considered an infringing act with respect to the human-readable program upon which it is based."[127] What difference then will there be between the rights of a person who owns the computer program copyright in a machine-readable version of a program, and the person who owns the copyright in the original human-readable version of that program? Both will be authorised to reproduce their respective programs in both machine and human-readable form.[128] Thus, wherever computer program copyright is held by someone other

---

124   *Ibid.,* p. 81, para. 1.1.
125   *Ibid.,* p. 82, paras. 2.2, 2.3.
126   *Ibid.,* p. 82, para. 3.2(c).
127   *Ibid.,* p. 84, para. 6.1.
128   It is true that, from a purely technical perspective, it is much easier to compile and assemble source code than to disassemble and decompile object code.

than the owner of the copyright in the human-readable version, it will make no sense to speak of either person having any "exclusive rights."[129]

The purported distinction between the terms of protection for each type of program may also be illusory. On the one hand, the White Paper states that programs in human-readable form will continue to be protected for the usual term of the life of the author plus fifty years.[130] On the other hand, after five years from the date of creation of a published human-readable program, "any person with access to the program in human-readable form may use it to make a machine-readable program" without infringing the copyright in either the human-readable program or any other machine-readable version of it.[131] Given that there will then be no restrictions whatever on what can be done with the machine-readable versions, what protection will be left for the owner of the source code?

A further difficulty with the proposed scheme is the fact that computer program copyright will not include "a right to use the program."[132] The stated reason for this is that "[t]here is no right to use under traditional copyright law"; the classic example cited is that the owner of the copyright in a printed cake recipe cannot prevent others baking the described cake.[133] This analogy, while good as an illustration of the distinction between ideas and their expression,[134] is totally inapposite in the context of "use" rights. For example, when a source code program is compiled into object code, the conversion of the program from the higher to the lower level language occurs quite mechanically and automatically.[135] To reverse the cake analogy, it is as though the placing of a recipe book in an oven results automatically in a cake being baked!

Thus, at least in the general terms in which it has been set out in the White Paper, the proposed special scheme of copyright protection for programs seems highly problematic. It is to be hoped that, after further consideration, the drafters of Canada's new Copyright Act will achieve a

---

129   As the draft provisions purport to do: note 120 above, p. 83, para. 5.1.
130   Indeed, as the White Paper acknowledges, Canada is almost certainly obligated under its treaty obligations to maintain this minimum term for such programs. *Ibid.*, p. 79.
131   *Ibid.*, p. 82, para. 2.3.
132   *Ibid.*, p. 82, note.
133   *Ibid.*
134   Which is how it was originally used by the Supreme Court of Canada in *Cuisenaire v. South West Imports*, [1969] S.C.R. 208, 40 Fox. Pat. C. 81, 57 C.P.R. 76.
135   Davidson (Chairman), "Protecting Computer Software: A Comprehensive Analysis" (1983), 4 Ariz. State L.J. 611-784. The essential difference between a cake recipe and source code is that the former is merely symbolic, whereas the latter is both symbolic and mechanical.

result which will ensure effective and workable copyright protection for all original programs regardless of the forms in which they are expressed or media in which they are fixed.

4.2.3   The Current Scope of Copyright Protection

Meanwhile, in the courts, while no cases have yet been decided at trial, various injunctions have been granted in interlocutory proceedings to restrain defendants from infringing the copyright in video games. In *Midway Mfg. Co. v. Bernstein*[136] the plaintiff alleged copyright infringement in three of its video games, "Galaxian," "Pac-man" and "Rally-X." At an *ex parte* hearing the plaintiff obtained an "Anton Piller" order which included an interlocutory injunction forbidding further infringement.[137] An "Anton Piller" order was also granted in *Nintendo of Amer. Inc. v. Coinex Video Games Inc.*[138] where the Federal Court of Appeal found the plaintiff to have "an extremely strong *prima facie* case" in its allegations of copyright infringement.[139] Similarly, in *Bally Midway Mfg. Co. v. Coinex Video Games Inc.*,[140] Addy J. granted an interlocutory injunction to restrain the defendants from infringing copyrights in "Ms. Pac-Man," "Super Pac-Man" and "Galaxian." In *Chin-Can. Communications Ltd. v. Chinese Video Centre Ltd.*,[141] the same judge refused to make an "Anton Piller" order but did issue an interim injunction to restrain infringement of videogame copyrights.

In *Spacefile Ltd. v. Smart Computing Systems Ltd.*, the plaintiff sought both an injunction to restrain infringement of copyright in a software package, and a ruling that one of the defendants was in contempt of court for violating an earlier consent order.[142] The court found that the latter defendant, who was a former employee of the plaintiff, was marketing a software system which was "an adaptation of the plaintiff's system incorporating much of it."[143] The court disposed of the issue of the extent to which copyright can subsist in software in the following abrupt manner:

---

136   [1983] 1 F.C. 510, 67 C.P.R. (2d) 112 (Fed. T.D.).
137   In a subsequent hearing *inter partes* the injunction was set aside on the ground that the plaintiff had failed to make a full disclosure of material facts when the order was obtained.
138   [1983] 2 F.C. 189, 69 C.P.R. (2d) 122, 34 C.P.C. 108, 46 N.R. 311 (Fed. C.A.).
139   69 C.P.R. (2d) at 130.
140   (1983), 71 C.P.R. (2d) 105 (Fed. T.D.).
141   (1983), 70 C.P.R. (2d) 184 (Fed. T.D.).
142   (1983), 75 C.P.R. 281 (Ont. H.C.).
143   *Ibid.*, at 282.

The manual is in printed form. The source code and the programmes are electronically recorded on discs but are capable of, and have been, printed from them. They are original ideas expressed in a particular form. They are proper subject-matter of copyright.[144]

Accordingly, an interlocutory injunction was granted to restrain further copyright infringement, although the court refused to find the defendant in contempt due to doubts as to whether the earlier consent order had been violated.[145]

Other courts have adopted a rather more cautious approach to program copyright issues. In *Atari Inc. v. Video Amusements of Can. Ltd.*,[146] an application for an interim injunction restraining the defendants from infringing the plaintiff's copyright in certain games was refused. Jerome A.C.J. found there to be a triable issue as to the applicability of copyright to computers and their programs. In *Apple Computer Inc. v. Computermat Inc.*,[147] the plaintiff alleged that the defendants had infringed its copyrights in certain operating system programs. The defendants did not deny copying the programs but argued that operating systems are not copyrightable. Hughes J. noted that the copyrightability of computer programs had yet to be determined at trial and, accordingly, refused to grant interlocutory relief.[148]

The most thorough judicial examination of the issues to date, albeit still only in an interlocutory judgement, is found in *IBM Corp. v. Ordinateurs Spirales Inc. Spirales Computers Inc.*[149] In that case IBM was successful in its application for an interlocutory injunction to restrain the defendants from infringing the copyright in one of its operating systems, the IBM PC Basis Input Output System (BIOS). In rejecting a defence argument that copyright could not subsist in the program concerned, Reed J. reviewed the growing number of Commonwealth decisions in which program copyright claims had been upheld, including the then very recent ruling of the full bench of the Australian Fede. ¹ Court in the *Apple v. Computer Edge* case.

Counsel for the defence had raised all of the major theoretical objections to software copyright:[150] the claim that copyright statutes

---

144   *Ibid.*
145   *Ibid.*, at 283.
146   Fed. T.D. Jerome A.C.J., 8 Dec. 1982 (unreported), summarized at 19 A.C.W.S. (2d) 4.
147   (1983), 75 C.P.R. (2d) 26, 1 C.I.P.R. 1 (Ont. H.C.).
148   The judge did, however, order the defendants to lodge with the court a bond to secure the sum of $100,000 in favour of the plaintiff pending the outcome of the action, and also required them to keep accounts of sales of the allegedly infringing software: 75 C.P.R. (2d) at 33.
149   (1984), 2 C.I.P.R. 56 (Fed. T.D.)
150   See chapter 2, above.

should be interpreted restrictively; the debate concerning the merger of ideas and their expression; the characterization of programs as machine parts; the communication issue; and the problem of fixation of programs in read only memory. On the question of statutory interpretation, Reed J. found no authority for a restrictive subject matter test and favoured the flexible approach to copyright legislation adopted by Fox and Lockhart JJ. in the Australian *Apple* appeal.[151]

Regarding the merger of idea and expression, he agreed with the Third Circuit's finding in *Apple v. Franklin* that, provided the idea on which a program is based can be expressed in other ways, no merger will have occurred.[152] Nor was Reed J. convinced by the classification of the operating system embedded in a chip as a machine part:

> Its permanent mounting within the machine is for convenience only. It can be removed and another replaced for it if desired. An analogy in my view would be to the role of a cassette tape in a tape recorder. Information is recorded on a tape in a fashion analogous to information being embedded in the chip – both operate in conjunction with the respective machines for which they are designed but are not a part of the machine.[153]

The judge considered rather more difficult the defendants' claim that copyright could not subsist in object code programs as they are not intended to communicate either information or instructions to human beings.[154] However, this argument he found to be countered by the general principle that "[c]opyright is essentially concerned with the expression of ideas in composition or language rather than with the function or purpose of those ideas."[155] Moreover, he noted that the plaintiff had published the program in both source and object code in the Technical Manual, and thus there undoubtedly existed "a written version of the program in its object code manifestation."[156]

Reed J. then turned to the question of whether IBM's program had been reduced to material form, as required by the *Can. Admiral* deci-

---

151   Note 149 above, at 61-2. See part 4.1.4, above.

152   *Ibid.,* at 63. See section 3.5, above.

153   *Ibid.,* at 65. Reed J. quoted in support the Third Circuit's comparison of programs with videotapes and phonorecords. For a discussion of the limitations of this analogy see section 2.3, above.

154   *Ibid.,* at 65-6, as apparently required by *Hollinrake v. Trusswell,* [1894] 3 Ch. 420.

155   *Ibid.,* at 66, quoting Lockhart J. in *Apple v. Computer Edge.* See section 4.1.4, above. Although not mentioned by Reed J., Canadian support for the proposition that a literary work need not be intended "for the imparting of information" can be found in *Bulman Group Ltd. v. "One-Write" Accounting System Ltd.* (1982), 16 B.L.R. 16, 62 C.P.R. (2d) 149, 132 D.L.R. (3d) 104 (Fed. T.D.).

156   2 C.I.P.R. at 66-7.

sion.[157] He found this criterion also to have been satisfied by the publication of both the source code and the object code in the Technical Manual supplied with the program. The fact that the BIOS program "cannot be read by the human eye in its reproduced state" he did not consider a problem.[158] The distinction between reproductions and adaptations was only discussed briefly. Reed J. noted that Fox J. in the Australian *Apple* ruling had decided that the ROM version of the program in issue in that case was a reproduction of an adaptation of the original source code. Reed J., however, considered "the better view" in such circumstances to be that "the 'chip' version of the code is a reproduction in material form."[159] By this he presumably meant a reproduction of the original source code. In any event, he was satisfied that, especially given the fact that the defendants' copying of the program was blatant, the plaintiff had demonstrated not merely an arguable but a *prima facie* case of copyright infringement.[160]

It is also interesting to note the way in which the other requirements for interlocutory relief were met. Despite the immense difference in "the comparative size of the two protagonists," IBM succeeded in demonstrating that damages at trial might be an inadequate remedy and that the balance of convenience lay in its favour. The court found that "withholding an injunction would open the floodgates to extensive activity by others," potentially leading to what counsel for IBM had described as "death by a thousand cuts."[161] There was also evidence to suggest that, due to the defendants' "inadequate" accounting procedures, IBM might never be able to prove its damages.[162] Even if damages could be proved, since they were also being sued by other parties alleging copyright infringement, Reed J. felt there was "at least some possibility" that the defendants might go out of business before a final resolution of IBM's action against them.[163] Finally, the judge commented that, in cases where copying is blatant, "it is appropriate to consider a less stringent test of potential damage, than would otherwise be the case."[164]

---

157   *Ibid.* See section 4.2.1, above.

158   *Ibid.,* at 68.

159   *Ibid.,* at 69.

160   *Ibid.*

161   *Ibid.,* at 70.

162   *Ibid.,* at 71.

163   *Ibid.,* at 71-2.

164   *Ibid.,* at 72. For support he referred to *Universal City Studios Inc. v. Zellers Inc.* (1983), 73 C.P.R. (2d) 1 at 10 (Fed. T.D.), and *Apple Computer Ltd. v. Franklin Computer Corp.,* 714 F. 2d 1240 (1983).

Although it has no doubt been viewed by owners of software in Canada as an encouraging development, the IBM decision is of little weight as a precedent. It is perhaps unfortunate that, as in the United Kingdom, interlocutory decisions continue to be made while the significant issues surrounding copyright protection of software have never been argued fully in a trial, let alone on appeal. Moreover, it may yet be some time before the general revision of Canada's copyright law promised in the 1984 White Paper comes to fruition. In the absence of specific statutory guidance, judges will continue to be faced with the unenviable task of attempting to fit the technology of the 1980s into the legal framework of the 1920s.

Chapter 5

Patents for Programs and Program-Related Inventions

5.1 Policy Issues

5.1.1 Arguments For and Against Patent Protection for Computer Programs

The primary objective of patent protection is generally thought to be to encourage inventiveness. An economic incentive is offered to inventors by way of a limited monopoly on the exploitation of their creations, while at the same time a requirement that inventions be fully disclosed avoids to some extent unnecessary duplication of effort.[1] In the specific context of computer programming, David Bender argued in 1968 that:

> An efficient system of patent protection would replace the incentive to conceal with an incentive to publish. If effective protection exists, incentive to invest in programs will be augmented by the prospect of royalties, and widespread use will be made of the fruits of investment. If the only available form of protection is secrecy, however, program hoarding will reduce the utility of new programs and choke off the sort of technical dialogue that nourishes the art.[2]

A great deal of water has passed under the bridge since these words were written and it is now clear that programmers have more to choose from than simply patents or trade secrets.

Copyright is gradually emerging as the primary framework of protection for proprietary interests in software. Compared to patents, copyright protection costs nothing to obtain and is relatively inexpen-

---

1   Indeed the word patent has its roots in the Latin word "patere," which means "to be open," although it should be noted that Letters Patent were at one time granted without a specification and thus without disclosure.
2   Bender, "Computer Programs: Should They Be Patentable?" (1968), 68 Columbia L.R. 241-59 at 246.

sive to enforce. The requirement of "originality" for copyright works is far less stringent than the additional requirements of novelty and unobviousness pertaining to patentable inventions. Indeed, once it is established as a matter of law that forms of expression used in computer programs can attract copyright protection, then copyright will subsist automatically in virtually anything a programmer writes. In marked contrast to this, only a minute fraction of all program-related inventions would ever pass the rigorous tests used in most jurisdictions for determining patentable subject matter.

Yet, where it can be obtained, a patent has significant advantages for an inventor over other available forms of protection. For example, unlike copyright, which only protects the form of expression of a work, a patent covers the underlying content of an invention. A patent thus establishes a far broader monopoly for an inventor than an author of a copyright work can ever obtain. Unlike copyright, a patent protects against independent creation. A grant of a patent may also be beneficial to an inventor in facilitating licensing.[3]

Yet obtaining a patent is often a lengthy and expensive process and enforcement may bring still greater problems. Also, given the relatively short life of many programs, an application delay of perhaps two to three years may be highly significant, and the considerable cost of obtaining a patent is likely to limit access by small software houses to the benefits of such protection. Not surprisingly, in the United States it has been large corporations such as the major oil companies which have spearheaded the campaign for patent protection to be extended to cover software-related inventions.[4]

Apart from concerns about the practical effects of patents in terms of monopolistic practices and concentration of market power, the pos-

---

3   Bender, *Computer Law: Evidence and Procedure* (New York: Matthew Bender, 1983), p. 4A-69. It is interesting to observe how Bender's enthusiasm for program patents waned in the one and a half decades following his 1968 article. In his 1983 work he listed only four advantages but ten disadvantages of patent protection for software, at pp. 4A-68-74.

4   The vigorous patent activity by companies involved in seismic data processing has been well documented by Moskowitz, "The Metamorphosis of Software-Related Invention Patentability" (1982), III Computer/Law J. 273-336. More generally, Hugh Brett has observed that the increased number of patent applications made by major corporations "has changed what was originally regarded as an individual right to a corporate weapon." The system is open to abuse by those with substantial resources who can afford to take out patents for inventions which they then do not bother to exploit, and applications may be filed "to confuse competitors, and even to defeat innovation." "The patent system - what future role in the creation of wealth?,"[1983] E.I.P.R. 83-4.

sibility of patenting computer programs and program-related inventions raises significant theoretical questions as to the proper scope of patent laws. A patent is supposed to give an inventor control over the underlying concept of an invention. Nevertheless, there are many ideas and principles which should always remain unrestrictedly in the public domain. As far as computer related inventions are concerned, legislators, courts and commentators have paid considerable attention to two specific aspects of this issue. One is the possible preemption of mathematical formulae (algorithms). The other is the extension of patent protection to processes of calculation which are analogous to those carried out by the human brain (mental steps).

5.1.2 Abstract Algorithms and Mental Steps

Our primary concern here is with *software* patents, but it is important to note in passing the situation regarding hardware. There is no fundamental objection to and nothing at all new about patent protection in respect of computer hardware. Perhaps the earliest computer patent was that granted in 1649 by Louis XIV to Blaise Pascal for the following invention:

> a machine by means of which all kinds of computations can be made: addition, subtraction, multiplication, with integers and fractions . . . without the use of writing pen or counting frame, by a method which is much more simple, more easy to learn, more rapid to use, and less tiresome to the mind than the other ways of calculation, used until now, and which aside from these advantages has that of being free of any danger of error, thus fulfilling the prime requirement of all calculation.[5]

Pascal's computer was of course purely mechanical, and he was clearly only receiving a patent on it as a *machine* which facilitated conventional calculations. There was no question of any monopoly on the abstract methods of calculation themselves.

Mechanical "computers" were eventually superseded by electro-mechanical, electrical and finally electronic computers. In a modern digital computer, many of the functions which in Pascal's computer were carried out mechanically, and which in early electronic computers were achieved by means of "hard-wired" programs, are now based in software.

At the heart of a piece of computer software is an algorithm,[6] a

---

5   Pascal, *Oeuvres* (1904-14), v. 2:399, quoted in Prager, "Examination of Inventions From the Middle Ages to 1836" (1964), 46 J.P.O.S. 268-91 at 281.

6   The words "program" and "algorithm" are often used synonymously. "Algorithm" is in fact a corruption of "algorism," itself derived from the name of the ninth-century Arab mathematician who is reputed to have invented the Arabic system of numeration. *The Oxford Dictionary of Computing* (Oxford: Oxford University Press, 1983), p. 11.

dictionary definition of which is "a series of instructions or procedural steps for the solution of a specific problem."[7] It is well established in the United States, England and Canada that ideas and principles in the abstract, or mathematical expressions of the same are not proper subject matter for patent protection.[8] Thus, if algorithms are merely mathematical expressions of abstract ideas, they must be unpatentable. Nor, it is argued, should protection be available for computer programs which merely implement such algorithms.

Gemignani[9] has suggested, however, that such a view of the theoretical appropriateness of patent protection for algorithms is too crude and simplistic. He concedes that it would be absurd to allow patents on such fundamental concepts as the law of gravity or the principles of addition. He argues, however, that such laws and principles would tend to be unpatentable anyway as in their broad form they lack the requisite element of utility.[10] To assume that all algorithms are merely expressions of abstract mathematical principles and thus automatically unpatentable is to paint with too broad a brush for two reasons. Firstly, a "distinction must be drawn between the metasystem that tells us why the algorithm works and the algorithmic process itself."[11] Thus, the fact that a method of calculation conforms to certain mathematical principles does not make it coextensive with those principles. Secondly, why should mathematical formulae be singled out for special treatment when all inventions depend to some extent on existing laws of nature? Gemignani has suggested the following more subtle analysis of the distinction between laws of nature and inventions:

> One ... can attempt to distinguish between what is discovered, in the sense of something that actually preexists its finding, and what is invented, which does not exist until its inventor creates it. Even if one adopts the Platonic view that global mathematical theories or systems exist a priori, this does not preclude the possibility of someone working in the context of those systems from inventing an algorithm, as opposed to discovering it. Inventors, after all, work within the constraints of the "real world." They do not, indeed cannot, ignore the laws of nature; they rather use these laws to their own advantage. If a mathematical system is part of the same "real world," why cannot an algorithm likewise be a bona fide invention?[12]

---

7   Chandour, *The Penguin Dictionary of Computers* (Hammondsworth: Penguin Books, 1977), p. 30. Judicial interpretations of the word have varied considerably and have been the source of considerable confusion. See section 5.2 below.
8   See sections 5.2, 5.3, 5.4 below.
9   "Should Algorithms be Patentable?" (1982), Jurimetrics J. 326-36.
10   *Ibid.*, at 329.
11   *Ibid.*
12   *Ibid.*, at 330.

Whatever the merits of this argument, an extension of patent protection to cover algorithms *per se* would require a significant departure from the established practices of the patent offices and courts in the United States, England and Canada.

The second major theoretical objection to program patents lies in the "mental steps" doctrine. This too is not terribly convincing. The early American cases outlining this doctrine, which dates back at least forty years, essentially held that "any human activity in the performance of a process renders the claim nonstatutory even when the patent application attempts to claim what otherwise should have been statutory subject matter."[13] The rationale for the rule was that, in a process which involved human intervention, the scope for subjective judgements would render the process unpatentable on account of vagueness.[14]

In 1968 the United States Patent and Trademark Office issued guidelines which effectively ruled out applications for program patents on the ground that processes which could be implemented by mental steps were not patentable.[15] The logic of ever applying this doctrine to computers seems dubious. In fact, computers do not make subjective judgements at all; the procedures they implement are entirely determined.[16] Thus, regarding the actual method by which a computer adds together, Bender has observed that it is "mere terminology" that "obscures the fact that the machine's data transformation is non-intellectual in nature. There is no mental step involved at all."[17] Moreover, as Hayhurst has argued, even if we do treat the operation of a program as being analogous to a process of mental calculation, the appropriateness of the mental steps doctrine remains questionable:

> Computers are adapted to out-perform the brain. Where an inventor has devised a "mental" process performable by a computer but not practically performable by a human brain, should patent protection not be possible? The computer has been utilised to make the impossible practicable. Should patent laws not reward this achievement?[18]

Yet, despite earlier suggestions to the contrary, in the United States the Court of Custom and Patents Appeals has stated that it considers it to be

---

13   *Ex Parte Read,* 123 U.S.P.Q. 446 (P.O. Bd. App., 1943).

14   See Comment, "The Mental Steps Doctrine" (1981), 48 Tenn. L.R. 903-17 at 911.

15   855 *Off. Gaz. Pat. Off.* 829 (1968). The Guidelines also required that patentable processes operate to change physical substance. See discussion in Moskowitz, note 4 above at 284.

16   *In re Prater,* 415 F. 2d 1378 at 1402 (C.C.P.A., 1968); *In re Musgrave,* 431 F. 2d 882 at 890 (C.C.P.A., 1970).

17   Note 2 above, at 257.

18   "Pythagoras and the Computer," [1982] E.I.P.R. 223-27 at 223.

beyond question that claims drawn to "purely mental steps" are non-statutory.[19]

5.1.3 The Status of Program-Related Inventions

At present there is little doubt that patent protection is not available for computer programs as such in the United States, England or Canada. But the question of program patents cannot be disposed of so easily. While a particular program as a set of computer instructions in whatever form may not be patentable, the status of a piece of apparatus or process or method of manufacture which utilizes such a program is a quite different matter.

Drawing the line between a program *per se* and an invention in which that program is implemented will not always be straightforward. For example, will the fact that an applicant has described some form of "post-solution activity" be sufficient to render patentable a claimed invention the core of which is a computer program? What is the position where hardware is constructed which replicates exactly the function of a piece of software? In such a situation would it make sense to allow a patent in respect of the former version of a program but not the latter?

As with copyright, there has been far more judicial consideration in the United States than elsewhere of these and other issues arising from attempts to obtain directly or indirectly patent protection for programs. Much of the litigation in the field in the past two decades has served to exacerbate rather than relieve uncertainties as to the availability and extent of patent protection for programs and program-related inventions. Nevertheless, in recent years, the Patent Office and the courts have steadily refined the criteria to be applied to computer-related claims. This is not to say, however, that the boundaries of patent protection for program-related inventions have been thoroughly mapped.

---

19   *In re Chatfield*, 191 U.S.P.Q. 730 at 735 (C.C.P.A., 1976). Eight years previously the Court had found that patent protection for a process was "not precluded by mere fact that the process could alternatively be carried out by mere mental steps." *Prater*, note 16 above, at 1389.

5.2 United States Patent Law

5.2.1 General Requirements For Patent Protection and Early Supreme Court Rulings

Under the United States Patent Act,[20] an invention can only be patented if it falls within one of four categories of statutory subject matter. These are "process, machine, manufacture, or composition of matter, or any new and useful improvement thereof. . . ."[21] Moreover, four further specific criteria must be satisfied. The invention must be new,[22] useful,[23] unobvious,[24] and original.[25] Once obtained, patent protection lasts for seventeen years.[26]

Most of the debate regarding program patents has focussed on the preliminary question of whether a computer program or program-related invention can constitute statutory subject matter for a patent. It has long been established in the United States that scientific truths and principles, and mathematical expressions of such truths and principles, are not patentable.[27] This basic issue arose in 1972 in the Supreme Court's first ruling on a program patent application, *Gottschalk v. Benson*.[28] The Court had to decide whether a method for converting binary-coded decimal (BCD) numerals into pure binary numbers was proper subject matter for a patent. Mr. Justice Douglas, for the Court, reached the following conclusion:

> It is conceded that one may not patent an idea. But in practical effect that would be the result if the formula for converting BCD numerals to pure binary numbers were patented in this case. The mathematical formula involved here has no substantial practical application except in conjunction with a digital computer, which means that

---

20   35 U.S.C. (1976), enacted by Congress pursuant to its power to "promote the Progress of Science and the Useful Arts." (U.S. Constitution, Art. 1, s. 1, cl. 8).

21   *Ibid.*, s. 101.

22   *Ibid.*

23   *Ibid.*

24   *Ibid.*, s. 103: "A Patent may not be obtained . . . if the differences between the subject matter sought to be patented and the prior art are such that the subject matter as a whole would have been obvious at the time the invention was made to a person having ordinary skill in the art to which said subject matter pertains."

25   *Ibid.*, s. 102: "A person shall be entitled to a patent unless . . . (f) he did not himself invent the subject matter sought to be patented."

26   *Ibid.*, s. 154.

27   *Mackay Radio & Tel. Corp. of Amer.*, 306 U.S. 86 (1939); *In re Castelet*, 562 F. 2d 1236 (C.C.P.A., 1977).

28   409 U.S. 63 (1972).

if the judgement below is affirmed, the patent would wholly pre-empt the mathematical formula and in practical effect would be a patent on the algorithm itself.[29]

The Court concluded that an algorithm, or mathematical formula, should be treated like a law of nature and it cited earlier cases in support of the general rule that "[p]henomena of nature, though just discovered, mental processes, and abstract intellectual concepts are not patentable, as they are the basic tools of scientific and technological work."[30] Until very recently, this general exclusion of algorithms from protection had not been seriously challenged in the subsequent jurisprudence. Rather, the debate shifted for a decade or so to the question of patent protection for software-related inventions, instead of for programs *per se.*

The Supreme Court's next consideration of program patents came in the 1978 case of *Parker v. Flook*.[31] Flook's application concerned an improved method for updating "alarm limits" during catalytic conversion processes. The Patent Examiner's rejection of the application was reversed by the Court of Customs and Patent Appeals,[32] which ruled that "since the mere solution of the algorithm would not constitute infringement of the claims, a patent on the method would not pre-empt the formula."[33] Accordingly, the invention did not fall foul of the *Benson* exclusion but was found to be proper subject matter for a patent.

In restoring the Examiner's ruling, the Supreme Court did admit that "[t]he line between a patentable 'process' and an unpatentable 'principle' is not always clear."[34] Moreover, the Court recognized that the inclusion in a process of a law of nature or a mathematical algorithm was not necessarily fatal for patent purposes,[35] and that Flook was not seeking to "wholly pre-empt the mathematical formula" used in his process.[36] However, the Supreme Court was not convinced by Flook's argument that his application could be distinguished from Benson's simply because of the presence of "post-solution activity" (*i.e.,* the adjustment of the alarm limit):

The notion that post-solution activity, no matter how conventional or obvious in itself, can transform an unpatentable principle into a patentable process exalts form over substance. A competent draftsman could attach some form of post-solution activity to almost any mathematical formula: the Pythagorean theorem would not have been patentable, or partially patentable, because a patent application contained a

29   *Ibid.,* at 71-72.
30   *Ibid.,* at 67.
31   437 U.S. 584 (1978).
32   *In re Flook,* 559 F. 2d 21(1977).
33   Note 31 above, at 587.
34   *Ibid.,* at 589.
35   *Ibid.,* at 590.
36   *Ibid.,* at 589.

final step indicating that the formula, when solved, could be usefully applied to existing surveying techniques.[37]

The Supreme Court thus made it clear that it would not tolerate the dressing-up of unstatutory claims in terms of post-solution activity. Rather, the "proper analysis" must look to whether the "process as a whole" is new and useful.[38] Applying this test to the facts of *Flook*, the Supreme Court found it "absolutely clear that respondent's application contains no claim of patentable invention."[39]

5.2.2   The Court of Customs and Patent Appeals' Interpretation of *Benson* and *Flook:* The *Freeman-Walter* Two-Step Test

Despite the apparent finality of the Supreme Court's rulings in *Benson* and *Flook*, the evolution of patent protection for programs and program-related inventions has been erratic in the extreme. Looking back on the developments to 1980, Gemignani depicted the following scenario:

> The plot has all of the elements of a comic opera with four principal characters: the Patent Office, which steadfastly turns down every application for a patent on a computer program; the court of Customs and Patent Appeals, which has fought for program patents in the face of increasing opposition from the Supreme Court; the Supreme Court, itself confused and trying to apply "nineteenth century legal notions to computer technology without understanding the technology,"[40] which keeps reversing the court of Customs and Patents Appeals without directly confronting the issue of program patentability; and Congress, which, despite anxious pleas from the Supreme Court to resolve the issue by statute, does nothing.[41]

Congress has still not intervened, and the Patent Office and the courts have continued to muddle through as best they can.

Following *Benson*, the Court of Customs and Patent Appeals developed in the case of *In re Freeman*[42] a two-pronged test for determining whether a computer-related invention qualifies as statutory subject matter under section 101 of the Patent Act. The first stage requires a determination of whether the claim directly or indirectly recites an

---

37   *Ibid.*, at 590.
38   *Ibid.*, at 591.
39   *Ibid.*, at 594.
40   Davis, "Computer Programs and Subject Matter Patentability" (1977), 6 Rutgers J. of Computers Tech. & L. 1-25 at 14.
41   Gemignani, "Legal Protection for Computer Software: The View from '79" (1980), 7 Rutgers J. of Computers, Tech. & L. 269-312 at 292.
42   573 F. 2d 1237 (C.C.P.A., 1978).

"algorithm as defined in *Benson*.[43] If the answer is "yes" then the court must decide whether the claim taken in its entirety "wholly preempts that algorithm."[44] On the facts of *Freeman,* the Court of Customs and Patent Appeals found that a system for typesetting which used a computer and a conventional phototypesetter passed the test and qualified as statutory subject matter.[45]

Following the Supreme Court's ruling in *Flook,* the second leg of the *Freeman* "two-step" test was modified somewhat in the case of *In re Walter*.[46] Under the test as reformulated, once it has been established that a claim directly or indirectly recites an algorithm, the following analysis must be made of the claim "as a whole":[47]

> If it appears that the mathematical algorithm is implemented in a specific manner to define structural relationships between the physical elements of the claim (in apparatus claims) or to refine or limit claim steps (in process claims), the claim passes muster under s. 101. If, however, the mathematical algorithm is merely presented and solved by the claimed invention, as was the case in *Benson* and *Flook,* and is not applied in any manner to physical elements or process steps, no amount of post-solution activity will render the claim statutory; nor is it saved by a preamble merely reciting the field of use of the mathematical algorithm.[48]

On the facts, Walter's claimed invention for processing seismic exploration data was found to be merely an improved method of calculation to be used in seismic prospecting. The specific end use (*i.e.,* the post-solution activity) did not transform the claims into statutory subject matter.[49] By no longer requiring literal pre-emption of the algorithm to defeat the applicant, the *Walter* court's formulation of the second prong of the *Freeman* test brought the test into line with the Supreme Court's ruling in *Flook.*

5.2.3   The Supreme Court's Rulings in *Diehr* and *Bradley*

In 1981 the Supreme Court dealt with two further computer-related inventions in the cases of *Diamond v. Diehr*[50] and *Diamond v. Bradley*.[51]

---

43   *Ibid.,* at 1245. In *Benson* the Supreme Court defined an algorithm as "a procedure for solving a given type of mathematical problem," 409 U.S. 63 at 65. The *Freeman* court stressed that a mathematical formula dressed up in "words which mean the same thing" would still be treated as an algorithm, 573 F. 2d at 1246.

44   *Ibid.,* at 1245.

45   *Ibid.,* at 1247.

46   618 F. 2d 758 (C.C.P.A., 1980).

47   *Ibid.,* at 767.

48   *Ibid.*

49   *Ibid.,* at 770-1.

50   450 U.S. 175 (1981).

51   450 U.S. 381 (1981).

The *Diehr* case concerned a claim for "a process for molding raw, uncured synthetic rubber into cured precision products."[52] The cure time was calculated according to "well-known time, temperature and cure relationships."[53] What was new about Diehr's method was that measurements obtained from constant monitoring of the temperature inside the mould were fed into a computer. The computer then repeatedly recalculated the cure time and signalled the optimal opening time for the press.

The Patent and Trademark Office construed the claim as basically being for a computer program, and on the basis of *Benson* ruled it to be non-statutory subject matter.[54] The Court of Customs and Patent Appeals disagreed and instead found the claim to be directed to an improved process for moulding rubber articles.[55] It was thus patentable.

By a five to four majority, the United States Supreme Court upheld the Court of Customs and Patent Appeals' ruling. Rehnquist J., for the majority, noted that three years earlier the Supreme Court had rejected Flook's claim for a method of computing an "alarm limit" because "[a]n alarm limit is simply a number and the Court concluded that the application sought to protect a formula for protecting this number."[56] However, Diehr's claim could be distinguished as follows:

> In contrast, the respondents here do not seek to patent a mathematical formula. Instead, they seek patent protection for a process of curing synthetic rubber. Their process admittedly employs a well-known mathematical equation, but they do not seek to pre-empt the use of that equation. Rather, they seek only to foreclose from others the use of that equation in conjunction with all of the other steps in the claimed process. . . . Obviously, one does not need a "computer" to cure natural or synthetic rubber, but if the computer use incorporated in the process patent significantly lessens the possibility of "overcuring" or "undercuring," the process as a whole does not thereby become unpatentable subject matter.[57]

---

52 For commentaries see: Casenote, "Patent Law . . . Diamond v Diehr" (1981), 13 St. Mary's L.J. 420-39; Blumenthal, "Supreme Court Sets Guidelines for Patentability of Computer Related Inventions: Diamond v. Diehr" (1981), 63 J.P.O.S. 117-22; Moskowitz, "The Patentability of Software Related Inventions After Diehr and Bradley" (1981), 63 J.P.O.S. 222-32; Recent Developments, "Patent Law . . . Diamond v Diehr" (1981), 48 Tenn. L.R. 1042-66; Casenote, "Diamond v Diehr II" (1982), 23 South Tex. L.J. 224-33; Note, "Algorithm Patentability After Diamond v Diehr" (1982), 15 Indiana L.R. 713-32; Note, "Patent Law: Patentability of a Process That Includes a Programmed Digital Computer: The Court Invents a New Standard – Diamond v Diehr" (1981), 7 U. Daytona L.R. 157-68; Stout, "Protection of Programming in the Aftermath of Diamond v Diehr" (1983), IV Computer L.J. 207-42.

53 *Ibid.*

54 *In re Diehr,* 602 F. 2d 982 at 985 (C.C.P.A., 1979).

55 *Ibid.,* at 988.

56 Note 52 above, at 186.

57 *Ibid.,* at 187.

Thus, the Supreme Court used the *Diehr* case as an opportunity to begin to break away from the restrictiveness of their earlier ruling in *Benson*. This break could not be achieved without a somewhat unnatural transition from the simplicity of a general exclusion to the more subtle analysis of each computer-related claim in its entirety. In particular, it is not entirely clear why the use made of the numbers computed in the Diehr process was not discounted as post-solution activity. It will be recalled that in *Flook* the Supreme Court had stressed that no mere reference to a useful application in a claim for an algorithm could render the claim statutory.[58]

The dissent in *Diehr*, which was rather longer than the majority opinion, did draw attention to the apparent artificiality of the distinction which the majority had purported to draw between Flook's claims and those of Diehr. Stevens J., who wrote the dissent, noted that the majority was only able to find Diehr's claim to be statutory by reading it as being for "a method of constantly measuring the actual temperature inside a rubber moulding press."[59] Yet there was nothing new about either the measuring devices used or the method of measuring the temperature.[60] Moreover, Stevens J. pointed out that the Court of Customs and Patent Appeals had not disturbed the finding of the Patent and Trademark Office Board of Appeals, that:

> the only difference between the conventional methods of operating a moulding press and that claimed in [the] application rests in those steps which relate to the calculation incident to the solution of the mathematical problem or formula used to control the mold heater and the automatic opening of the press.[61]

Thus, for the minority, a "fair reading of the entire application" made it clear that the invention was nothing more than "a method of using a digital computer to determine the amount of time that a rubber molding press should remain closed."[62] This Stevens J. found to be "strikingly reminiscent of the method of updating alarm limits that Dale Flook sought to protect."[63]

The Supreme Court was certainly in danger of falling into the trap which it had itself anticipated of exalting form over substance.[64] Nevertheless, *Diehr* gave the Patent Office and the Court of Customs and Patent Appeals the long awaited green light to assess program-related

---

58   See text accompanying notes 37-38, above.
59   Note 52 above, at 206.
60   *Ibid.*, at 207-08.
61   *Ibid.*, at 208.
62   *Ibid.*
63   *Ibid.*, at 209.
64   *Parker v. Flook*, 437 U.S. 584 at 590 (1978).

inventions on their merits and opened the door to a more discriminating analysis of the statutory subject matter question.

As a companion case to *Diamond v. Diehr,* the Supreme Court heard argument in the case of *Diamond v. Bradley.*[65] *Bradley* concerned an appeal from a ruling by the Court of Customs and Patent Appeals that a piece of firmware qualified as statutory subject matter under section 101. Unfortunately, the opportunity for the Supreme Court to clarify this important area of patent law was lost when an equally divided court affirmed the Court of Customs and Patent Appeals' decision without making any comment as to the merits of the case.[66]

Bradley and Franklin's invention was entitled a "Switch System Base Mechanism." It provided an improved method for changing data stored in temporary locations known as "scratchpad registers."[67] The Patent Office rejected the claims as being directed to a mathematical algorithm which fell foul of the rule in *Benson,*[68] and the Board of Appeals affirmed. In allowing the inventors' appeal, the Court of Customs and Patent Appeals found that the Board had confused "*what* the computer does with *how* it is done."[69] A computer inevitably uses "mathematical operations" to manipulate data, but "[o]f importance is the significance of the data and their manipulation in the real world, *ie what* the computer is doing."[70] The Court found the claimed invention to be "a combination of hardware elements – a machine."[71] For the purposes of section 101 it was no different from "a strictly mechanical adding machine."[72] The Court then applied the *Freeman* two-step test and concluded that no mathematical formula or method of calculation was "either claimed as such or essential to the vitality of the claims."[73]

By allowing a patent in respect of firmware, which shares characteristics with both hardware and software, the Court of Customs and Patent Appeals stepped closer to a position whereby certain uses of algorithms in and of themselves could qualify for patent protection. As will be seen, a further movement towards this position has since occurred in the case of *In re Pardo.*[74]

---

65   450 U.S. 381.
66   *Ibid.,* Chief Justice Burger had excused himself from the case.
67   *Re Bradley,* 600 F. 2d 807 (C.C.P.A., 1979).
68   *Ibid.,* at 809. The examiner misread *Benson* on this point as holding that all computer program and program-related inventions are nonstatutory.
69   *Ibid.,* at 811 (emphasis supplied).
70   *Ibid.,* at 812 (emphasis supplied).
71   *Ibid.,* at 813.
72   *Ibid.,* at 812.
73   *Ibid.,* at 813.
74   685 F. 2d 912 (C.C.P.A., 1982).

One further point which was clarified in *Diehr* and *Bradley* was that the determination of statutory subject matter should be regarded as quite separate from the issues of novelty (section 102) and non-obviousness (section 103).[75] Of these two further criteria, only the issue of non-obviousness has yet reached the Supreme Court.[76] Despite the relaxation of the statutory subject matter requirements which *Diehr* and *Bradley* signalled, this preliminary issue has continued to be a major focus of litigation. However, as more claims pass the statutory subject matter test, it is likely that attention will gradually shift to questions of novelty and unobviousness.

5.2.4 Developments Since Diehr: A New Challenge to the Supreme Court?

In October 1981, the Patent and Trade Mark Office issued new Guidelines setting out patent examining procedures for program-related inventions.[77] The Guidelines confirmed that the *Freeman-Walter* two stage test would continue to provide the framework for investigations of patentability. In future, however, claims directed to a computer program would only be deemed non-statutory "if, when considered as a whole, they merely recite a mathematical algorithm, or a method of calculation."[78]

A year later, the United States Court of Customs and Patent Appeals merged with the United States Court of Claims to become the United States Court of Appeals for the Federal Circuit. Before that date, however, the Court of Customs and Patent Appeals had dealt with four computer-related patent cases in the light of *Diamond v. Diehr*.[79]

The first, *In re Taner*,[80] concerned claims relating to a method of seismic exploration involving simulated energy waves. The claims were rejected by both the Examiner and the Board of Appeals on the dual grounds that the claimed subject matter was nonstatutory and that the claimed invention was "obvious." The Court of Customs and Patent Appeals disagreed on both counts. Looking at the claims as a whole, the Court found them to "set forth a *process*" which constituted statutory subject matter.[81] Although an algorithm was directly recited in the

---

75   450 U.S. 175 at 190; 600 F. 2d 807 at 812.
76   *Dann v. Johnston*, 424 U.S. 219 (1976).
77   Patent and Trademark Office, *Manual of Patent Examining Procedures*, s. 2110.
78   *Ibid.*
79   See Milde, "Life After Diamond v. Diehr: The CCPA Speaks Out on the Patentability of Computer-Related Subject Matter" (1982), 64 J.P.O.S. 434-56.
80   681 F. 2d 787 (C.C.P.A., 1982).
81   *Ibid.*, at 790.

claims, the Court did not share the Board's view that "appellants seek to patent that algorithm in the abstract."[82] In reaching this conclusion, the Court distinguished *Walter*[83] (which had also concerned seismic signals) and overturned its decision in *Christianson*[84] in which it had rejected a method claim on the basis of a narrower interpretation of *Benson.* On the secondary question of obviousness, the Court found that earlier seismic wave inventions did not anticipate Taner's method.

On August 5, 1982, the Court handed down two more decisions on software-related claims, *In re Pardo*[85] and *In re Abele.*[86] *Pardo* dealt with the first step of the *Freeman-Walter* test and with an issue of obviousness, while *Abele* dealt with the second step of the test.

Pardo and Landau's application concerned a piece of operating software which rearranged formulae into a proper order for execution in certain calculations. The specification described the invention as an "algorithm" and for the Board of Appeals that alone was enough evidence of its unpatentability.[87] The Board also ruled that the claimed invention was obvious.[88] The Court of Customs and Patent Appeals disagreed on both these issues.

Crucial to the Court's reversal was its definition of "algorithm." Pardo and Landau had in fact filed their patent application before the Supreme Court had even decided *Benson,* and thus before the limited interpretation of "algorithm" had been developed in that and subsequent decisions. Thus the applicants' use of the word to describe their invention was hardly an admission that they were claiming nonstatutory subject matter.[89] Rather, the Court of Customs and Patent Appeals stressed that the *Freeman-Walter* test only applied to *mathematical* algorithms.[90] Even the Examiner in the present case had acknowledged that the claimed algorithm was not mathematical in nature. The Court went further and ruled that, in terms of generality of application, the claimed invention, as in *Bradley,* was no more restrictive than a claim for a general purpose adding machine:

> Appellants' method claims are directed to executing programs in a computer. The method operates on any program and any formula which may be input, regardless of

---

82   *Ibid.*
83   618 F. 2d 758 (C.C.P.A., 1980).
84   478 F. 2d 1392 (C.C.P.A., 1973).
85   684 F. 2d 912 (C.C.P.A., 1982).
86   684 F. 2d 902 (C.C.P.A., 1982).
87   Note 85 above, at 914.
88   *Ibid.,* at 915.
89   *Ibid.,* at 916.
90   *Ibid.*

mathematical content. That a computer controlled according to the invention is capable of handling mathematics is irrelevant to the question of whether a mathematical algorithm is recited by the claims.[91]

Thus in future, the Patent Office will have to look much more closely at what any so-called "algorithm" used in a claimed invention actually is and does.

The Court also disagreed on the second issue, obviousness. The Board of Appeals had taken judicial notice that the invention was obvious and thus cited no evidence in support of its rejection on this ground. The Court found, however, that "the skill of a person of ordinary skill in either computer programming or design is not a proper subject for judicial notice today, no matter how simple a claimed invention may seem in hindsight."[92] Rather, the Board should have determined the prior art, the differences between the prior art and the claimed invention, and the level of ordinary skill in the art at the time of the invention.[93] In a field which changes as rapidly as computer programming, the issue of obviousness may prove critical in future cases. What is obvious to people skilled in the art today may have been merely science fiction even a few years ago.

The distinction between mathematical and non-mathematical algorithms arose again in the case of *In re Abele*. The claimed invention was an improved technique of computer tomography (CAT Scanning) "whereby the exposure to X-ray is reduced while the reliability of the produced image is improved."[94] The Examiner rejected the claims on the basis of a narrow reading of *Parker v. Flook*. He concluded that, apart from certain mathematical calculations, all the steps of the method and apparatus claims were well known or "merely a necessary antecedent step to provide values for solving the mathematical equations."[95] This reasoning was firmly rejected by the Court of Customs and Patent Appeals which found this interpretation of *Flook* to have been rejected already on many occasions, including by the Supreme Court in *Diamond v. Diehr*.

The Board of Appeals also ruled the claims unstatutory but relied instead on the *Freeman-Walter* test in doing so. In particular, the Board found that the claims did not implement the mathematical algorithm "in a manner to define structural relationships between physical elements in the apparatus claims or to refine or limit claim steps in the process

---

91   *Ibid.*
92   *Ibid.*, at 917.
93   As required by *Graham v. John Deere Co.*, 383 U.S. 1 (1966).
94   Note 86 above, at 903.
95   *Ibid.*, 904.

claims."[96] On appeal, this approach too was rejected by the Court, which instead opted for a far broader reading of *Walter*. In the Court's opinion, the purpose of the two-part analysis should be understood as follows:

> The goal is to answer the question "What did applicants invent?" If the claimed invention is a mathematical algorithm, it is improper subject matter for patent protection, whereas if the claimed invention is an application of the algorithm section 101 will not bar the grant of a patent.[97]

Applying this analysis to the facts, the court found that some of the claims passed the test, while others failed.[98]

The last of the four decisions by the Court of Customs and Patent Appeals following *Diamond v. Diehr* was *In re Meyer and Weissman*.[99] The claimed invention was a "process and an apparatus for identifying locations of probable malfunction in a complex system," in this case the human brain.[100] Data gathered from a series of standard tests was fed into a computer which then, *inter alia,* displayed results on a screen. The invention was basically a diagnostic or memory aid for a physician. Its purpose was "replacing, in part, the thinking processes of a neurologist with a computer."[101] Both the Examiner and the Board rejected all claims as being directed to a mathematical algorithm and thus being nonstatutory under the *Benson* test.[102]

While it upheld the decision of the Board, the Court of Customs and Patent Appeals was careful to qualify the basis on which the application was rejected. The status of mathematical algorithms and mental processes was addressed directly. The Court stressed again that scientific principles and laws of nature could not be patented, but pointed out that not all mathematical algorithms fell into this category:

> [S]ome mathematical algorithms and formulae do not represent ideas or mental processes and are simply logical vehicles for communicating possible solutions to complex problems. The *presence of a mathematical algorithm or formula in a claim is merely an indication that a scientific principle, law of nature, idea or mental process may be the subject matter claimed and, thus, justify a rejection of that claim under 35 USC 101; but the presence of a mathematical algorithm or formula is only a signpost for further analysis.*[103]

Thus it is not the presence of an algorithm, even of a mathematical algorithm, which matters, but rather what the algorithm represents. The

---

96   *Ibid.,* 905.
97   *Ibid.*
98   *Ibid.,* at 907.
99   215 U.S.P.Q. 193 (1982).
100   *Ibid.,* at 196.
101   *Ibid.,* at 198.
102   *Ibid.,* at 196.
103   *Ibid.,* at 197 (emphasis supplied).

Court was thus stressing once again that content and not form will be determinative. Exactly the same principles of interpretation are to be applied to a claim representing a mental process.[104]

Thus in its four final rulings on the patentability of computer related inventions, the Court of Customs and Patent Appeals made a concerted effort to look beyond form and semantics to content and purpose. A subsequent example of this more discriminating type of approach by a lower court can be seen in *Paine, Webber v. Merrill Lynch*.[105]

The plaintiffs in that case sought a declaratory judgement of non-infringement, invalidity and unenforceability of a patent held by Merrill Lynch. The patent in issue related to data processing methodology and apparatus for operating a cash management account system (CMA).[106] The specifications of the patent set out the schematic flow chart of the CMA, but they did not include a description of any apparatus for running the system. Paine Webber argued that the apparatus claims must fail as the recited "means" for performing certain functions referred "only to the functional steps rather than to specific apparatus or structure."[107] Moreover, Paine Webber alleged that the method claimed "merely describes a series of manipulative steps that can be performed by hand with the aid of paper, pencil and telephone."[108]

The Delaware District Court rejected these objections as being irrelevant to the central issue of whether the CMA constituted patentable subject matter under section 101 of the Act. What mattered was not "the label of the claims" but whether they included statutory subject matter.[109] Turning then to the substantive question of patentability, the court noted that the "mental steps" argument against protection had been discredited and that "computer programs are recognized as being

---

104   *Ibid.*, at 198.
105   *Paine, Webber, Jackson & Curtis Inc. v. Merrill Lynch, Pierce, Fenner & Smith Inc.*, 564 F. Supp. 1358 (D. Del., 1983).
106   The "CMA," otherwise known as a "Securities Brokerage – Cash Management system," provided a combination of three financial services: a brokerage security account, several money market funds and a charge/chequing account. *Ibid.*, at 1361-2.
107   *Ibid.*, at 1365.
108   *Ibid.*, at 1366.
109   The court made reference to *Application of Maucorps*, 609 F. 2d 481 at 485 (1979) in which the Court of Customs and Patent Appeals had noted that, whether an invention is claimed as an apparatus or process is often an exercise in drafting, and that those principles used to determine whether a patent claims statutory subject matter apply equally whether an invention is claimed as an apparatus or process. Note 105 above, at 1366.

patentable" provided that they "meet the same requirements as other inventions."[110]

Chief Judge Latchum used the phrases "computer program" and "computer algorithm" interchangeably, but was careful to distinguish both from "mathematical algorithms":

> Unfortunately, the term "algorithm" has been a source of confusion which stems from different uses of the term in the related, but distinct fields of mathematics and computer science. In mathematics, the word algorithm has attained the meaning of recursive computational procedure and appears in notational language, defining a computational course of events which is self contained, for example, $A^2 + B^2 = C^2$. In contrast, the computer algorithm is a procedure consisting of operation [sic] to combine data, mathematical principles and equipment for the purpose of interpreting and/or acting upon a certain data input. In comparison to the mathematical algorithm, which is self-contained, the computer algorithm must be applied to the solution of a specific problem.[111]

It might be said that this new definition of "computer algorithm," with its built-in requirement of post-solution activity, is nothing more than a semantic trick to avoid the pitfalls of the *Benson* case and objections to claims directed to "purely mental steps." Such a criticism of the judgement would be unfair, however, given the court's careful evaluation of the content and substance of the disputed claims rather than merely their form or wording.

In the absence of Supreme Court intervention, the task of further clarifying the boundaries of patent protection for programs and program-related inventions will fall to the new Court of Appeals for the Federal Circuit. It is to be hoped that the Court will continue to utilize the more flexible and refined test for algorithm patentability which has been developed in cases like *Pardo* and *Paine Webber*. Due to the need to satisfy the novelty and unobviousness requirements, together with the cost of obtaining a patent, there is still unlikely to be a flood of applications for patent-related inventions. Regardless of how relaxed the statutory subject-matter test becomes, copyright will almost certainly remain the primary source of protection for programs as such. Nevertheless, greater flexibility at the examining stage may encourage developers of truly innovative programs to seek patent protection for "computer algorithms" far more frequently than they have done in the past.

---

110   *Ibid.*
111   *Ibid.*, at 1366-7.

5.3 United Kingdom Patent Law

5.3.1 The 1977 Patents Act and the European Patent Convention

Under section 1 of the Patents Act 1977,[112] a patent may only be granted for an invention which is new,[113] involves an inventive step,[114] and is capable of industrial application.[115] Under section 1(3) certain things are expressly excluded from protection:

> [T]he following (among other things) are not inventions for the purposes of this Act, that is to say, anything which consists of –
> (a) a discovery, scientific theory or mathematical method;
> (b) a literary, dramatic, musical or artistic work or any other aesthetic creation whatever;
> (c) a scheme, rule or method for performing a mental act, playing a game or doing business, or a program for a computer;
> (d) the presentation of information . . . .

The exclusions are qualified to the following extent:

> the foregoing provisions shall prevent anything from being treated as an invention for the purposes of this Act only to the extent that a patent or an application for a patent relates to that thing as such.[116]

Thus, while section 1(2) apparently precludes the grant of a patent for any program *per se*, as a result of the caveat the question of protection for program-related inventions has been left wide open. As American courts have discovered, drawing a line between these two categories is easier said than done.

Section 1(5) empowers the Secretary of State to vary by order (subject to approval by both Houses of Parliament) the list of exclusions in section 1(2) "for the purpose of maintaining them in conformity with developments in science and technology." With regard to the patentability of programs *per se*, a relaxation seems unlikely. For one thing, the exclusion of programs from protection brings United Kingdom law in line with the European Patent Convention (EPC).[117] Moreover, the

---

112   25-26 Eliz. 2, c. 37.
113   Section 1(1)(a).
114   Section 1(1)(b).
115   Section 1(1)(c).
116   Section 1(2).
117   1973, arts. 52 and 57. Article 52 provides:
     52(1) European Patents shall be granted for any inventions which are susceptible of industrial application, which are new and which involve an inventive step.
     52(2) The following in particular shall not be regarded as inventions within the meaning of paragraph 1: (a) Scientific theories and mathematical methods; (b)

Banks Committee,[118] which reported on the British Patent System in 1970, was firmly opposed to patents for programs and recommended that:

> A computer program, that is: a set of instructions for controlling the sequence of operations of a data processing system, in whatever form the invention is presented e.g. a method of programming computers, a computer when programmed in a certain way and where the novelty or alleged novelty lies only in the program; should not be patentable.[119]

What then of patent protection for computer-related inventions? The objection of the Banks Committee was to claims in which "the invention lies merely in the program itself and does not result in any new process or product. . . ."[120] The Committee felt that such claims should be distinguished from "inventions . . . which involve the use of a program." The latter should be patentable provided the invention "does not merely reside in the details of the program."[121]

A similar approach can be seen in the *Guidelines for Examination in the European Patent Office.* In determining inventiveness generally, examiners are urged to "disregard the form or kind of claim and concentrate on the content in order to identify the novel contribution which the alleged 'invention' claimed makes to the known art."[122] This point is elaborated with specific reference to computer-related inventions thus:

> If the contribution to the known art resides solely in a computer program, then the subject matter is not patentable in whatever manner it may be presented in the claims. For example, a claim to a computer characterised by having the particular program stored in its memory or to a process for operating a computer under the control of the program would be as objectionable as a claim to the program *per se* or the program when recorded on magnetic tape.[123]

Is there any room under this approach for flexibility? For instance, might it be possible to draw a distinction between "operating" and "applications" software? Might a patent still be granted for a program

---

Programs for Computers.

52(3) The provisions of paragraph 2 shall exclude patentability of the subject matter or activities referred to in that provision only to the extent to which a European Patent relates to such subject matter as such.

All EEC Member States except Denmark have ratified the EPC, and all except Ireland and Denmark have enacted parallel national legislation.

118 *Report of the Committee to Examine the Patent System and Patent Law: The British Patent System* (London: HMSO Cmnd. 4407, 1970).

119 *Ibid.*, para. 487.

120 *Ibid.*, para. 486.

121 *Ibid.*

122 Chapter IV, "Patentability," para. 2.2.

123 *Ibid.*, para. 2.1.

which alters the manner in which a computer functions *qua* computer, rather than simply being for adapting a computer for use in a particular context?

It is obviously significant that both the European Patent Convention and the British Patents Act only exclude computer programs from protection where claimed "as such."[124] This restriction might be avoided if it were possible to construe a claim to a piece of operating software as being an improvement to a computer as a machine. An analogous situation is discussed in the *Guidelines for Examination in the European Patent office:*

> [A] gramophone record distinguished solely by the music recorded thereon would not be patentable; if, however, the form of the groove were modified so that the record, when used with an appropriate pickup mechanism, functioned in a new way (as in the first stereo record), there could be patentable subject matter.[125]

This line of reasoning is similar to that which has recently been applied to program claims by the United States Court of Customs and Patent Appeals.[126]

5.3.2   Court Decisions

In the United Kingdom, the patentability of program-related inventions has not yet been argued in a reported case concerning a patent applied for after 1 June 1978, the date when the 1977 Act came into force. The issue was, however, canvassed in five cases arising under the 1949 Patents Act. Under section 101(1) of that Act, the test for patentability was whether an alleged invention was a "manner of new manufacture" or "new method or process of testing."

In *Re Slee and Harris's Application,*[127] the alleged invention was an improved method of solving sets of simultaneous linear equations with the use of a known computer. The main benefit of the alleged invention was that it would make it possible for a number of processing operations ("iterations") to be conducted simultaneously rather than consecutively, thus substantially reducing the time taken to solve problems. Two separate applications were made and, for both, the threshold issue of patentability was considered at a preliminary hearing. The first two claims of the first application, together with a third claim submitted

---

124   EPC, art. 52(3); UK Patents Act, s. 1(2).
125   Note 122 above, para. 2.2.
126   *E.g., Diamond v. Bradley,* 450 U.S. 381 (1981); *In re Pardo* 684 F. 2d 912 (C.C.P.A., 1982). See 5.2.3, 5.2.4, above.
127   [1966] R.P.C. 194.

during the hearing, were essentially for a method of operating a computer in the improved manner. The examiner rejected all three claims on the basis that the "end product" of the methods claimed was "merely intellectual information" and as such did not come within section 101 of the Act.[128] A fourth claim, which was for the computer as programmed to operate in the prescribed manner, did not meet with this objection as it could be regarded as being directed to "a machine which has been temporarily modified."[129]

The specification of the second application was "substantially the same" as the first, but the claims were directed to the "programming means" by which the computer was to be controlled.[130] The examiner was aware of the fact that such "means" might be no more than a printed sheet of paper and as such might not be deemed patentable. However, he allowed this second application also to proceed on the ground that a "serious and relevant argument" could be made for regarding the means as analogous to a cam used to control the operation of a machine.[131]

The first computer-related case to come before the Patents Appeal Tribunal was *Badger Co. Inc.'s Application*.[132] The alleged invention was a method of mechanically designing and producing, with the aid of a computer and a plotter, a visual drawing of a piping system. In the Patent Office the hearing officer concluded that the applicant's were merely claiming "a method of using, programming and operating a computer," and that the product of this method, like the product in *Slee and Harris's Application*, was "merely intellectual information."[133] Accordingly, the officer refused to allow the application to proceed and observed that he did "not envisage any kind of permissible amendment which could overcome this difficulty."[134]

The Patents Appeal Tribunal disagreed. Lloyd-Jacob J. identified two potentially novel features in the application: "the preparation, tabulation and codification" of data to be fed into the computer and plotter, and "the conditioning of the operating mechanism so as to permit the computation to proceed in the manner desired."[135] While the former feature could not be patented, a claim directed to the latter was

---

128 *Ibid.*, at 197.
129 *Ibid.*, at 198.
130 *Ibid.*
131 *Ibid.* For reasons not related to the preliminary issue of s. 101 patentability, Slee and Harris's application did not in fact proceed to grant.
132 [1970] R.P.C. 36.
133 *Ibid.*, at 38.
134 *Ibid.*
135 *Ibid.*, at 39-40.

not *a priori* unallowable. The judge suggested two possible forms which an acceptable claim might take and eventually the application was accepted with claims drawn up on those lines.[136]

Gevers' Application concerned data processing apparatus (a computer) for recording the registration of word trade marks, and means for controlling such apparatus (punched cards).[137] In the Patent Office the Superintending Examiner found the alleged invention to be "a scheme or plan which, although it may be ingenious and useful, is not a patentable invention."[138] An appeal to the Patents Appeal Tribunal was allowed. Graham J. had absolutely no doubt that "data processing apparatus, which is . . . constrained to function in a particular way and produce a particular result" was a manner of manufacture for patent purposes.[139] The judge was equally convinced that a punched card could also properly be claimed as a manner of manufacture. As a control element in a computer, a punched card should be treated in the same way as conventional mechanical control devices such as cams and carburettors. Once again, an application with appropriately drawn claims was subsequently accepted.

The disputed claims in the next reported case, *Burroughs Corp.'s Application,* related to "a method of transmitting data over a communication link between a central computer and certain of a ring of outlying slave computers connected to it."[140] At the Patent Office the Superintending Examiner rejected the claims, relying once again on the ruling in *Slee and Harris's Application* to the effect that a process which had no product other than intellectual information could not constitute a manner of new manufacture.[141]

The appeal to the Patents Appeal Tribunal was heard by Graham and Whitford JJ. who rejected the rather simplistic approach taken by the Superintending Examiner. Graham J. stressed the importance of looking beyond the form of any claim to its substance:

[I]t is not enough to take a narrow and confined look at the "product" produced by a method. Of course, if a method is regarded purely as the conception of an idea, it can always be said that the product of such a method is merely intellectual information. If, however, in practice the method results in a new machine or process or an old machine giving a new and improved result, that fact should in our view be regarded as the

---

136 The successful claims were directed to "1. A process for conditioning the operation of a computer and associated plotter of known types to produce . . ." and "2. A computer of known type arranged to produce." *Ibid.,* at 41.
137 [1970] R.P.C. 91.
138 *Ibid.,* at 93.
139 *Ibid.,* at 98.
140 [1974] R.P.C. 147.
141 *Ibid.,* at 152.

"product" or the result of using the method, and cannot be disregarded in considering whether the method is patentable or not. Method claims of this kind have been held to be patentable in many cases.[142]

Thus the correct test for acceptance was whether the claim in question was "clearly directed to a method involving the use of apparatus modified or programmed to operate in a new way."[143] This test was found to have been satisfied and the application was remitted to the Patent Office for further consideration.[144]

The Patent Appeal Tribunal's final reported consideration of the status of program patents under the 1949 Patents Act came in *Int. Business Machines Corp.'s Application*.[145] In allowing a patent for a standard computer programmed in a novel way, Whitford J. reaffirmed the principle that "an inventive concept, if novel, can be patented to the extent that claims can be framed directly to an embodiment of the concept in some apparatus or process of manufacture."[146] In the instant case, there was no doubt that the computer itself was not novel. However, the Tribunal found that the claims were not in fact directed to the computer as such, and the apparatus comprising the computer programmed to carry out a particular system had sufficient novelty to merit protection.

The decision in *Slee and Harris's Application* left as an open question the possibility of patent protection for programs *per se* under the 1949 Act. This avenue has now been closed for the foreseeable future by the express exclusion of programs from the definition of statutory subject matter under the 1977 Act. Much clearer under the old Act, however, was the availability of protection for computers programmed in a particular manner and thus more generally for program-related inventions. While the issue has yet to come before the courts, there is no obvious reason why, in principle, such protection should not also be available under the new Act.

---

142   *Ibid.*, at 158.
143   *Ibid.*, at 160.
144   The judges anticipated but rejected the possible complaint that to allow this claim would be to "open the door to methods of operating simple calculators or cover academic mathematical solutions" *Ibid.*, at 160. Graham J. did, however, suggest that, provided they were embodied in some physical form, computer programs *per se* might be patentable (at 161). This route has, of course, now been closed off by s. 1(2)(c) of the 1977 Patents Act.
145   [1980] F.S.R. 564.
146   *Ibid.*, at 573.

5.4 Canadian Patent Law

Under the Canadian Patent Act[147] a patent can be issued for an "invention,"[148] defined in section 2 as:

> any new and useful art, process, machine, manufacture or composition of matter, or any new and useful improvement in any art, process, machine, manufacture or composition of matter.[149]

Section 28(3) contains the important limitation that "[n]o patent shall issue for . . . any mere scientific principle or abstract theorem." This limitation is not as directly applicable to software as the United Kingdom Act's exclusion of "a program for a computer."[150] The ruling out of protection for mathematical algorithms in the abstract does, however, cast doubt on the patentability of computer programs implementing such algorithms. Yet, as under the United Kingdom statute, an invention which entails the use of a program or which consists of a known computer programmed to operate in a particular way need not necessarily be barred from protection.

The precise implications of sections 2 and 28(3) for programs and program-related inventions have been the subject of speculation for some time. In January 1971, the Economic Council of Canada argued on policy grounds that patent protection for computer programs "would not be appropriate in Canada at the present time."[151] In December of the same year, the Patent Appeal Board handed down its first reported ruling in a program-related case, *Re Waldbaum's Application*.[152] The Applicant had devised a program for operating a known data processor in a new and unobvious way to process information about the traffic density on trunk telephone lines. He had claimed as an invention not the computer program itself, but rather his new method or process of controlling the computer and the novel use to which it was being put.

The Patent Appeal Board expressed its very definite agreement with the Patent Office's view that a program could not be patentable subject matter in itself. However, the Board identified the central issue

---

147   R.S.C. 1970, c. P-4.

148   *Ibid.*, s. 28(1).

149   *Ibid.*, s. 2.

150   1977 Patents Act, s. 1(3).

151   *Report on Intellectual and Industrial Property* (Ottawa: Information Canada, 1971). The main arguments given against patent protection were the administrative problems (and cost) of establishing novelty and the difficulty of policing protection (pp. 102-3). The critical issue of possible protection for program-related inventions was not even mentioned in the Report.

152   *Re Application No. 961,392* (1971), 5 C.P.R. (2d) 162.

in *Waldbaum* as being "whether a computer that is programmed in one way is a machine which is different from the same computer when programmed in another way."[153] The Board concluded that there was a difference and that, provided it operated in a new and unobvious manner, a computer programmed in a particular manner could indeed be patented.[154]

This decision seemed to leave considerable scope for the patenting of program-related inventions. However, when the Patent Appeal Board again considered a program-related invention in 1978, it laid down a rather stricter set of criteria for determining patentability. In *Schlumberger's Application*,[155] the claimed invention related to oil and gas exploration and consisted of a computer-operated process for deriving and analyzing measurements obtained from boreholes sunk into the earth. In the Patent Office, the application was rejected by the Commissioner of Patents. He took the view that Schlumberger was trying to claim a "monopoly on a computer programme" and thus the application must fail as "such a programme, even if it were new and useful, is not an invention within the meaning of s. 2 of the *Patent Act*."[156]

The Patent Appeal Board agreed that the claimed invention was not patentable and outlined its new position on program-related inventions as follows:

1. Claims to a computer program *per se* are *not* patentable;
2. Claims to a new method of programming a computer are *not* patentable;
3. Claims to a computer programmed in a novel manner, *expressed in any and all modes*, where the novelty lies solely in the program or algorithm, are *not* directed to patentable subject matter under Section 2 of the Patent Act;
4. Claims to a computing apparatus programmed in a novel manner, where the patentable advance is in the apparatus itself, are patentable; and
5. Claims to a method or process carried out with a specific novel computing apparatus devised to implement a newly discovered idea are patentable.[157]

While certainly much narrower than the criteria laid down in *Waldbaum*, this new position of the Board regarding program-related inven-

---

153 *Ibid.*, at 166.
154 Accordingly, the Patent Appeal Board had no objection to the following: claims defining "a data processor which is programmed or controlled so as to operate in a new and unobvious manner . . . ."; claims "directed to a method for controlling the operation of a computer . . ."; "a claim defining a process for conditioning the operation of a data processor . . ."; a claim defining "a process coomprising a new use of a stored programme data processing apparatus." . . . *Ibid.*, 168-9.
155 106 C.P.O.R. at xviii (P.A.B., 1970).
156 Quoted in the Federal Court of Appeal (1981), 56 C.P.R. (2d) 204 at 205.
157 106 C.P.O.R. at xxv.

tions was "not entirely negative."[158] However, a novel use for a novel program would not in itself constitute patentable subject matter.

The Schlumberger Corporation appealed to the Federal Court of Appeal, arguing that it was not seeking to patent a program as such.[159] Rather, the claimed invention was a machine-operated calculation process for extracting useful information from some measurements. This process used a computer program to speed things up. While the definition of "invention" in the Patent Act might indeed be read as excluding programs as such, there was nothing in the Act to indicate that an invention involving a computer must also be ruled out.

The Federal Court of Appeal did not seem to disagree with this argument but nevertheless dismissed Schlumberger's appeal. The Court looked closely at the "invention" which Schlumberger was attempting to patent and concluded that it was "merely the discovery that by making certain calculations according to certain formulae, useful information could be extracted from certain measurements."[160] Leaving aside the computer, the calculations and formulae were clearly unpatentable as being "mere scientific principle[s] or abstract theorem[s]."[161] That being the case, the use of a computer to execute the calculations could not render patentable what would otherwise be unpatentable.[162]

Despite the restrictiveness of the statutory subject-matter test set out by the Patent Appeal Board in *Schlumberger,* it should not be assumed that the door has been closed to patents for program-related inventions in Canada. What can be deduced with some certainty from the Court of Appeal's ruling in the case is that a patent will not be issued for the mere computerization of a process of calculation. On the other hand, an invention which is in itself new and useful will not be excluded from protection merely because it includes a computer program. It remains an open question whether the courts will in the future allow claims for the computerization of a process or method which has a tangible output (*i.e.,* not merely the result of a calculation).

An appeal to the Federal Court of Canada is currently pending in another computer program-related case. The case concerns an applica-

---

158   Hayhurst, "Industrial Property" (1979), 11 Ottawa L.R. 391 at 404.

159   *Schlumberger Can. Ltd. v. Commr. of Patents* (1981), 56 C.P.R. (2d) 204 at 205, 38 N.R. 299. Leave to appeal to S.C.C. refused (1981), 63 C.P.R. (2d) 261n.

160   *Ibid.,* at 206.

161   *Ibid.,* quoting *Gottschalk v. Benson,* 409 U.S. 63 (1972). For a discussion of the degree of concordance between the Federal Court's ruling in *Schlumberger* and the jurisprudence developed by the U.S. Supreme Court see August, "Patentability of Computers and their Programs in Canada" (1982), 14 Bull. Pat. & T.M. Inst. of Can. 923-37.

162   "[T]he fact that a computer is or should be used to implement discovery does not change the nature of that discovery." Note 159 above, at 206.

tion, originally filed in 1973, for a patent to protect a "Securities Valuation System."[163] The claimed invention made it possible to calculate and display the value of an investment portfolio using a computer programmed in a particular way. In January 1977, a Patent Office Examiner ruled that the claims did not disclose statutory subject matter and refused to allow the application to proceed. An appeal to the Patent Appeal Board was heard in May 1982. The Board accepted the applicant's argument that inventions involving computers were not necessarily excluded from patent protection, but stressed that "developments including computers are not brought within the terms of the Patent Act simply because a computer is used in their implementation."[164] The general status of program-inventions since *Schlumberger* was then summarised by the Board in the following terms:

> In computer-related subject matter unless the actual physical aspects are patentable or unless the inherent capabilities of a computer have been combined with another system, which is already on its own merits within a statutory field of invention and thereby produce either a new tangible result or an improvement to a tangible result, then, the Board considers, it is very difficult to find a patentable invention. We take the view that a process or procedure for using a known computer to process information, without further integration of that information into some practical system, is not patentable subject matter within Section 2 of the Patent Act. To state what we understand from *Schlumberger*: this is why computers were invented.[165]

Turning to the application before it, the Board found that, although the claimed invention was described as being a computer system and a method for operating that system, the true subject matter of the application was the computer programs which were used in the system. Such programs, however original, could not in themselves ever be patented. The Board remitted the application to the Commissioner of Patents who ruled that the claims did not contain patentable subject matter.[166]

The precise manner in which computer-related patent claims are drafted will often be critical. In the "Securities Valuation System" case the Patent Appeal Board placed considerable emphasis on the fact that, at one point in the application, there was a reference to "the computer programs comprising the invention."[167] If the applicant's appeal now proceeds to the Federal Court it will be interesting to see if such wording again proves fatal. In any event, it is perhaps unfortunate that the case is

---

163   (1984), 112 C.P.O.R. v. (P.A.B.). The time scales in this case are a good example of the logistic problems of patent litigation.

164   *Ibid.*, at vi.

165   *Ibid.*, at vii.

166   *Ibid.*, at ix.

167   *Ibid.*

so similar to *Schlumberger's Application* in that in both cases the allegedly inventive processes and methods merely produced a mathematical conclusion. A program-related invention with a tangible end product might have a greater chance of success.[168]

168   Indeed in the "Securities Valuation Case" the Board distinguished the application before it from *Diamond v. Diehr* as follows: "In this case . . . the process being claimed occurs entirely within the computer system and the end result is not a real change in a tangible thing, it is still, at the end of the claimed process, merely information. There is no further integration into a practical process as in *Diehr*. We do not see, therefore, how the *Diehr* case assists Applicant. It points the other way." *Ibid.*, at viii.

Chapter 6

Trade Secrets, Confidentiality, and Contractual Protection of Programs and Data

6.1 The Legal Foundations of Trade Secrecy and Confidentiality

6.1.1 Equity, Contract, Tort or Property?

Although copyright has its origin in the common law it has now almost entirely become, as patent law has always been, a creature of statute. Consequently, although issues of legal principle do arise when copyright and patent concepts are applied to software, questions regarding the scope of such protection are in essence matters of statutory interpretation. In marked contrast, the law relating to trade secrets and confidentiality is generally lacking in any settled conceptual base. Even in the United States, where most states have enacted legislation to deal specifically with trade secrets, the doctrinal foundations of the rights which are derived from trade secret law are still disputed by both courts and commentators.

This is not to say that trade secret protection for software is unobtainable at present. On the contrary, some commentators have suggested that it is probably the most widely used of all the legal protections currently available.[1] Yet the uncertain conceptual basis of such rights has significant implications for the breadth of protection which can be secured and for the types of remedies which are available.

Secrecy rights have variously been attributed to equity, contract, tort and property. Regarding the first of these, equity, an old English

---

1   Bender, "Trade Secret Protection of Software" (1970), 38 Geo. Wash. L.R. 909-57; Bender, *Computer Law: Evidence and Procedure* (New York: Matthew Bender, 1983); Tapper, *Computer Law*, 3rd ed. (London and New York: Longman, 1983).

couplet attributed to Sir Thomas More states that "Three things are to be helpt in Conscience: Fraud, Accident and things of Confidence."[2] Thus, in certain circumstances equity will require a person who has promised to do so to keep a secret. Accordingly, a court may grant an injunction to restrain a promisor from breaking a promise, or award an injured party damages where a confidence has been breached.

Protection for confidential information may also be governed by contract law. By means of an express or implied covenant a party to a contract may be bound not to disclose certain information to third parties without authorization. Such terms will commonly be included in a programmer's contract of employment and can also be found in software licensing agreements. Where covenants are explicit, contractual protection of trade secrets may seem to have an advantage over equitable remedies in that the scope of protection is at least clearly defined. Moreover, confidential information which would not qualify as a trade secret may be protected contractually.[3] However, few of the covenants commonly used in employment contracts and licence agreements have been tested in the courts, and it may well be that many are too broad to be enforceable. Meanwhile, at the other end of the scale, a covenant which is drawn too narrowly might actually have the effect of limiting the scope of protection which would otherwise be available in equity. Thus, the law of contract may be significant in defining the scope of trade secret protection. It does not however provide the primary foundation for such protection. Courts have made it clear that an obligation of confidence can arise even in the absence of any express or implied contractual relationship.[4]

A third possibility is to locate trade secrecy and confidentiality in tort law. In the United States the generally accepted definition of trade secrets is that found in the Restatement of Torts,[5] while in England the Law Commission has recommended the creation by statute of a new tort

---

2   1 *Rolle's Abridgement* 374, quoted by Megarry J. in *Coco v. Clark,* [1969] R.P.C. 41.

3   *Cybertek Computer Products v. Whitfield,* 203 U.S.P.Q. 1020 at 1023 (Cal. Sup. Ct., 1977).

4   *Saltman Enrg. Co. v. Cambell Enrg. Co.,* [1963] 3 All E.R. 413n, 65 R.P.C. 203 at 211; *Seager v. Copydex,* [1967] 2 All E.R. 415, [1967] R.P.C. 349 at 368; *Schauenburg Indust. Ltd. v. Borowski* (1979), 25 O.R. (2d) 737, 8 B.L.R. 164, 50 C.P.R. (2d) 69, 101 D.L.R. (3d) 701 (H.C.).

5   *Restatement of Torts,* s. 757, comment b (1939). Section 757 was omitted from the 2nd Restatement in 1979. However, in *Amoco Production Co. v. Lindley,* 609 P. 2d 733 (S.C. Okla., 1980), the court observed that the omission was "because in the opinion of the editors the law of trade secrecy has developed independently into a body of law in its own right, separate from its origins in tort law. The tort premises are nonetheless an integral part of the developed case law of trade secrets."

of breach of confidence.[6] In addition, the law relating to unfair competition, which is at least analogous to tortious liability,[7] can be viewed as a source of protection for trade secrets.

Finally, a trade secret can be regarded as property, the misappropriation of which might give rise not only to civil remedies such as conversion damages, but also criminal sanctions such as fines and imprisonment. This construction of trade secrets is inevitably controversial due to the potential operation of the criminal law, yet it is precisely the availability of enforcement "teeth" which makes the proprietory model attractive to software developers.[8]

6.1.2 Judicial Attitudes

Courts on both sides of the Atlantic have on the whole been reluctant to recognize property rights as the primary basis for remedying what are essentially breaches of confidence. In an oft-quoted passage in *DuPont Power Co. v. Masland*[9] Mr. Justice Holmes stated in 1917 that:

> The word property as applied to trademarks and trade secrets is an unanalyzed expression of certain secondary consequences of the primary fact that the law makes some rudimentary requirements of good faith. Whether the plaintiffs have any valuable secret or not the defendant knows the facts, whatever they are, through a special confidence that he accepted. The property may be denied but the confidence cannot be. Therefore the starting point for the present matter is not property or due process of law, but that the defendant stood in confidential relations with the plaintiffs, or one of them.

Similarly, in England Lord Denning, in *Fraser v. Evans*,[10] explained the basis of remedies for breach of confidence thus:

> [T]he court will, in a proper case, restrain the publication of confidential information. The jurisdiction is based, not so much on property or on contract, but rather on the duty to be of good faith. No person is permitted to divulge to the world information which he has received in confidence, unless he has just cause or excuse for doing so. Even if he comes by it innocently, nevertheless, once he gets to know that it was originally given in confidence, he can be restrained from breaking that confidence.

---

6   Working Paper, *Breach of Confidence* (London: HMSO, 1974); Report No. 110, *Breach of Confidence* (London: HMSO Cmnd. 8388, 1981).

7   ˙Dworkin, "Unfair Competition: Is the Common Law Developing a New Tort?" [1979] E.I.P.R. 241.

8   See the discussion of criminal sanctions in chapter 7 below.

9   244 U.S. 10 at 102 (1917).

10   [1969] 1 Q.B. 349, [1969] 1 All E.R. 8 at 11 (C.A.). In the earlier trade secret case of *Seager v. Copydex*, note 4 above, at 368, Lord Denning had already stated that "The law on this subject does not depend on any implied contract. It depends on the broad principle of equity that he who has received information in confidence shall not take unfair advantage of it."

In North America, however, the proprietory model for the legal protection of confidential information continues to enjoy a degree of popularity. Some judges still seem to think in terms of property or at least quasi-property rights and, over the past two decades, many American jurisdictions have expressly criminalized the misappropriation of trade secrets. In Canada also there have been moves to extend the scope of criminal sanctions in the area of confidential information. Such innovations are clearly predicated on a proprietory construction of trade secrets.

What, then, is the conceptual basis of the law in this area? Confusing though it may seem, equity, contract, tort and property may all have an important role to play in the protection of confidential information. One general taxonomy is, however, crucial. As Tapper has observed:

> some of the fog which surrounds this whole area might be dispelled by emphasising more consistently the distinction between proprietary concepts based upon the secrecy of the content of the information which generally give rise to real remedies, and confidential concepts based upon considerations of good faith between parties which generally give rise to personal remedies.[11]

Thus "trade secrets" as a form of intellectual *property* should be distinguished from duties of confidentiality founded on broad equitable and tortious principles. The law of contract may come into play in modifying both types of protection. It is unfortunate that these distinctions have not been consistently recognized or applied by either North American or English judges.

The scope of trade secrecy and confidentiality as sources of protection for software and data will now be outlined. The implications of the treatment of information as property merit further consideration and will be discussed separately in the context of possible criminal sanctions for theft of programs and data.[12]

6.2 The Scope of Protection Offered by Trade Secrecy and Confidentiality

6.2.1 Potential Breadth of Application

Trade secrecy and confidentiality potentially offer extremely broad protection. Unlike the operation of copyright and patent law, the general

---

11   Tapper, note 1 above, p. 31.
12   See chapter 7, below.

applicability of trade secrecy and confidentiality to software is well established.[13] A number of other advantages should be noted. Whereas neither copyright nor patents can protect ideas and principles in the abstract, there are no similar restrictions on what can be classified as confidential information. Moreover, protection is immediate, requires no formalities, and can continue indefinitely. The secrecy of the information must of course be maintained, and this may be an onerous burden. However, some secrets, such as the recipes for Coca-Cola and Kentucky Fried Chicken, have been successfully protected for considerable periods of time. Trade secrets and confidentiality also offer more comprehensive protection than either copyright or patents. Regarding software, for example, the idea underlying a computer program, the expression of that idea in flow chart, source or object code and related notes and documentation can all be protected.

Trade secret and confidentiality rights are also broad in terms of the types of infringement against which protection is offered. Misappropriation of a trade secret by any means, including memory alone, may be actionable. It is true that in the United States the Supreme Court on one occasion observed that "equity has no power to require a man to wipe clean the slate of his memory."[14] However, a close reading of that case makes it clear that relief was denied because on the facts there had been no breach of confidence and not because the disputed subject matter had been memorized.[15] Moreover, in a more recent ruling which dealt directly with misappropriation of software, a California court had no reservations in finding that "documentation need not be taken in order to establish liability. . . . [A]ppropriation by memory will be proscribed under the same circumstances as an appropriation via more tangible means."[16]

Similarly in England, while at one time the courts did not recognize any cause of action where confidential information was appropriated by memory alone,[17] this restriction no longer seems to exist. Thus, in *Amber Size and Chemical Co. v. Menzel*, Astbury J. commented:

---

13   See sections 5.3 and 5.4, above.

14   *Peerless Pattern Co. v. Pictorial Review Co.*, 132 N.Y.S. 37 at 39 (1911).

15   Bender, "Trade Secret Protection of Software" (1970), 38 Geo. Wash. L.R. at 940. Bender refers to *Rabinowitz v. Dasler*, 78 U.S.P.Q. 163 (1948), where the Supreme Court quoted the passage from *Peerless* yet still granted relief in a situation where appropriation was by memory.

16   *Cybertek Computer Products v. Whitfield*, 203 U.S.P.Q. 1020 at 1025 (Cal. Sup. Ct., 1977).

17   *E.g., Merryweather v. Moore*, [1892] 2 Ch. 518.

How can it possibly matter whether the servant learns the process by heart or writes it down? It is an equal breach of confidence to use or disclose it in either case.[18]

Other English and Commonwealth courts have since taken a similarly expansive view of the scope for acts infringing confidence.[19]

6.2.2   Restrictions on Scope: Rights of Employees and the Need to Preserve Secrecy

Reliance on trade secrecy and confidentiality to protect valuable information is not without its problems. While the misappropriation of specific secrets, perhaps even by memory alone, may be actionable, an employer cannot prevent a former employee from using his or her general skills and experience when moving on to a new job. Since employment mobility is high in the software industry, this qualification on the scope of protection may be very significant.[20] A programmer who has developed a software package for one employer will usually be able to write similar programs for a subsequent employer in considerably less time.

As with copyrights and patents, there is a broad policy issue at stake here concerning the free flow of information. In deciding the scope of trade-secret protection in a specific case, courts will bear in mind the general desirability of useful knowledge being disclosed.[21] The narrower policy question concerns the competing interests of employers and employees. As one American court put it:

> [I]n trade secret litigation, courts are looking at the equities of the given set of circumstances out of which the claimed trade secret arises. The courts are then balancing those equities between the right of the company to use its employees and resources to its utmost advantage against the right of the highly developed mind and skill of the employee.[22]

In seeking a balance, courts have tended to rely on distinctions between generic and specific information, with protection being available only for the latter.[23]

---

18   [1913] 2 Ch. 239 at 242.
19   *E.g., Printers and Finishers Ltd. v. Holloway (No. 2),* [1965] 1 W.L.R. 1, [1964] 3 All E.R. 731; *Westminster Chemical N.Z. Ltd. v. McKinley,* [1973] N.Z.L.R. 651; *Faccenda Chicken Ltd. v. Fowler,* [1984] 1 I.R.L.R. 61.
20   *E.g.,* in 1982, job turnover in California's Silicon Valley averaged 24%. Taylor, "Protecting Corporate Secrets," Time (Sept. 19, 1983).
21   *Structural Dynamics Corp. v. Enrg. Dynamics Corp.,* 401 F. Supp. 1102 at 1110 (E.D. Mich., 1975).
22   *Amoco Production Co. v. Lindley,* 609 P. 2d 733 at 745 (S. Ct. Okla., 1980).
23   *Telex Corp. v. IBM Corp.,* 510 F. 2d 894 at 929 (10th Cir., 1975); *Northern Office Microcomputers v. Rosenstein,* [1982] F.S.R. 124 at 140; *Faccenda Chicken Ltd. v. Fowler,* note 19 above, at 65-6. See sections 6.3.6 and 6.4.4 below.

The extent of equitable protection for confidential information essentially depends on the nature of the relationship which gives rise to the confidentiality. Remedies for misappropriation of trade secrets, however, will only be granted where a court is satisfied that a plaintiff has taken adequate steps to preserve secrecy. This burden on the plaintiff in an action may be onerous, and "often entails establishing that affirmative and elaborate steps were taken to insure that the secret claimed would remain so."[24] Precautions will usually be necessary on two fronts. Firstly, courts will expect a trade secret holder to take reasonable care to ensure that there is adequate "in-house" security for confidential programs. This will usually include both physical and security measures and the regulation of employees' access to and use of the confidential information. Secondly, secrecy must be maintained externally, that is, once software has been distributed on the market by sale or otherwise. Secrecy may be lost through widespread distribution of a software package without effective controls on its use, or alternatively due to "reverse engineering."

In the American courts there have already been a number of cases dealing specifically with the protection of software by trade secrecy or confidentiality. On the whole, existing doctrines have been applied with little apparent difficulty. In England and Canada there has been little litigation specifically in this area. However, if and when judicial comment appears, it is unlikely that there will be many surprises. As in the United States, protection of software and data as confidential information fits fairly easily into the existing legal framework.

6.3 Trade Secrets and Confidentiality in the United States

6.3.1 The Relationship between State Trade Secret Legislation and Federal Patent and Copyright Laws

In the United States, while patents and copyrights are governed by federal law, the protection of trade secrets is constitutionally the prerogative of the states. However, where federal and state laws purport to cover common subject matter, federal law will prevail. Since the subject matter of trade secrets will quite often also be patentable or copyrighta-

---

24   *Amoco Production Co. v. Lindley,* note 22 above, at 743.

ble, there is a possibility that trade secret laws enacted by states will be wholly or partly pre-empted by federal patent and copyright legislation.

In the case of patents, in 1964 the United States Supreme Court twice held that, just as a state could not directly encroach on the federal patent jurisdiction, neither could it do so indirectly by granting protection which was in conflict with federal patent laws.[25] For almost a decade the implications of these decisions for state trade secret laws remained uncertain, but in 1974 the Supreme Court clarified the matter somewhat in *Kewanee Oil v. Bicron.*[26] The majority of the justices who heard that case found there to be no conflict between an Ohio trade secret statute and the federal patent law such that the former would be pre-empted. On the contrary, the court observed that "Trade secret law and patent law have co-existed in this country for over one hundred years. Each has its particular role to play, and the operation of one does not take away from the need for the other."[27] In a subsequent case dealing with computer-related trade secrets,[28] the Tenth Circuit expressly applied the Supreme Court's ruling in *Kewanee* to refute an assertion that federal patent law pre-empted state trade secret protection.

The position regarding copyright is less clear. Section 301(a) of the 1976 Copyright Act provides that "all legal or equitable rights that are equivalent to any of the exclusive rights that are within the general scope of copyright . . . are governed exclusively by this title." This sweeping pre-emption provision is, however, immediately qualified in section 301(b) as follows:

> Nothing in this title annuls or limits any rights or remedies under the common law or statutes of any state with respect to . . .
>
> (3) activities violating legal or equitable rights that are not equivalent to any of the exclusive rights within the scope of copyright as specified by section 106.

The implications of this section for trade secret legislation were discussed by an Illinois District court in *Warrington Assoc. v. Real-Time Engineering Systems.*[29] The court noted the *Kewanee* decision regarding patent pre-emption and observed that "the congruence and, concomitantly, the likelihood of preemption, between patent and trade secret law is stronger than between trade secret and copyright law".[30] More specifically, the court had no doubt that the protection afforded by

---

25   *Sears Roebuck & Co. v. Stiffel Co.*, 376 U.S. 225 (1964); *Compco Co. v. Day-Bright Lighting*, 376 U.S. 234 (1964).

26   416 U.S. 470 (1974), reversing 478 F. 2d 1074 (6th Cir., 1973).

27   *Ibid.*, at 493.

28   *Telex v. IBM*, note 23 above.

29   216 U.S.P.Q. 1024 (N.D. Ill., 1981).

30   *Ibid.*, at 1026.

trade secrets was not "equivalent"[31] to that provided by copyright law since the former is far broader, protecting "the very ideas" of an author. The court then considered the legislative history of the Copyright Act and concluded that Congress had not viewed the new Act as pre-empting "the common law of trade secret misappropriation."[32] As a further distinction between copyright and trade secrets, the court noted that, at common law, "the trade secrets tort is premised on concepts of trust and confidentiality, and not copying."[33]

Nevertheless, the fields of trade secrecy and copyright are by no means mutually exclusive and the implications for secrecy of copyright publication of trade secret material must be borne in mind. In its discussion of the broader relationship between copyright and trade secrets the *Warrington* court commented:

> While disclosure of the expression does not vitiate rights secured by copyright law, that same disclosure may well strip the underlying idea of its originality and thus its status as a trade secret. To a certain degree the two respective rights in intellectual property interact. To the extent a work has been copyrighted and published, the chances of unpriviliged disclosure may increase. But the mere fact that an expression is copyrighted does not, in and of itself, disclose the trade secret or eliminate its mantle of confidentiality.[34]

This conclusion that limited publication does not necessarily destroy secrecy is consistent with an earlier ruling of the same district court. In *Management Science Amer. v. Cyborg Systems Inc.*[35] a computer program with a copyright notice affixed had been licensed to 600 licencees, but no registration had been made for copyright purposes. The court found the plaintiff's trade secret claims not to be barred as a matter of law.[36]

The first appeal court ruling on a trade secret preemption issue relating to software copyright came in *Technicon Medical Information*

---

31   As per Copyright Act 1976, s. 301(b).
32   The court quoted the following passage from the House Committee Report: "The evolving common law rights of 'privacy', 'publicity' and 'trade secrets' ... would remain unaffected so long as the causes of action contain elements such as an invasion of personal rights or a breach of trust or confidentiality." (H. Rep. No. 94-1476, 94th Cong., 2d Sess. at 132 (1976)).
33   Note 29 above, at 1026.
34   *Ibid.*
35   6 Comp. L. Serv. Rep. 921 (N.D. Ill., 1978).
36   Similarly, in the subsequent case of *BPI Systems v. Leith* a Texas district court found no pre-emption where the software package in question was "not copyrighted," presumably meaning not registered for copyright purposes: 532 F. Supp. 208 at 211 (1982).

System v. Green Bay Packaging.[37] The plaintiff in that case claimed that the defendants had misappropriated certain trade secrets contained in software manuals. The defendants moved for summary judgement on the ground that the plaintiff had published the documents in question and was thus estopped from claiming that they contained trade secrets. While agreeing that "general publication of a trade secret will destroy the trade secret," the trial court refused to conclude as a matter of law that "the mere affixing of a copyright notice to the Manuals voids any claim of secrecy."[38] The Seventh Circuit likewise concluded that neither the affixing of a statutory copyright notice, nor the publication of the documents estopped the plaintiff from "subsequently asserting that such documents have not been generally published, but instead contain subject matter which is trade secret."[39]

Thus the practice, followed by many software houses, of seeking double protection by affixing copyright notices to programs as a backup measure in case secrecy is lost, may sometimes be effective. However, whether or not the dissemination of a software package with a copyright notice affixed will defeat a trade secret claim will remain a question of fact in each case. Certainly publication, be it "limited" or otherwise, will be considered as one of a number of factors which might indicate a loss of secrecy.

6.3.2   Applicability of State Trade Secret Laws to Software and Data

The Restatement of Torts describes a trade secret in the following terms:

> any formula, pattern, device or compilation of information which is used in one's business and which gives him an opportunity or advantage over competitors who do not know or use it.[40]

This definition, which has been adopted by most states, is certainly expansive. As one court has observed, "a trade secret in the broad sense consists of any unpatented idea which may be used for industrial or

---

37   687 F. 2d 1032 (1982). Cert. den. 103 S. Ct. 732 (1983).

38   211 U.S.P.Q. 343 at 347 (E.D. Wis., 1980).

39   Note 37 above, at 1039. Note that this case was actually decided under the 1909 Act. The *ratio* would probably hold equally good today, but compare *Videotronics Inc. v. Bend Electronics,* 564 F. Supp. 1471 at 1477 (D. Nev., 1983), where a district court ruled that "[b]ecause the court has found that the plaintiff's property interest in the electronic video device is covered by the Copyright Act, relief under the state common law doctrines of misappropriation and trade secret cannot obtain here."

40   *Restatement,* s. 757, comment b.

commercial purposes."[41] The general availability of trade secret protection for software and data has never seriously been in doubt.[42] However, "secrecy" must be established and maintained to ensure that information capable of protection continues to qualify as a trade secret. The nature of this requirement merits some attention.

While stating that "an exact definition of a trade secret is not possible," the Restatement of Torts stresses that "a substantial element of secrecy must exist, so that, except by the use of improper means, there would be difficulty in acquiring the information."[43] In determining whether a person's information qualifies as a trade secret the following factors will be relevant:

> (1) the extent to which the information is known outside of his business; (2) the extent to which it is known by employees and others involved in his business; (3) the extent of measures taken by him to guard the secrecy of the information; (4) the value of the information to him and to his competitors; (5) the amount of effort or money expended by him in developing the information; (6) the ease or difficulty with which the information could be properly acquired or duplicated by others.[44]

As this list makes clear, "secrecy" is a rather loose concept, and is certainly a relative term. The first factor in the list refers simply to the extent to which the information in question is generally known. Information which is public knowledge, or at least common knowledge in the relevant industry, can not constitute a trade secret.[45] However, while courts sometimes speak in terms of "novelty" as a pre-requisite for trade secrecy,[46] it is now well established that "novelty and uniqueness are not a requirement for trade secret protection."[47]

In *Jostens v. Nat. Computer Systems*,[48] the Supreme Court of Minnesota made the following comments about the type of information which can be claimed as secret.

> Courts agree that trade secrets lie somewhere on a continuum from what is generally known in a field to what has some degree of uniqueness, although there need not be the

---

41   *Sinclair v. Aquarius Electronics,* 116 Cal. Rptr. 654 at 658 (1974).
42   In the *Amoco* case, for example, the Supreme Court of Oklahoma commented that there was "no question that under applicable law a computer program could be classified as a trade secret." 609 P. 2d 733 at 743 (1980).
43   *Restatement,* s. 757, comment b at 6.
44   *Ibid.*
45   *Sperry Rand Corp. v. Petronix,* 311 F. Supp. 910 at 913 (E.D. Pa., 1970).
46   *Data General Corp. v. Digital Computer Controls Inc.,* 357 A. 2d 105 at 110 (Del. Ch., 1975).
47   *Structural Dynamics Corp. v. Enrg. Dynamics Corp.,* 401 F. Supp. 1102 at 1110 (1975). See also *Sinclair v. Aquarius,* note 41 above, at 658; *Univ. Computing v. Lykes-Youngstown,* 504 F. 2d 518 at 532 (5th Cir., 1974).
48   318 N.W. 2d 691 (S.C. Min., 1982).

degree of uniqueness or originality required for patent or copyright protection. Within these limits, courts have suggested a variety of further limitations. Some measure of discovery is required. Mere variations on general processes known in the field which embody superior advances are not protected. But unique principles, engineering, logic and coherence in computer software may be accorded trade secret status. And a trade secret may modify and improve standard models to a point at which the newer version is unique in the industry.

Further, generally known computer elements may gain trade secret protection from the nature of their combination.[49]

Thus, a court may be prepared to adopt a very flexible approach in deciding whether information is "generally known" or whether it is sufficiently "novel," in the broad sense of the word, to qualify for trade secret protection. Since secrecy is a relative term, "partial" or "qualified" secrecy will often be enough to secure protection. The fourth and fifth factors listed in the Restatement focus on the deemed value of information and the cost to the owner of developing it. Thus courts should consider the competitive edge which the information gives and the costs of acquiring that information. Software and data will be evaluated in much the same way as any other putative trade secrets.

However, the factors pertaining to the maintenance of secrecy both internally (2 and 3) and externally (6), present special problems in the software context. The three most significant threats to secrecy are likely to be inadequate internal security, the distribution of software without sufficient controls on use, and the possibility of "reverse engineering." Each merits a brief discussion.

6.3.3   Maintaining Secrecy Internally

Given that certain information is capable of acquiring the status of a trade secret, courts will look at the care which has been taken to preserve the secrecy of that information. A heroic effort may not be necessary, but courts will expect supposedly valuable information to be handled as such. In a case concerning computer programs which had been written for engineering applications, *Structural Dynamics v. Engineering Designs,*[50] a Michigan district court concluded that, although the company in question "did not use the ultimate in policing measures, the professional caliber of its employees, and the nature of its development work made heavyhanded measures unnecessary."[51] Thus, the nature of the information for which protection is sought and the circumstances sur-

---

49   *Ibid.,* at 698-9 (citations omitted).
50   See note 47 above.
51   *Ibid.,* at 1117.

rounding its use will be significant in determining an appropriate level of security.

While "heavyhanded measures" were deemed unnecessary in the *Structural Dynamics* case, the court in *Com-Share v. Computer Complex*[52] was clearly impressed with the thoroughness of the security measures taken by the plaintiff in that case, concluding that "the utmost caution" had been exercised by the plaintiff in protecting the secrecy of its time-sharing software. Com-Share's security measures included a confidentiality notice on each page of its program listings, built-in passwords in its systems and the keeping of tapes and symbolics locked when not in use.[53]

It is possible that a company's response to a perceived security threat will be considered judicially as an overreaction, as was the case in *Telex v. IBM*.[54] Following attempts by Telex to appropriate IBM's trade secrets, IBM claimed substantial damages including a figure of $3 million for "increased extraordinary security costs." This latter part of the claim, allegedly for the use of "guards, television cameras, sensors, locks, safes, computer controlled access system, and the like,"[55] was allowed by the trial court but struck down on appeal. The Tenth Circuit found that Telex's principal strategy for obtaining IBM's secrets had been to lure key employees away from IBM with offers of substantial salary increases and bonuses. As Telex was clearly "not climbing fences or breaking down doors," IBM could not demonstrate that its increased security costs were the proximate result of Telex's actions.[56]

In addition to assessing physical security measures, courts may look at the adequacy of non-disclosure agreements signed by employees having access to confidential information.[57] They may also consider whether sufficient steps have been taken both to identify to employees material which is confidential and to remind them of their obligations to maintain secrets. In *Jostens v. Nat. Computer Systems*, for example, the Supreme Court of Minnesota found that the plaintiff's "failure to take reasonable precautions to protect the confidentiality of what it now claims to be secret was such that the defendant employees could not be expected to have known what was confidential and what was not."[58]

---

52   338 F. Supp. 1229 (E.D. Mich., 1971).

53   *Ibid.,* at 1234.

54   367 F. Supp. 258 (N.D. Okla., 1973); reversed 510 F. 2d 895 (10th Cir., 1975).

55   510 F. 2d at 933.

56   *Ibid.*

57   See Gilburne and Johnston, "Trade Secret Protection For Software Generally and in the Mass Market" (1982), III Computer/Law J. 211-72 at 222-4.

58   318 N.W. 2d 691 at 700 (1982).

6.3.4   Controlling the Use of Distributed Software

The problems of maintaining secrecy escalate once software or data are sold or leased. Where material is sold outright, the scope for the exercise of proprietary controls is minimal and the main hope for secrecy lies in practical measures to safeguard against reverse engineering.[59] However, where material is distributed under licence agreements, certain obligations can be imposed on customers to respect the confidentiality of the software or data.

In *J & K Computer Systems v. Parrish,*[60] the plaintiff sought to recover damages and enjoin former employees and a company founded by them from using or disclosing its confidential computer programs. The trial court found in favour of the plaintiff and awarded damages of $7,500 in respect of an accounts receivable program. On appeal, the defendants argued, *inter alia,* that that particular program had been revealed to certain customers and was "therefore not protectible."[61] The appeal court disagreed:

> The record . . . shows that the plaintiff endeavoured to keep its accounts receivable program secret. Plaintiff's employees and customers were informed of the secret nature of the program. The program was marked with the following legend ". . . Authorized Use By Licence Only." That a few of the plaintiff's customers had access to the program does not prevent the program from being classified as a trade secret where the plaintiff was attempting to keep the secret and the program is still unavailable to the computer trade as a whole.[62]

Thus, just as limited publication of a trade secret will not necessarily destroy secrecy, likewise limited dissemination of trade secret material need not be fatal, provided it is done in confidence.

Where software or data are distributed on a mass scale, however, it seems inevitable that at some point a claim to "secrecy" would become untenable. Yet the issue of secrecy should remain a question of fact in each case, and mass distribution will not in itself create a legal presumption that secrecy has been lost.

6.3.5   Reverse Engineering

"Reverse engineering" essentially entails "starting with the known product and working backwards to divine the process."[63] Trade secret

59   See section 6.3.5 below.
60   642 P. 2d 732 (S. Ct. Utah, 1982).
61   *Ibid.,* at 735.
62   *Ibid.*
63   *Sinclair v. Aquarius,* 116 Cal. Rptr. 654 at 666 (1974).

protection does not guard against such reverse engineering of a product by anyone who has obtained it by legitimate means. Thus in *Analogic Corp. v. Data Translation Inc.*, the court commented that "a device which has been described in trade journals and placed on the market is generally open to duplication by skilled engineers."[64] The possibility of reverse engineering is not, however, an excuse for improper conduct whereby secrets are obtained by means of a breach of confidence. A court will still look at whether "improper means were used to discover the secret."[65]

Where a secret has been improperly obtained, however, courts may take into account the feasibility of reverse engineering in determining an appropriate remedy. In particular, reference is often made to the so-called "head-start" doctrine whereby "the appropriate injunctive period is that which competitors would require after public disclosure to develop a competitive machine."[66] In the *Analogic* case the court gave the following rationale for this principle:

> [D]efendants who have wilfully attempted to profit through violation of a confidential relationship need not be placed in as good a position as other honest competitors . . . . The plaintiff is entitled to have its trade secrets protected at least until others in the trade are likely, through legitimate business procedures, to have become aware of these secrets. And even then the defendants should not be permitted a competitive advantage from their avoidance of the normal costs of invention and duplication.[67]

The emphasis is thus very much on accountability for unjust enrichment and a significant factor in assessing damages will be the amount of money which a defendant has saved because of misappropriation of a plaintiff's trade secrets.[68]

6.3.6 Rights and Obligations of Employees

The public policy interest in employee mobility may significantly impinge on the scope of both implied and express non-disclosure covenants. While courts have recognised that employers may have a legiti-

---

64   *Analogic Corp. v. Data Translation Inc.*, 358 N.E. 2d 804 (S. Ct. Mass., 1976). The *Data General* court stated the principle thus: "an imitator is always entitled to copy a device containing alleged trade secrets through a process of reverse engineering in which the use of protected design drawings are not employed." 357 A. 2d 105 at 110 (Del. Ch., 1975).

65   *Chicago Lock v. Fanberg*, 676 F. 2d 400 at 404 (9th Cir., 1982).

66   *Winston Research Corp. v. Minnesota Min. & Mfg. Co.*, 350 F. 2d 134 at 142 (9th Cir., 1965).

67   *Analogic Corp. v. Data Translation*, note 64 above, at 808.

68   See Klippert, *Unjust Enrichment* (Toronto: Butterworths, 1983), pp. 228-9 for a discussion of the restitution aspects of the *Telex v. IBM* case.

mate interest in maintaining control over valuable developments resulting from research they have funded, post-employment restraints may
place an employee in the paradoxical position of being "restrained,
because of his increased expertise, from advancing further in the industry in which he is most productive."[69]

In *Amoco Production v. Lindley,*[70] the plaintiff sought to restrain a
former employee from using any part of a computer program which was
designed for well log analysis in oil and gas exploration and was developed by him during his employment with Amoco. An *ex parte* restraining order was made and at trial a temporary injunction was issued
barring Lindley from using any part of the "Lindley II System." On
appeal, the Supreme Court of Oklahoma found that Amoco had not
discharged the burden of proving that the computer system in question
was a trade secret.[71] Thus, the company had no common law claim to
restrain disclosure by Lindley. Amoco claimed, however, that Lindley
was in any event in breach of a clause contained in his contract of
employment whereby he had agreed: "to disclose promptly and in writing . . . all inventions or discoveries capable of use in connection with the
business of COMPANY . . . and agrees not to disclose same to others,
except as required by his employment, without consent of company."[72]
The appeal court construed this clause narrowly, however, as applying
only to patentable inventions and concluded that "[t]he software system
is not an invention, so on the sole basis of the contract Mr. Lindley could
disclose it, or use it for his own benefit."[73]

The *Amoco* court distinguished the case of *Structural Dynamics v.
Engineering Mechanics*[74] in which a Michigan district court had found a
computer program not to be a trade secret but had ruled that three
former employees of the plaintiff could nevertheless be restrained from
using the program due to a contractual non-disclosure provision. In that
case the non-disclosure clause, which the *Amoco* court considered "exc-
eptionally broad,"[75] barred the former employees from divulging "to any
person, firm or corporation . . . any privileged or confidential information, trade secret, or other proprietory information including but not

---

69   *Wexler v. Greenberg,* 160 A. 2d 430 at 434 (S. Ct. Pa., 1960).
70   609 P. 2d 733 (S. Ct. Okla., 1980).
71   *Ibid.,* at 743. "There has to be evidence that indeed the secret was a secret, and that
      evidence is not before the court."
72   *Ibid.,* at 736.
73   *Ibid.,* at 743. Note, however, that the court was relying on pre *Diamond v. Diehr*
      jurisprudence as to patentability. See section 5.2, above.
74   401 F. Supp. 1102 (E.D. Mich., 1975).
75   Note 70 above, at 745.

limited to the experimental and research work of the corporation, its methods, formulae, drawings or appliances."[76] It is by no means certain that other courts faced with covenants as broad as this would find them enforceable.[77]

6.4 Trade Secrets and Confidentiality in England and Canada

6.4.1 The Basis of the Common Law Remedy

Unlike in the United States, there are no statutory provisions dealing with trade secrets in England or Canada. Perhaps for this reason, the distinction between trade secrets and duties of confidentiality has not had as much significance as in American jurisprudence. Certainly English and Canadian courts have been less troubled with the finer points of classification of trade secrets as property or otherwise.[78]

On the contrary, the common law action for breach of confidence seems to be quite firmly grounded in equity and the basis of relief can be stated quite simply. In the words of Lord Denning in *Seager v. Copydex:*[79]

> The law on this subject . . . depends on the broad principle of equity that he who has received information in confidence shall not take unfair advantage of it. He must not make use of it to the prejudice of him who gave it without obtaining his consent.

Working from this broad principle, English courts have developed a fairly straightforward framework to delimit the scope of the relief available in equity. In *Coco v. Clark,*[80] Megarry J. set out the following three requirements for a successful action for breach of confidence:

---

76   Note 74 above, at 1112.

77   The scope for post-termination restrictive covenants is curtailed by statute in some states. *E.g.,* s. 16600 California Business and Professional Code: "Except as provided in this chapter, every contract by which anyone is restrained from engaging in a lawful profession, trade or business of any kind is to that extent void." See Milgrim, (1978)*Trade Secrets* App. D-1; Brooks, "Agreements with Consultants and Employees and Registering Copyrights in Computer Software" *in* Practicing Law Institute, *Computer Law 1982: Acquiring Computer Goods and Services,* v. 1, pp. 9-302.

78   However, there is a faint possibility that in Canada the existence of a contractual term governing confidentiality might preempt an action based in equity. See Vaver, "Civil Liability for Taking or Using Trade Secrets in Canada" (1981), 5 Can. Bus. L.J. 253-301 at 263-4.

79   [1967] 2 All E.R. 415, [1967] R.P.C. 349 at 368.

80   [1969] R.P.C. 41 at 47.

First, the information itself . . . must have the "necessary quality of confidence about it." Secondly, that information must have been imparted in circumstances importing an obligation of confidence. Thirdly, there must be an unauthorized use of that information to the detriment of the party communicating it.

The application of these three criteria to confidences relating to computer programs and data presents, in theory at least, no special problems. So far there have been no reported cases in England or Canada dealing specifically with programs or data, although some of the implications of confidentiality for the software industry have been highlighted by a ruling of the Supreme Court of South Africa.[81] Before this case is discussed, however, the general implications of the three-pronged *Coco v. Clark* test will be outlined.

6.4.2   Confidentiality and Relative Secrecy

Information having the "necessary quality of confidence" was negatively defined by Lord Greene in *Saltman v. Campbell*[82] as "not . . . something which is public property and public knowledge." This test of confidentiality only makes obvious sense if applied objectively. Yet in *Schering Chemicals Ltd. v. Falkman Ltd.,*[83] Shaw L.J. stated that "ethics and good faith"[84] were the critical factors, and that "It is not the law that where confidentiality exists it is terminated or eroded by adventitious publicity."[85] This view has however been strongly criticised by the Law Commission[86] which found the approach of Shaw L.J. to be

unacceptable, since, taken to its logical conclusion, it would mean that information once acquired in confidence could not be used by the acquirer even though the information was, at the time of acquisition, or had later come, into the public domain.

As one commentator has put it, an adoption of the approach taken in the *Schering* case "would impose a unique disability for the recipient to which others would not be subject."[87]

The more reasonable and better established view is probably that secrecy is "a question of degree depending upon the particular case."[88]

---

81   *Northern Office Microcomputers v. Rosenstein,* [1982] F.S.R. 124. See section 6.4.4, below.

82   (1948) 65 R.P.C. 203 at 215.

83   [1982] Q.B. 1, [1981] 2 All E.R. 321 (C.A.).

84   *Ibid.,* at 338.

85   *Ibid.,* at 339.

86   *Breach of Confidence* (London: HMSO, Cmnd. 8388, 1981), p. 132.

87   Hull, "Recent Developments in the Law of Breach of Confidence, "The Law Soc. Gaz. (15 June 1983), 1537-9 at 1539.

88   *Franchi v. Franchi,* [1967] R.P.C. 149 at 153.

Two recent cases, one Canadian and one English, illustrate the practical application of such a "relative secrecy" approach. In *Ridgewood Resources Ltd. v. Henuset*,[89] the plaintiff alleged that the defendant had used confidential information in deciding to purchase certain oil lands. On this basis the plaintiff claimed that he was entitled to "a minimum 10 per cent interest" in the lands.[90] The case turned on whether the information in question was sufficiently confidential. The Alberta Court of Appeal firmly rejected the plaintiff's suggestion that an obligation of confidence could arise even though the information communicated was in the public domain. Rather, the court stressed that "[b]oth elements, secrecy of the information and the circumstances of confidential disclosure, must co-exist."[91] On the facts, the court found that the first element had not been proved:

> The information in this case did not have "the necessary quality of confidence about it." It was known to only a small group, but the community in which the information would have any significance was itself a small group. . . . Among prospective purchasers of oil lands, the information was in the public domain. . . . The communication of information which is in the public domain, though not known to the recipient, does not (apart from contract) make the recipient liable for its use.[92]

Similarly, in the recent case of *Sun Printers v. Westminster Press*,[93] the English Court of Appeal found that a onetime confidential report had lost its confidentiality through coming into the hands of too many interested readers. The report, prepared by an independent commission, dealt with possible reductions in the plaintiff's workforce. Copies were distributed to management and union officials. The defendant's appeal against an injunction restraining publication succeeded because, although "there was in the beginning a stipulation of confidence . . . as distribution became wider . . . a stage was reached where the seal of confidence was broken."[94]

A similar test would probably be applied in a case concerning "secret" computer programs or data. Whether distribution, even on a large scale, will be fatal for secrecy will depend on the size of the community which would be significantly interested in the information, and on the steps taken to pass on obligations of confidence to recipients.

---

89   (1982), 18 Alta. L.R. (2d) 68, 35 A.R. 493 (C.A.). Leave to appeal to S.C.C. refused (1982), 43 N.R. 90, 36 A.R. 450.
90   *Ibid.*, at 69.
91   *Ibid.*, at 76.
92   *Ibid.*, at 76-7.
93   (1982), 126 S.J. 260 (C.A.).
94   *Ibid.*

It is easy to see why an essentially objective test should be applied in establishing the extent to which information is "secret." It might be thought, however, that subjective factors would prove crucial to an assessment of the obligations imposed by a relationship of confidence. Yet even here the courts may use objective criteria in the existence and scope of duties of confidentiality. Thus, in *Coco v. Clark*,[95] Megarry J. set out the following test:

> It seems to me that if the circumstances are such that any reasonable man standing in the shoes of the recipient of the information would have realized that upon reasonable grounds the information was being given him in confidence, then this should suffice to impose upon him the equitable obligation of confidence.[96]

However, courts will be reticent to find obligations of confidence based purely on circumstances, for in such situations they are "being asked to enforce what is essentially a moral obligation."[97]

6.4.3   Remedies For Misuse

Where a breach of confidence has been established, in assessing the appropriate relief, courts will look at the advantage which a defendant has gained through his or her wrongful conduct. Courts in the Commonwealth have developed a "springboard" doctrine which is quite similar to the American "head-start" basis of assessment. Roxburgh J. first suggested the principle in *Terrapin v. Bldrs.' Supply Co.*:[98]

> As I understand it, the essence of this branch of the law, whatever the origin of it may be, is that a person who has obtained information in confidence is not allowed to use it as a spring-board for activities detrimental to the person who made the confidential communications and spring-board it remains even when all the features have been published or can be ascertained by actual inspection by any member of the public. . . . the possessor of the confidential information still has a long start over any member of the public.

By adopting this attitude courts have made it clear that they are concerned not merely to protect secrets, but also to protect "the information gathering process."[99] Yet, as the Law Commission observed, the springboard doctrine seems at first sight to be inconsistent with the principle

---

95   [1969] R.P.C. 41 at 48.

96   For a discussion of the extent to which courts will impose an obligation where none was implied see Vaver, "Civil Liability for Taking or Using Trade Secrets in Canada" (1981), 5 Can. Bus. L.J. 253-301 at 275-6.

97   *House of Spring Gardens v. Point Blank*, [1983] F.S.R. 213 at 253, *per* Costello J. (H. Ct. Ireland).

98   [1967] R.P.C. 375 at 391 (Ch. 1959); [1960] R.P.C. 128 (C.A.).

99   Landy, "The Protection of Trade Secrets in Canada", 12 Pat. & T.M. Inst. of Can. Bull. 712 at 725.

that, once information is in the public domain, it can no longer be protected as "confidential." The Commission concluded that there is no inconsistency here, provided a gloss is added to the "public domain" principle so that it reads as follows:

> [O]bjection cannot be taken to a claim for an injunction in proceedings for breach of confidence in respect of the use of information on the sole ground that the information in question is in the public domain, so long as, by reason of the defendant's having use of the information in breach of confidence before it entered the public domain, he would, unless restrained, enjoy an advantage over those who have had to obtain the information through its public release.[100]

As in the United States, the "spring-board" doctrine is only a starting point for determining the scope of relief. Courts will also consider such factors as the degree of culpability of a defendant's behaviour,[101] and the need to foster competition in a particular industry.[102]

In this context of remedies for breach of confidence, a particularly difficult issue concerns the extent to which an innocent third party recipient can be restrained from using confidential information. There have been cases where courts have restrained recipients of information obtained in breach of confidence who have had no notice of the breach.[103] A more frequent judicial conclusion, however, has been that, where a third party receives confidential information, an obligation of non-disclosure will only take effect from the time at which that person becomes aware of the original confidence.[104]

6.4.4 Rights and Obligations of Employees

As in the United States, courts will enforce both express and implied covenants of non-disclosure, but usually only where they are sufficiently specific and where the employee is made fully aware of his or her obligations. In *Searle v. Celltech,*[105] the plaintiff company was engaged

---

100   *Breach of Confidence,* (London: HMSO, Cmnd. 8288, 1981), para. 6.70.
101   *Schauenburg Indust. v. Borowski* (1979), 25 O.R. (2d) 737, 8 B.L.R. 164, 50 C.P.R. (2d) 69, 101 D.L.R. (3d) 701 (H.C.).
102   *Fisher-Karpark Industries v. Nichols* [1982] F.S.R. 351 (Ch. Div.).
103   *Polyresins Ltd. v. Stein-Hall Ltd.,* [1972] 2 O.R. 188, 5 C.P.R. (2d) 183, 25 D.L.R. (3d) 152; *Butler v. Bd. of Trade,* [1971] 1 Ch. 680, [1970] 3 All E.R. 593. See Durie, "Wheatley v. Bell: Confidential Information – Property or Not?" [1983] E.I.P.R. 194-195.
104   *E.g.,* see comments of Lord Denning in *Fraser v. Evans,* [1969] 1 Q.B. 349, [1969] 1 All E.R. 8 at 11 (quoted in section 5.1.2, above). In its 1981 Report, the Law Commission felt that the obligation should take effect from the point at which a third party knows or ought to know of the original obligation of confidence. See note 100, above.
105   [1982] F.S.R. 92.

in research and development in genetic engineering, a field which, like software development, is characterized by fierce competition, rapid product obsolescence and high job mobility. One of the defendants, Carey, was a former employee of the plaintiff who had terminated his contract of employment in order to set up a new company backed by another defendant, the National Enterprise Board (NEB). The plaintiff sought an injunction to restrain Carey from using or disclosing to the NEB the names, aptitudes, characters and specializations of any of the plaintiff's other research staff. Injunctive relief was refused and an appeal failed on the ground that an obligation of confidentiality had not been established. Brightman L.J. commented:

> In my opinion, if an employer seeks to restrain his ex-employee from making use of know-how acquired by him during the course of his employment, the employer's evidence should specifically identify the secret which he claims to be his property, and explain exactly how knowledge of that secret came into the possession of the employee in such circumstances that the conscience of the employee was affected so that it would be unconscionable of the employee to make use of the information for his own purposes. These conditions are not even arguably satisfied in the present case.[106]

In addition to these criteria, another of the judges stressed the general desirability of free competition in the employment market as a further reason for limiting judicial intervention in such cases.[107]

The case of *Northern Microcomputers v. Rosenstein*[108] has already been discussed in chapter 4 in the context of copyright law. Having decided that copyright did indeed subsist in the contested suite of computer programs and that the respondent was the copyright owner, the Supreme Court of South Africa then addressed the separate issue of whether the respondent should be restrained from exploiting his copyright because he had misappropriated the applicant's trade secrets. In dealing with the threshold issue of the relationship between copyright and trade secrets, the court found that the fact that copyright vested in Rosenstein did not give him "the right to disregard the obligation which the common law imposes upon him to respect his employers' trade secrets."[109] In this regard, the court found persuasive section 41(3) of the South African Copyright Act which provides that "nothing in the Act shall affect the operation of any rule of equity relating to breaches of trust or confidence."[110] Even apart from this statutory provision

---

106   *Ibid.*, at 109.
107   *Ibid.*, at 93 *per* Cumming-Bruce J.
108   [1982] F.S.R. 124 (S. Ct. S. Africa, 1981).
109   *Ibid.*, at 137.
110   Marais J. said of the section, "If it does not save the express or implied rights of employers to have their employees respect their trade secrets, it is difficult to

however, Marais J. felt that:

> It would be contrary to well-known principles of statutory construction to read the Copyright Act as abolishing, or derogating from, the common law rights of an employer unless express language, or the clearest of necessary implications, compelled such a reading.[111]

The Court then addressed the substantive issue of whether the programs in suit were in fact trade secrets. As to the possibility of trade secret protection, the court held it "to be plain" that programs could be so protected.[112] The more difficult issue was where to draw the line "between the use by an employee of his own skill, knowledge and experience, and the use by him of his employer's trade secrets."[113] Marais J. favoured the following balance:

> Generally speaking, [the employee] cannot be prevented from using his own skill and experience to attain a particular result, merely because it is a result which he has achieved before for a previous employer. I say, generally speaking, because one can conceive of cases where the result sought to be achieved is so elusive that only a solution of the kind which legend has it prompted Archimedes to say "Eureka" will do, and the employee has been engaged specifically to find it. In such a case, it may well be that the employee who has evolved the solution may have to refrain from solving it in the same way for a future employer.[114]

On the facts, the court found that the use of computers to provide accounting and administrative systems for doctors and dentists could "hardly be described as inspired."[115] Thus, although he was enjoined from directly copying the programs he had developed, Rosenstein was not restrained from developing similar software in the future:

> If respondent were permitted simply to copy [the programs] he would be unfairly nullifying the advantage of the "long start" over anyone else to which applicants are entitled. To that limited extent, the suite of programmes is, in my opinion, a trade secret. . . . But it does not follow from this that respondent may not again apply his mind to the development of a suite of programmes to cater for the accounting and

---

conceive of any field of application which it might have." (*Ibid.*, at 137-8). The wording of s. 41(3) of the South African statute is identical to s. 46(6) of the United Kingdom Copyright Act 1956. Similarly, s. 45 of the Canadian Copyright Act, which excludes any non-statutory claim to copyright, adds the caveat that "nothing in this section shall be construed as abrogating any right or jurisdiction to restrain a breach of trust or confidence."

111 Note 108 above, at 138.

112 *Ibid.* In support, the judge quoted from Tapper's *Computer Law* (1978 ed.), p. 30 (". . . no reasonable doubt that such programmes are eligible for this sort of protection . . ."). Marais J. added a caveat that, to be protected, a program must not be "commonplace."

113 Note 108 above at 138.

114 *Ibid.*, at 139.

115 *Ibid.* Indeed, competing systems were already on the market.

financial needs of doctors and dentists, or that, if he does, he must wipe clean from the slate of his memory (as if that were possible) any recollection he may have of the things which it seemed to him were appropriate for inclusion in such a suite of programmes, or of appropriate formulae, or the like. To accept the contrary view would halter respondent's use of his own training, skill and experience to an unacceptable degree.[116]

In this way the court sought to balance the trade secret holder's right to a head-start against the program author's right to continue to apply his expertise in the business of software development.

The rights and obligations of employees in relation to confidential information were recently reviewed by the English High Court in the case of *Faccenda Chicken Ltd. v. Fowler.*[117] Mr. Justice Goulden found that, subject to any express agreement, information acquired by an employee during the course of employment will, from the point of view of confidentiality, fall into one of three classes. The first is information which, "because of its trivial character or its easy accessibility from public sources of information" is not confidential at all. This can be disclosed by an employee or former employee to anyone, "even his master's competitor."[118] The second class is made up of:

information which the servant must treat as confidential (either because he is expressly told it is confidential, or because from its character it obviously is so) but which once learned necessarily remains in the servant's head and becomes part of his own skill and knowledge applied in the course of his master's business. So long as the employment continues, he cannot otherwise use or disclose such information without infidelity and therefore breach of contract. But when he is no longer in the same service, the law allows him to use his full skill and knowledge for his own benefit in competition with his former master.[119]

To some extent, however, the use of such information by a former employee may be regulated by an express term of a contract of employment.[120]

These two classes of information are to be contrasted with the third category comprising "specific trade secrets so confidential that, even though they may necessarily have been learned by heart and even though the servant may have left the service, they cannot lawfully be used for anyone's benefit but the master's."[121] On the facts of the case, the court found that the plaintiff's sales information fell into the second category. As the plaintiff had failed to impose appropriate restrictive covenants,

---

116   *Ibid.*, at 140.
117   [1984] 1 I.R.L.R. 61.
118   *Ibid.*, at 65.
119   *Ibid.*
120   *Ibid.*
121   *Ibid.*, at 66.

its former employees were at liberty to use the sales information for their own purposes.[122]

A limitation of the analysis in the *Faccenda* case is that it does not address the possibility of information starting in one category and moving to another after a period of time has elapsed. For example, information which is highly confidential at the time of an employee's departure from a company might become steadily less sensitive as competitors catch up on any "headstart" which that company might have. Thus, over time, information might shift from the third of Goulding J.'s categories to the second, or from the second to the first. Any obligation of confidence binding an ex-employee might accordingly be reduced or terminated.

6.5 Contractual Aspects

6.5.1 Software Development and Source Code Escrow Deposits

Questions regarding rights of ownership in software developed by employees have already been discussed, and mention has been made of the common law and statutory checks on the scope for contractual regulation of such rights.[123] Ownership disputes may also arise where software development is contracted out to an independent programmer or software house. In such instances it is generally in the interests of both the party commissioning and the party writing the software to enter into an express and unambiguous agreement establishing from the outset their respective rights and obligations. The general provisions of such contracts are beyond the scope of the present discussion.[124] Suffice it to say, however, that the ownership of all intellectual property rights in any existing documentation and in the software which is to be developed should be agreed from the start. Moreover, formal assignments or confirmatory assignments of intellectual property rights and confidentiality agreements should be executed where appropriate.

---

122 *Ibid.* Goulding J. observed that the plaintiff "is inviting me to strain the proper limits of the law regarding abuse of confidential information in order to make good its own omission to impose restrictive obligations on those who serve it."

123 See sections 6.2.2, 6.3.6, 6.4.4, above.

124 See, however, Morgan and Stedman, *Computer Contracts,* 2nd ed. (London: Oyez Longman, 1984), chapter 3.

Somewhat different issues arise where a software house retains intellectual property rights in a program and either directly licenses one or more end users, or licenses a distributor to market a program. The software house will typically wish to retain exclusive control over the source code version of the program and will accordingly only license the object code. Where a program is licensed for distribution, the software house will also be concerned to impose obligations on a distributor to take all steps necessary to protect its intellectual property rights in the software. Thus, for example, a software distribution licence will normally obligate a distributor to affix appropriate copyright notices on all copies which are sublicensed.[125]

The end user or distributor will have rather different concerns regarding the software house's proprietary rights in the software. In particular, where access is to be limited to the object code version of a program, the distributor may insist that the software house enter into an escrow arrangement whereby the source code and any documentation necessary for its maintenance are deposited with a third party. The escrow agent will then be required to keep the deposited materials secure and confidential pending the occurrence of one or more specified events, the most common being an act of insolvency on the part of the software house.[126] On, or at some specified time after, the occurrence of the specified contingency, the escrow agent will be authorised to release the deposited materials to the distributor or, if appropriate, to any end user.[127]

Though conceptually straightforward, for both technical and legal reasons an escrow arrangement may be problematic.[128] Due to the frequency with which some programs are modified and updated, a distributor or end user will be concerned as to whether the escrow agent has been supplied with the latest version of the source code and supporting documentation. Indeed, more generally, where the escrow agent merely provides a safe deposit facility, the distributor may have no way of knowing that anything at all of value has been deposited by the software

---

125 Statements may also be included regarding the retention of all present and future patent rights and the preservation of trade secrets contained in the software.

126 The specified event might, however, simply be any failure by the software house to maintain or update the software.

127 For an example of a software escrow agreement (for use in the U.K.) see Morgan and Stedman, note 124 above, Appendix H.

128 Nycum, Kenfield and Keenan, "Debugging Software Escrow: Will it Be There When You Need It?" (1984), IV Computer/L.J. 441-63; Fraser and Grasset, "Keeping Software a Trade Secret", [1984] *Computer Law* 43-46; "Source Code Escrow Agreements" [1984] *Computer Law* 55-56.

house. These concerns can be alleviated, at least in part, by arranging for the escrow agent, or an independent expert, to verify all materials which are deposited. Such procedures will, however, add to the cost of the escrow arrangement. More significantly, the software house may be reluctant to make the disclosure of confidential or trade secret information contained in the source code or supporting documentation which will be necessary for verification to occur.[129] A further source of practical uncertainty exists where one of the criteria for release of the deposited materials is failure on the part of the software house to maintain the program adequately. The parties may well disagree as to whether such a failure to maintain has occurred. An arbitration clause may thus be necessary to provide a means for resolving factual disputes.[130]

A source code deposit arrangement is also likely to have legal implications which may make it both less straightforward and less attractive than it might at first appear. For example, various provisions of bankruptcy law in the United States, England and Canada may cast doubt on the effectiveness of a transfer of intellectual property rights which is contingent on the insolvency of the software house. Indeed, it may be that to keep the source code out of the reach of a receiver or trustee in bankruptcy, the deposit will have to be made with an independent third party who is neither an agent of the software house nor an agent of the developer or end user.[131] Moreover, the potential liabilities of the intermediary who holds the source code may be very considerable. A premature release of the deposited materials might jeopardise valuable trade secrets owned by the software house. On the other hand, a failure to accede to a legitimate request for access made by a distributor or end user might also give rise to a substantial claim for damages to compensate for an inability to maintain or upgrade software.

Despite these potential difficulties, the deposit of source code and supporting documentation with a third party may be the only means of keeping the code confidential, while ensuring that the licencee is not left ultimately without software support.

6.5.2 Mass Market Licensing

Where software is designed or at least customised for a specific end user, a software house will often be in a strong position both to impose and enforce contractual obligations relating to intellectual property

---

129 Nycum, Kenfield and Keenan, *ibid.*, at 448.
130 *Ibid.*, at 450-1.
131 Thus producing an arrangement which may not be a "true escrow" at all. *Ibid.*, at 452.

rights. For example, in *S & H Computing v. SAS Inst.*,[132] a company which, contrary to a provision of a licence agreement, used a program on a non-designated central processing unit and made unauthorised copies was found to be in breach of contract. Less certain, however, is the availability of such protection in the context of mass-marketed programs.

Software packages designed for business and home computers are often "sold" in circumstances, such as by mail order, in which it may not be feasible for the licensor to obtain signed licence agreements at the point of distribution. The customer generally receives a sealed package containing a diskette or other storage medium on which a program is recorded together with supporting documentation. Clearly visible under the plastic wrapper there is usually a "licence agreement," headed by a statement in large letters to the effect that a person opening the package will be deemed to have agreed to all the terms and conditions of the licence. The terms typically include a statement that the end user or licensee agrees to respect all proprietary rights of the licensor and, in particular, will not make unauthorised copies of the program.[133] Moreover, the licence is generally stated to be "non-transferable" or "non-assignable," with the licensor retaining "exclusive rights" to the software and with use of the program restricted to a single computer terminal. There is also commonly a sweeping disclaimer of warranties, and a purported exclusion of all liabilities other than a commitment for a short period of time to replace any defective storage media.

The enforceability of many of the provisions of such "licences" may be doubtful. The licensor may be subject to general common law restrictions on the imposition of terms by a dominant party using a standard form contract.[134] Moreover, specific consumer protection provisions may be applicable, especially where programs are to be used on home computers.[135] Some commentators have suggested that many of the terms of typical "shrink-wrap" licences are manifestly unreasonable

---

132   568 F. Supp. 416 (M.D. Tenn., 1983).

133   The making of archival copies of a program is, however, often permitted and the making of minor modifications and the merger of the program with other specified programs may also be authorised.

134   See Rakoff, "Contracts of Adhesion: An Essay in Reconstruction" (1983), 96 Harvard L.R. 1174.

135   *E.g.*, in the U.S., UCC 2 and state consumer protection legislation, and in the U.K. Unfair Contract Terms Act 1977 and Supply of Goods and Services Act 1982. See Cooper, "Forming and Enforcing 'Tear Me Open' Licenses" paper prepared for Practicing Law Institute, Computer Law Institute, Nov 3-5, 1983 (unpublished).

and, if challenged, would probably not be upheld by courts, at least in the United States.[136]

Thus, while they may be effective devices for protecting intellectual property rights in programs distributed on a limited scale, trade secrecy, confidentiality and licensing methods may be of limited use in situations where software is mass marketed. Indeed, attempts to compel end users to sign licence agreements may collide with a general marketing objective of facilitating distribution on a broad scale and through a variety of channels. Despite enforcement difficulties, copyright will therefore be the primary means of protecting programs which are widely distributed.

---

136   *E.g.*, Schwartz, "Who Owns Your Business Software?" in Business Computing (Jan. 1984), 52-5.

Chapter 7

Criminal Law Protection of Programs and Data

7.1 The Scope Of Criminal Sanctions

7.1.1 Computer Abuse and Computer Crime

On both sides of the Atlantic the spectre of "computer crime" has loomed quite large in recent years. Yet estimates of the annual cost of computer-related crime vary widely,[1] and it seems impossible to determine with any precision how much substance there is behind the ghost.[2] Although by its nature not readily susceptible to proof or disproof, the conventional wisdom seems to be that the vast majority of computer-related crimes remain either undiscovered or unreported by their victims.[3] There is also a widespread tendency, especially in sensational news reporting, for all suspicious or clearly mischievous incidents of computer-related damage or loss to be dubbed indiscriminately "computer crime," regardless of whether any actual criminal offence has been committed.

The reality is probably that, although they may be reprehensible in some way, many of the "wrongs" which the unscrupulous may perpetrate with or through a computer system are not actionable as crimes, and indeed may not be legally actionable at all. Thus, an important distinc-

---

1 Lamb, "Computer Thieves Steal £2.5 Billion a Year," *New Scientist* (7 July 1983), 11-19; Canada, House of Commons Sub-Committee on Computer Crime, *Proceedings* Issue 4 (Ottawa: Supply and Services Canada, 1983), Testimony of Peter Ward at 5-7; *Computer Crime: Expert Witness Manual* (Washington: U.S. Dept. of Justice, 1980).

2 Canada, House of Commons Sub-Committee on Computer Crime, *Proceedings* Issue 15 (Ottawa: Supply and Services Canada, 1983), Testimony of Susan Nycum at 14.

3 Parker, *Crime By Computer* (New York, 1976); O'Grady, "Holding Back the Three Millisecond Crime Wave" Computing (May 31, 1984), at 24-25.

tion must be made between "computer abuse" and "computer crime."[4] The present discussion will be focussed mainly on the latter, much narrower, category of legally recognised criminal offences, and an assessment of the criminal sanctions currently available in the United States, England and Canada for theft of, or other unlawful interference with, computer programs and data.[5] Computer abuse will be considered to the limited extent that it has been specifically criminalised in the United States.

As a preliminary point, however, it is worth noting some of the advantages and disadvantages for the program or data owner of invoking criminal sanctions as compared to civil remedies. First, there is the potential deterrent value of prosecution. While there is considerable doubt as to the efficacy of criminal sanctions in deterring offenders generally,[6] it may be that "white-collar" criminals will tend to adopt a more calculated approach to punishment and where the stakes are high they may at least treat the risk of prosecution as a significant commercial factor.[7] Secondly, although interlocutory orders can be obtained with speed in some civil cases, criminal prosecutions are generally disposed of more quickly than civil actions. Thirdly, if the appropriate public prosecuting authority can be persuaded to initiate proceedings, a conviction can be obtained at little or no expense to the owner of the programs or data in question.[8]

The fact that most criminal prosecutions are publicly backed, however, is also the source of some significant disadvantages in pursuing criminal rather than civil remedies. For one thing, the involvement in

---

4   See Nycum, "Criminal Law Aspects of Computer Abuse" (1976), 5 Rutgers J. Comp. & L. 271. In criminological circles there has been considerable debate as to the appropriateness and significance of the distinction between "abuses" and "crimes," especially in the context of organisational deviance and "white collar crime." See Sutherland, "Is White Collar Crime Crime?" (1945), 10 Am. Soc. Rev. 132-39; Tappan, "Who is the Criminal?" (1947), 12 Am. Soc. Rev. 96-102; Erman and Lindman, eds., *Corporate and Governmental Deviance* (New York: Oxford Univ. Press, 1978).

5   A discussion of hardware related crimes such as theft of micro-computers and criminal damage to computer systems is beyond the ambit of this book.

6   *E.g.,* Chambliss, "Types of Deviance and the Effectiveness of Legal Sanctions" (1967), Wisconsin L.R. 703-719; Tullock, "Does Punishment Deter Crime?" (1974), 36 The Public Interest 103.

7   By all accounts the introduction of severe penalties for certain intellectual property infringements in Hong Kong rapidly had a marked effect on the level of piracy there.

8   The owner may be put to some limited expense in furnishing evidence and generally assisting in the preparation of the prosecution case. Moreover, the cost saving advantage is not, of course, available in the case of a private prosecution.

the criminal process of the "victim" of a criminal offence tends to be quite peripheral, and important decisions about the conduct of a case are generally taken by the police or public prosecutor.[9] Moreover, although compensation orders can sometimes be obtained following a criminal conviction, the outcome of criminal sentencing is usually of no direct benefit to the victim of an offence. Finally, the police or other public prosecutory body may be reluctant to become involved in cases which they consider to be essentially concerned with private commercial disputes.

7.1.2   Methods of Protecting Programs and Data With the Criminal Law

There appear to be three ways in which computer programs and data can be brought under the aegis of the criminal law. First, traditional property rights may be interpreted in such a way as to render programs or data susceptible to theft. A second possibility, which has proved quite popular with American legislators, is the creation by statute of offences specifically related to unauthorised interference with software or data.[10] A third approach is indirect protection by way of penal sanctions attaching to breaches of intellectual property rights.

The application of property concepts to computer programs and data is, however, problematical. Divorced from any tangible media in which they are stored, programs and data are essentially information which can be gathered, held, retrieved, manipulated and communicated via a computer system. At first sight, the proposition that a piece of information can be "stolen" makes little sense. At common law in England, for example, theft has traditionally been understood in terms of a taking without authority of a tangible object belonging to another person with the intent to permanently deprive that person of it. Yet an item of information can be learned, and thus effectively appropriated, without anything being physically taken or interfered with. How in such circumstances can there be an intent to permanently deprive? A partial reply to such arguments is that the essence of an owner's property right at common law is not so much the possession of a tangible object as the power of control over a thing, be it tangible or otherwise. Nevertheless,

---

9   For a general discussion of the way in which offences are taken over by the state see Christie, "Conflicts as Property" (1977), Br. J. of Criminology.

10   See section 7.2.3, below.

the common law definition of theft has often proved "hopelessly inadequate" for dealing with rights in information.[11]

Though in many respects unsatisfactory, an analysis based on the form of storage rather than the substance of programs and data may provide a limited degree of criminal law protection. A prosecutor can sidestep the issue of whether information can be treated as property by charging theft of a tangible object in which the information is stored. A computer printout is an obvious example. Another line of attack has been to stretch existing definitions of property and treat a piece of information as property *per se,* usually on the ground that it is of demonstrable value to the owner. A more direct approach is the modification of existing theft statutes so as to expressly include computer programs and data within the statutory definition of property. This position can also be reached indirectly by attaching penal sanctions to intellectual property rights which already encompass computer programs and data. Finally, some jurisdictions have created a corpus of criminal law dealing specifically with "computer abuse" as a new area of legislative activity.

7.1.3   Procedural and Evidentiary Considerations

Significant practical and legal problems may arise where evidence relating to a criminal prosecution has been either stored in or generated by a computer. While a detailed discussion of procedural and evidentiary considerations is beyond the scope of this book, mention will be made of the main areas of difficulty. At the investigation stage, where the commission of an offence is suspected it may be technically difficult to ascertain what unlawful events in relation to programs and data, if any, have actually occurred. Traditional search and seizure techniques are not particularly well suited to the task of uncovering computer evidence. A person suspected of an offence will often be able to conceal or destroy, with the greatest of ease and without trace, evidential material held in digital form. Even the seizure by an investigatory authority of peripheral storage media such as disks and tapes will not necessarily uncover potentially incriminating material stored in, for example, ROMs (read only memories) or integral hard disks.

Moreover, once apparently incriminating "evidence" of a computer-related offence has been obtained, there may still be legal obstacles to its introduction in criminal proceedings. Although significantly

---

11   Hammond, "Quantum Physics, Econometric Models and Proprietory Rights in Information" (1981), 27 McGill L.J. 47-72.

eroded by various exceptions under which such material may be admitted in a trial, there remains in both English and North American jurisprudence a general exclusion of "hearsay" evidence. The basic rule is that an oral or written statement made by a person other than the witness currently testifying will not be admitted as proof of the facts contained in that statement.[12] *Prima facie,* computerised records would appear to fall foul of this test. Under American, English and Canadian law there are, however, circumstances in which certain business and other records may be admitted in evidence as direct proof of their contents. The extent to which computerised records can be brought under the aegis of such exemptions will be discussed briefly in the context of the criminal sanctions available in each jurisdiction.

7.2 Criminal Sanctions in the United States

7.2.1   Intellectual Property Offences

Under the Copyright Act 1976, stringent criminal sanctions can be imposed in cases where copyright has been infringed on a commercial basis.[13] The reproduction or distribution of at least a thousand infringing copies of a sound recording or sixty-five infringing copies of an audiovisual work can result in a fine of up to $250,000 or imprisonment for up to five years, or both.[14] In cases involving between one hundred and a thousand infringing copies of a sound recording or between seven and sixty-five infringing copies of an audiovisual work the maximum penalty is a $250,000 fine or up to two years imprisonment, or both.[15] In all other cases where copyright is infringed "wilfully and for purposes of commercial advantage or private gain" the maximum penalty is a $25,000 fine or imprisonment for up to one year, or both.[16] Thus, many infringers of copyrights in software or data could in theory be fined or imprisoned, and where an audiovisual work, such as a videogame, is infringed on a commercial basis the $250,000 fine and five years imprisonment limits would often be applicable. Penalties up to these latter

---

12   This does not, however, preclude the introduction of evidence of such statements simply for the purpose of proving that those statements were made, *E.g., Sub-ramaniam v. Public Prosecutor,* [1956] 1 W.L.R. 965 (P.C.).

13   17 U.S.C., s. 506 (as amended).

14   18 U.S.C., s. 2319(b)(1).

15   *Ibid.,* s. 2319(b)(2).

16   *Ibid.,* s. 2319(b)(3).

limits can also be imposed for knowingly trafficking in counterfeit labels which are affixed or designed to be affixed to certain works, which might encompass some types of software and data.[17]

No such criminal penalties are available for patent infringement, but prosecution for theft of trade secrets is possible in many states. For example, under the California Penal Code theft includes stealing, taking or carrying away any article representing a trade secret with the intent to deprive the owner of it.[18] Under that statute a person also commits an offence if he "[h]aving unlawfully obtained access to the article, without authority makes or causes to be made a copy of any article representing a trade secret".[19] Despite the broad definition of "article" in the statute, the application of these provisions to software or data may not, however, be straightforward. In *People v. Ward*,[20] an employee of a computer service bureau gained access by telephone to the system of a rival bureau. He then instructed the remote computer to transmit a copy of a particular program and arranged for the copy to be printed out at his office. The court found, obiter, that the impulses by means of which the program was transmitted to the computer at the defendant's office did not constitute an article due to their intangibility. The printed copy of the program, however, did qualify as an article and the defendant was accordingly convicted for taking the printout of the program listing. The case illustrates the importance of defining the rights to be protected in a manner appropriate to computer technology. Ward would presumably have been acquitted had he kept the program in an intangible form.[21]

7.2.2   Application of Established Criminal Laws

In a number of reported cases, successful prosecutions for theft of programs, data or other information have been brought under tradi-

---

17   *Ibid.*, s. 2318. The relevant works are copyrighted motion pictures or other audiovisual works, and phonorecords of copyrighted sound recordings.
18   Cal. Penal Code, s. 499(c).
19   *Ibid.*
20   3 C.L.S.R. 206 (Cal. Super. Ct., 1972). See Becker, "The Trial of a Computer Crime" (1980), II Computer/Law J., 441-56.
21   If a similar incident were to occur in California today, however, a conviction could probably be obtained under s. 502 of the Cal. Penal Code which provides, *inter alia*, that "[a]ny person who intentionally accesses or causes to be accessed any computer system or computer network for the purpose of (1) devising or executing any scheme or artifice to defraud or extort or (2) obtaining money, property, or services with false or fraudulent intent, representations, or promises shall be guilty of a public offence." "Property" is defined as including computer programs.

tional criminal statutes. In *Hancock v. State*[22] the accused appealed from a conviction for theft of various computer programs from his employer. He had attempted to sell the programs in question to a rival company for $5,000,000. A Texas appeal court rejected assertions by the defence that either the programs were not property and thus could not be stolen, or that if they were property the value of the programs was in any event less than the $50 threshold required under the relevant theft statute. Both arguments were also rejected by the Fifth Circuit, which agreed with the Texas Appeal Court's valuation of the programs on a market, rather than actual, basis.[23]

The question of valuation will always be difficult in such situations as programs and data are almost invariably worth a great deal more than any media in which they might be stored or paper on which they might be printed out. The problem is not peculiar to computer-related cases, however. In *U.S. v. Lester*,[24] the stolen articles were geophysical maps with no obvious market value. The Third Circuit ruled that "any reasonable method may be employed to ascribe an equivalent monetary value to the items."[25] An application of this principle can be seen in *U.S. v. Digilio*[26] where the value of certain documents was established by reference to a "thieves Market."[27]

In *U.S. v. Bottone*,[28] however, copies of documents were made without any tangible property being taken at all. Consequently, the court was forced to address directly the question whether the information contained in the documents *per se* could be stolen and transported as was charged.[29] Having established that the originals of certain documents would qualify as valuable goods, the court turned to the tricky question of whether mere copies of such documents were "goods" which had been "stolen, converted or taken by fraud."[30] The court took what seems to be a highly pragmatic position and ruled that:

---

22   402 S.W. 2d 906 (Tex. Cr. App., 1966).
23   379 F. 2d 552 (5th Cir., 1967).
24   282 F. 2d 750 (3rd Cir. 1960).
25   *Ibid.*, at 755.
26   538 F. 2d 972 at 979 (3rd Cir., 1976).
27   Similarly, in *U.S. v. Bottone*, 365 F. 2d 389 at 393 (1966), the Second Circuit stated, "we dismiss out of hand the contentions that secret processes for which European drug manufacturers were willing to pay five and six figures and in whose illicit exploitation appellants eagerly invested a large portion of their time and an appreciable amount of their fortunes was not worth the $5,000 required to subject them to federal prosecution."
28   *Ibid.*
29   The actual charge concerned transportation of stolen goods in interstate or foreign commerce.
30   Note 27 above.

> where the physical form of the stolen goods is secondary in every respect to the matter recorded in them, the transformation of the information in the stolen papers into a tangible object never possessed by the original owner should be deemed immaterial.[31]

Thus all the court required was that *some* tangible object be taken or transported.[32]

Subsequently, a rather similar approach was taken by a district court in *U.S. v. Lambert*.[33] There the court saw:

> no reason to restrict the scope of [the theft statute] to the theft of government paper and ink, or to unauthorized reproduction. The phrase "thing of value" . . . in conjunction with the explicit reference to "any record" covers the content of such a record.

The only caveat the court added was that it did not mean to suggest that the statute would cover "the unauthorised oral transfer of government information not found in government records."[34]

The limitations of this pragmatic type of approach to intangible property can, however, be seen in the case of *U.S. v. Seidlitz*.[35] Seidlitz was convicted of two counts of wire fraud relating to remote accessing of the computer system of his former employer, Optimum Systems, Inc. (OSI). On a number of occasions he had dialed up the OSI system in Maryland from his office in Virginia and commanded the computer to transmit to him substantial portions of the source code of a valuable program known as WYLBUR. He also gained access to the OSI computer from his home in Maryland.[36] Seidlitz was initially also charged with interstate transportation of stolen property, but an acquittal on this third count was granted during the trial as no tangible property had been taken.[37] The defence argued both at trial and on appeal that the wire fraud charges should also fail as the alleged scheme to defraud could not have been for the purposes of "obtaining money or property," as required by the relevant statute. Both courts disagreed, however, and found that WYLBUR was a trade secret of OSI and thus constituted "property" for the purposes of the wire fraud statute.[38]

---

31   *Ibid.*, at 393-4.
32   *Ibid.*, at 393. This requirement meant that "the statute would presumably not extend to the case where a carefully guarded secret formula was memorized, carried away in the recesses of a thievish mind and placed in writing only after a boundary had been crossed."
33   446 F. Supp. 890 at 895. (D. Conn., 1978).
34   *Ibid.*, note 6.
35   589 F. 2d 152 (4th Cir., 1978), *cert. denied* 441 U.S. 922 (1979).
36   589 F. 2d at 153-55.
37   *Ibid.*, at 155, note 12. The trial at first instance is discussed in Bequai, *Computer Crime* (Lexington, Mass.: D.C. Heath & Co., 1978), pp. 38-39.
38   589 F. 2d at 160.

Both the failure of the interstate transportation charge, and the somewhat tenuous basis on which the abstracted portions of the program were found to be property for wire fraud purposes, are indicative of the awkwardness of applying traditional proprietory concepts to programs and data. Moreover, as Bequai has observed, the prosecutors were fortunate that Seidlitz operated from his Virginia office and not merely his Maryland home as otherwise the wire fraud statute would also have been inapplicable.[39]

7.2.3   Computer Crime Legislation

a   Proposals for comprehensive legislation to deal with computer-related crime have been before the United States Congress in various forms since 1977.[40] In the meantime, the Counterfeit Access Device and Computer Fraud and Abuse Act of 1984 has criminalized access to or use of a computer without proper authorization in three specific situations. These are obtaining classified information relating to defense, foreign relations or nuclear materials and weapons; obtaining private financial information; and abusing federal government computers.[41] At the state level, over the last decade there has been a proliferation of laws enacted to cover various aspects of computer use and abuse,[42] and many of these statutes are quite far reaching in scope.

The Arizona Criminal Code, for example, legislates in the following broad terms against "computer fraud":[43]

> A person commits computer fraud in the first degree by accessing, altering, damaging or destroying without authorization any computer, computer system, computer network, or any part of such computer, system or network, with the intent to devise or execute any scheme or artifice to defraud or deceive, or control property or services by means of false or fraudulent pretences, representations or promises.[44]

More comprehensive still is Florida's Computer Crimes Act[45] which sets out three broad categories of computer-related offences. These are

---

39   Note 37 above.

40   See Note (Gonzales) "Addressing Computer Crime Legislation: Progress and Regress" (1983), 4 Computer L.J. 195-206.

41   18 USC s. 1030 (Public Law 98-473, 12 Oct. 1984).

42   Most are listed in Lautsch, "Digest and Analysis of State Legislation Relating to Computer Technology" (1980), 20 Jurimetrics J. 201-312. See also Krieger, "Current and Proposed Computer Crime Legislation" (1980), II Computer/Law J., 721-71.

43   Title 13 Criminal Code, Ariz. Rev. Stat. An.

44   *Ibid.*, s. 13-2316A. Second-degree computer fraud is committed by "intentionally and without authority accessing, altering, damaging or destroying any computer, computer system or computer network or any computer software, program or data contained in such computer, computer system or computer network." *Ibid.*, s. 13-2316B.

45   Fla. Stat. An., ss. 815.01-815.07.

"offences against intellectual property," "offences against computer equipment or supplies" and "offences against computer users."[46] These three classifications are not mutually exclusive, and the Act as a whole expressly leaves open the possibility of also invoking any other provision of the state criminal law.[47] Many other states have similarly broad computer crime statutes.

7.2.4 Evidentiary Considerations

Apart from any secondary questions as to the weight of such evidence, the principal theoretical objections to the admissibility of computer records are the hearsay and best evidence rules.[48] As far as hearsay is concerned, at the federal level and in most states a broad exception is made for business records. For example, the Federal Rules of Evidence render admissible:

> Records of regularly conducted activity - A memorandum, report, record, or data compilation, in any form, of acts, events, conditions, opinions, or diagnoses . . . if kept in the course of a regularly conducted business activity.[49]

The exception applies regardless of whether the maker of the record is in fact available as a witness.

At the state level, business records are generally admissible under either a specific statutory exemption or under the common law "shopbook" rule.[50] In terms of statutory exceptions to the hearsay rule, most states have adopted the 1936 Uniform Business Records as Evidence Act which, *inter alia*, provides that:

> A record of an act, condition or event, shall, in so far as relevant, be competent evidence if the custodian or other qualified witness testifies to its identity and to the mode of its preparation, and if it was made in the regular course of business, at or near the time of the act, condition or event, and if, in the opinion of the court, the sources of information, method and time of preparation were such as to justify its admission.[51]

This provision is essentially a codification of the established common law shop-book exception. Under that exception, a record could be admitted if made in the normal course of business, at or near the time of the

---

46   *Ibid.,* ss. 815.04-815.06.
47   *Ibid.,* s. 815.07.
48   For a fuller treatment of the evidentiary and procedural aspects of computer-related litigation in the United States see Bender, *Computer Law and Evidence* (New York: Matthew Bender, 1983); Bequai, *Computer Crime* note 37, above; Becker, "Trial of a Computer Crime" (1980), II Computer/Law J. 441-56.
49   Federal Rules of Evidence, Rule 803(6).
50   See McCormick, *Handbook of the Law of Evidence,* 2nd ed. (1972), para. 316.
51   9 Unif. L. Ann. 506 (1965). See Bequai, note 37 above, at 122-25.

transaction in question, by a person currently unavailable to testify who had personal knowledge of the event and no motive for falsifying the record.[52]

A further potential obstacle to the admission of computer records is the "best evidence" rule whereby, for example, if a document is to be tendered in evidence, the original rather than a copy should always be produced. At the federal level the rigour of this rule has been mitigated considerably by the codification of several broad exceptions.[53] These include proof of the contents of an "official record" by means of a certified copy,[54] and the introduction in evidence of summaries of "voluminous writings" where the individual documents would be admissable and the opposing party has had an opportunity to inspect them.[55] Both have been held applicable to computer generated evidence.[56]

7.3 Criminal Sanctions in the United Kingdom and Canada

7.3.1 Intellectual Property Offences

In both the United Kingdom and Canada the relevant statutes have established offences of criminal infringement of copyright and, to a more limited extent, offences in relation to patents.[57] Subject to the threshold issue of the subsistence of copyright in software,[58] and provided "guilty knowledge" can be proved, the offences relating to copyright infringement should be broad enough to cover most cases of software piracy conducted on a commercial footing. In the United Kingdom there has

---

52   As Bequai has pointed out, a problem with this exception in the context of computer evidence is that considerations of computer security may militate against computer operators being allowed much personal knowledge of the data they handle.

53   Federal Rules of Evidence, Rules 1001-1006.

54   Rule 1005.

55   Rule 1006.

56   In *King v. Murdoch Acceptance Corp.*, 222 So. 2d 393 (D. Miss., 1969), Rule 1005 was held applicable to a computer printout. In *Ed Guth Realty Inc. v. Gingold*, 315 N.E. 441 (N.Y., 1974), Rule 1006 was held applicable to statistical evidence which was in a computer-readable form.

57   UK: Copyright Act 1956, 4 & 5 Eliz. 2, c. 74, s. 21; Patents Act, 25-26 Eliz. 2, c. 37, s. 109-113. Canada: Copyright Act, R.S.C. 1970, c. C-30, s. 25; Patent Act, R.S.C. 1970, c. P-4, ss. 71-81.

58   See chapter 4 above.

been at least one conviction for criminal infringement of the copyrights in a program description and in a program operating manual.[59]

In both countries, however, the penalties which can be imposed following a conviction have tended to be, at least when compared to the position under the United States Copyright Act, only nominal.[60] Accordingly, in its 1977 Report, the Whitford Committee recommended that the penalties in section 21 of the Copyright Act should be raised to a more realistic level and also that "possession in the course of trade" should be made an offence.[61] With a general revision of the Copyright Act evidently still far from seeing the light of day, in 1982 and 1983 the Whitford recommendation was implemented in respect of penalties for offences relating to infringing copies of sound recordings and cinematograph films.[62] The Copyright Act 1956 (Amendment) Act 1982 amended section 21 of the principal Act by insertion of the following new subsection:

> Any person who, at a time when copyright subsists in a sound recording or in a cinematograph film, by way of trade has in his possession any article which he knows to be an infringing copy of the sound recording or cinematograph film, as the case may be, shall be guilty of an offence under this subsection.[63]

In the following year, the Copyright (Amendment) Act 1983 further amended section 21 so as to substantially increase the penalties which

---

59 *Times,* 26 July 1984, p. 3. Howard Austin pleaded guilty to and was convicted by magistrates of two offences under s. 21(1)(b) of the Copyright Act 1956. Guilty pleas were also accepted in respect of three offences under s. 1(1)(b) of the Trade Descriptions Act 1968 (applying a false trade description to goods), and one offence under s. 3 of the Forgery and Counterfeiting Act 1981 (using a false instrument).

60 Sections 21(7) and (8) of the U.K. Copyright Act provide for a maximum penalty of £50 or, on a second or subsequent conviction, up to two months imprisonment. Section 25 of the Canadian Copyright Act provides, *inter alia,* for a fine of $10 for each infringing copy dealt with, up to a maximum for a first time offender of $200 for one transaction. *Cf.* the heavy penalties which can be imposed under the U.S. Copyright Act (as amended), discussed in section 7.2.1, above.

61 *Report of the Committee to Consider the Law on Copyright and Designs* (London: HMSO Cmnd. 6732, 1977), para. 711. Both of these recommendations were accepted in principle by the government in its 1981 Green Paper, *Reform of the Law Relating to Copyright, Designs and Performers' Protection* (London: HMSO Cmnd. 8302, 1918). However, the government rejected a further proposal made by the Whitford Committee that the "guilty knowledge" requirement "should be abolished in such cases leaving the accused entitled to an acquittal if he is able to establish that he was not aware of and had no reasonable grounds to suspect that the acts complained of were acts done in relation to infringing copies" (para. 711). The government considered this latter change would "be going too far in that the law would then lean too heavily on the vast majority of honest traders" (Green Paper, p. 50).

62 The Copyright Act 1956 (Amendment) Act 1982 (1982, c. 35); The Copyright (Amendment) Act 1983 (1983, c. 42).

63 The Copyright Act 1956 (Amendment) Act 1982, s. 1.

can be imposed for offences relating to infringing copies of sound recordings and films.[64]

In July 1984 the Copyright (Computer Software) Amendment Bill was introduced in the House of Commons under the "ten minute rule" and was given its first and only reading.[65] In addition to amendments already discussed,[66] the proposed legislation would have added the words "or computer programme" after each occurrence of the words "cinematograph film" in the 1982 and 1983 amendment acts. Thus possession of infringing copies of software in the course of trade would potentially attract penalties of an unlimited fine and up to two years imprisonment.[67] Further draft legislation to amend the Copyright Act in relation to software was tabled as a private members' bill in the 1984-85 session of Parliament.[68]

7.3.2   Application of Established Criminal Laws

English judges have been much less willing than their American counterparts to overlook the logical obstacles to applying common law theft principles to the "stealing" of information. As for the Canadian courts, however, there is reason to believe that a pragmatic approach more like that taken by courts across the border will prevail. The root of judicial concern in England was well stated by Lord Upjohn in his dissenting judgement in *Boardman v. Phipps*.[69] Addressing the issue of whether confidential information could constitute trust property, he said:

> In general, information is not property at all. It is normally open to all who have eyes to read and ears to hear. The true test is to determine in what circumstances the information has been acquired . . . in the end the real truth is that it is not property in

---

64   The Copyright (Amendment) Act 1983, s. 1(3). £2,000 is the current maximum fine for offences sentenced summarily, as established by the Criminal Penalties etc. (Increase) Order 1984 (SI 1984 No. 447), s. 2(4) and Sch. 4. On conviction for certain offences under s. 21 of the principal Act the fine which may be imposed on indictment is potentially unlimited, although it will be governed in practice by the general principle that a fine should be within an offender's capacity to pay: *R. v. Churchill (No. 2)* [1966] 2 All E.R. 215 (CCA). A term of imprisonment for up to two years may also be imposed in some cases. See ss. 21(7A) and (7B) of the 1956 Act (as amended).

65   Ordered to be printed 24 July 1984. For the Bill's full title, see chapter 4 above, note 38.

66   See section 4.1.2, above.

67   As per Copyright Act 1956 (as amended), s. 21(7A). On penalties, see note 64 above.

68   See chapter 4 above, note 45 and accompanying text.

69   [1966] 3 All E.R. 721 at 759, [1967] 2 A.C. 46 (H.L.).

any normal sense, but equity will restrain its transmission to another if in breach of some confidential relationship.[70]

Other judges have echoed a general unease at any suggestion that the scope of property rights in intangibles be drastically extended.

In the case of *Oxford v. Moss*,[71] the question of whether confidential information could be stolen arose specifically. The defendant, a student at Liverpool University, had dishonestly obtained the proof of an exam he was soon to write. After reading the paper he returned it, and it was an agreed fact in the case that Moss never intended to steal the paper itself. The stipendiary magistrate who heard the case at first instance held that, although the defendant's conduct was clearly reprehensible and would be described by a layman as "cheating," nevertheless the confidential information which he obtained was not property for the purposes of the Theft Act.[72] The Divisional Court agreed and dismissed the prosecution's appeal.[73]

As for so called "trade secrets," it can be argued that they too are not property for Theft Act purposes. For one thing, as has often been noted, even if secrets are regarded as property they will still be "difficult to steal" since there is usually no intent to deprive the owner of them.[74] Section one of the 1978 Theft Act does now make it an offence to "by any deception dishonestly obtai[n] services" and at first sight this makes a proprietory construction of information "more hopeful."[75] But as Tettenborn has noted, there are two significant limitations to the scope of this provision.[76] The first is that it only applies in situations where information would otherwise be supplied "on the understanding that the benefit has been or will be paid for."[77] In other words, the information must potentially be "for sale." Trade secrets generally are not. The second problem is that the word "deception" as used in the Theft Act "almost certainly does not encompass deceiving a machine."[78]

---

70   *Ibid.*, at 759.
71   (1978) 68 Cr. App. R. 183.
72   The Theft Act 1968, s. 4(1), defined property as including "money and all other property, real or personal, including things in action and other intangible property."
73   More recently a Crown Court judge has confirmed that information is not recognised by the criminal law as property: *Times*, 14 Sept. 1983, p. 2. See Eisenschitz, "Theft of Trade Secrets," [1984] 4 E.I.P.R. 91-92.
74   Griew, *The Theft Acts 1968 & 1978,* 3rd ed. (London: Sweet & Maxwell, 1978), pp. 2-14 and 2-56.
75   Tettenborn, "Stealing Information" (1979), 129 New L.J. 967-68.
76   *Ibid.*, at 967.
77   Theft Act 1978, s. 1(2).
78   Tettenborn, note 75 above, at 967.

Further evidence of the reluctance of English judges to treat "intell-ectual property" as property which can be stolen can be seen in *Rank Film Distributors v. Video Information Centre.*[79] In that case the House of Lords noted, *per curiam,* that copyright infringement was not in itself theft[80] and that the risk of a prosecution under the Theft Act for theft of copyright could be "disregarded as remote."[81] Thus, in the absence of legislative intervention, which is not currently anticipated, it seems unlikely that the English criminal law will afford much protection against misappropriation of computer programs and data in situations where there is neither theft of a tangible object nor criminal infringe-ment of the Copyright Act.[82]

In Canada, however, there have recently been indications that the law may develop quite differently. In particular, the decision of the Ontario Court of Appeal in *R. v. Stewart*[83] may indicate that Canadian judges will eschew the reticence of their English counterparts and in-stead treat even information *per se* as property which can be stolen. At present, under section 283(1) of the Criminal Code, "anything whether animate or inanimate" is capable of being stolen. Courts have on a number of occasions attributed a fairly broad meaning to the word "anything." For example, in *R. v. Scallen,*[84] the British Columbia Court of Appeal held that "anything" need not be tangible or material and included a bank credit. Similarly, in *R. v. Hardy,*[85] the same court found the elements of theft to be complete where the accused caused a company to issue cheques to him as additional salary.

However, by far the broadest interpretation of the word "anything" is that recently promulgated by the majority of the Ontario Court of Appeal in *R. v. Stewart.*[86] The accused was charged with counselling mischief, counselling theft of confidential information and counselling fraud. As a "self-employed consultant," Stewart had been approached by a person associated with a trade union who requested him to obtain the

---

79   [1981] 2 All E.R. 76, [1982] A.C. 380.

80   *Ibid.,* at 81.

81   *Ibid.,* at 83.

82   Where more than one person is involved in the misappropriation, a charge of conspiracy may perhaps be sustained. See *Scott v. Metro. Police Commr.,* [1975] A.C. 819, [1974] 3 All E.R. 1032 (H.L.): conspiracy to contravene s. 21(1)(a) of the Copyright Act held to be a conspiracy to defraud.

83   (1982), 38 O.R. (2d) 84, 74 C.P.R. (2d) 1 at 4, 68 C.C.C. (2d) 305, 138 D.L.R. (3d) 73; reversed (1983), 42 O.R. (2d) 225, 35 C.R. (3d) 105, 24 B.L.R. 53, 74 C.P.R. (2d) 1, 5 C.C.C. (3d) 481, 149 D.L.R. (3d) 583 (C.A.).

84   [1974] 4 W.W.R. 345, 15 C.C.C. (2d) 441 (B.C. C.A.).

85   (1980), 25 B.C.L.R. 362, 57 C.C.C. (2d) 73 (C.A.).

86   Note 83 above *per* Houlden and Cory JJ.A.

names, addresses and telephone numbers of the employees of a hotel whom the union wished to organize. Stewart then approached an employee of the hotel, Hart, and offered to pay him to obtain the desired information by copying either personnel files or a computer printout of the payroll. Hart was not, however, to remove or tamper with the records themselves.

In the Ontario High Court, Krever J. found the accused not guilty on all three counts of counselling. On the question of whether information could be stolen, the judge concluded that "confidential information is not property for the purpose of the law of theft in Canada." To qualify as "anything" under section 283(1) of the Code "the thing, whether tangible or intangible, must be capable of being property."[87] He added:

> If this interpretation should be thought to be inadequate to meet the needs of modern Canadian society, particularly because of the implications for the computer age, the remedy must be a change in the law by Parliament. It is not for a court to stretch the language used in a statute dealing with the criminal law, to solve problems outside the contemplation of that statute.[88]

The majority in the Court of Appeal, however, preferred not to wait for legislative intervention. Instead, Houlden and Cory JJ.A. allowed the Crown's appeal from the acquittal on the charge of counselling the commission of theft. On the general policy level, Houlden J.A. observed that:

> The last half of the twentieth century has seen an exponential growth in the development and improvement of methods of storing and distributing information. I believe that s. 283(1) of the *Code* is wide enough to protect the interests of those who compile and store such information and to restrain the activities of those who wrongfully seek to misappropriate it.[89]

While he recognized that his view of information as property was not in accord with the ruling in *Oxford v. Moss,* Houlden J.A. relied instead on the earlier *Exchange Telegraph* cases[90] in which stock exchange quotations were classified as "property." Having concluded that the information concerning the hotel employees was property for the purposes of theft, he had no hesitation in also finding it to be property for the purposes of fraud.[91]

---

87   (1982), 138 D.L.R. (3d) 73 at 85.
88   *Ibid.*
89   Note 86 above, at 495.
90   *Exchange Telegraph Co. v. Gregory and Co.,* [1896] 1 Q.B. 147; *Exchange Telegraph Co. v. Central News Ltd.,* [1897] 2 Ch. 48; *Exchange Telegraph Co. v. London & Manchester Press Agency Ltd.* (1906), 22 T.L.R. 375.
91   (1983), 5 C.C.C. (3d) 481 at 496.

Cory J.A., concurring, also made reference early in his judgement to the broad policy issue at stake in the case:

> If questioned, a businessman would unhesitatingly state that the confidential lists were the "property" of his firm. If they were surreptitiously copied by a competitor or outsider, he would consider his confidential data to have been stolen. The importance of confidential information will increase with the growth of high technology industry. Its protection will be of paramount concern to members of industry and the public as a whole.[92]

The judge supported his conclusion that such protection already exists under section 283(1) of the Code by reference to three disparate sources. First, he referred to the American rulings in *Bottone* and *Lambert* as support for "the conclusion that information is property."[93] Secondly, he maintained that even if this proprietory construction of information *per se* failed, "[t]here still remains a right of property in confidential information which . . . falls within the wide definition of property contained in section 283(1)."[94] Finally, he argued that a copyright owner has a proprietary interest in his work and that this interest falls within section 283(1).[95] In *Stewart* Cory J.A. was confident that the list of hotel employees was "an unpublished work to which copyright attaches."[96] Thus, "when the accused counselled Hart to photograph or photocopy the confidential list, he counselled him to commit theft."[97]

In a fairly lengthy dissent, Lacourcière J.A. highlighted the serious difficulties created by the expansive interpretations of the Criminal Code's theft provisions adopted by his colleagues. Stewart's counsel had conceded in argument that, if Stewart had "counselled the removal of record cards or computer print-outs, *i.e.*, something physical and tangible, the offence of counselling theft would have been complete."[98] Yet on the facts it was clear that he had not done so. Lacourcière J.A. considered the plain meaning of the language of the *Code* together with decided cases and concluded that:

> Canadian courts have grafted a property concept on the definition of the words "anything whether animate or inanimate," and thus confidential information *per se* is not protected under the *Criminal Code*. I agree with Krever J.'s conclusion that it is for Parliament to broaden the criminal definition of the property concept if the needs of modern Canadian society require it.[99]

---

92   *Ibid.*, at 497.
93   *Ibid.*, at 497-98. For a discussion of those cases, see section 7.2.2, above.
94   *Ibid.*, at 498.
95   *Ibid.*, at 501.
96   *Ibid.*, at 500.
97   *Ibid.*, at 501.
98   *Ibid.*, at 486.
99   *Ibid.*, at 491.

Lacourcière J.A. also noted that English courts had made it clear that in their view information *per se* could not be stolen,[100] and that in Commonwealth jurisdictions remedies for misappropriation of trade secrets were founded in equity and not property.[101]

When the case was remitted to the trial court for sentencing, an absolute discharge was given. Stewart has nevertheless appealed against his conviction to the Supreme Court of Canada.[102] Unless overturned on appeal, however, the Ontario Court of Appeal's ruling may be taken as authority for the proposition that it is now a criminal offence in Canada to misappropriate any trade secrets or confidential information. Simple infringement of copyright may also be an offence.[103] Thus, by treating information *per se* as a kind of property, the majority departed radically from traditional Anglo-Canadian jurisprudence and may have greatly expanded the scope of the theft offence in Canada.

7.3.3 Computer Crime Legislation

In the United Kingdom, with one significant exception, there is no legislative action specifically aimed at any kind of "computer crime" or "computer abuse." The exception is the Data Protection Act which received the royal assent in July 1984 and will come into force in stages over a period of roughly three years.[104] The Act will impose a number of duties on computer users who handle "personal data."[105] Failure to comply with such obligations may constitute a criminal offence, and in some situations there will be no limit to the fine which may be ordered on conviction.[106]

In Canada, Parliament has considered two sets of draft amendments intended to bring certain types of "computer abuse" expressly within the ambit of the Criminal Code.[107] While of far broader application, the amendments were in part intended to close a loophole which

---

100   Citing *Oxford v. Moss* (1978), 68 Cr. App. R. 183, and *Rank Film Distributors v. Video Information Centre*, [1981] 2 All E.R. 76, [1982] A.C. 380 (H.L.).

101   (1983), 5 C.C.C. (3d) at 490-1.

102   Hertz, "Protecting Computer Systems with the Criminal Law" (1984), 1 Computer Law 1-5.

103   This would be a significant progression from the already established civil remedy of damages for conversion. See *Pro Arts Inc. v. Campus Crafts Holdings* (1980), 28 O.R. (2d) 422, 10 B.L.R. 1, 50 C.P.R. (2d) 230, 110 D.L.R. (3d) 366 (H.C.).

104   1984, c. 35. See generally section 8.3, below.

105   See section 8.3.3, below.

106   See section 8.3.6, below.

107   Bill C-677, 29-30-31 Eliz II, 1980-81-82; Bill C-19, 32-33 Eliz II, 1983-84.

came to light in 1980 in the case of *R. v. McLaughlin*.[108] In *McLaughlin*, the Supreme Court of Canada ruled that a student who had tampered with the University of Alberta's computer system could not be convicted of theft because of the limited meaning of the phrase "telecommunication facility" in the Criminal Code.[109] The decision highlighted the difficulty of stretching existing offence categories to cover acts of computer abuse and led to calls for legislative change from the Canadian Bar Association, the Canadian Information Processing Society and the Canadian Law Information Council.[110] Other voices were subsequently added to the chorus.[111]

In 1983 Parliament was presented with a private members bill, Bill C-667,[112] containing proposed amendments to the Criminal Code to deal with misappropriation of software and data. The amendments would have, *inter alia*, extended the definition of property in the Code expressly to include "computer software or programs, copies thereof, and retrievable computer data or information produced and stored in machine-readable form by any means."[113] Moreover, the definition of theft in section 283 would have been extended to cover the situation where a person "directs to his use or to the use of another person, all or part of a computer program or copy thereof or any computerized data,"[114] and mischief would have included destroying, damaging or altering a computer program or data "in a way that renders it useless or inoperative or diminishes its commercial or scientific value."[115]

Bill C-667 died on the order paper. In February 1984, however, the federal government introduced a package of proposed amendments to the Code containing provisions which, if enacted, would have established a far broader regime of computer-related offences than that pro-

---

108   [1980] 2 S.C.R. 331, [1981] 1 W.W.R. 298, 18 C.R. (3d) 339, 53 C.C.C. (2d) 417, 113 D.L.R. (3d) 186, 23 A.R. 530, 32 N.R. 350. See also *R. v. Marine Resources Analysts Ltd.* (1980), 41 N.S.R. (2d) 631, 76 A.P.R. 631 (Co. Ct.). Leave to appeal denied (1980), 43 N.S.R. (2d) 1, 81 A.P.R. 1 (C.A.).

109   The student had been charged under s. 287(1)(b) of the Code which provides that "everyone commits theft who fraudulently, maliciously or without colour of right, uses any telecommunication facility or obtains any telecommunication service."

110   Whan, "Computer Crime and R. v. McLaughlin" (1981), 18 C.R. (3d) 350-64 at 364.

111   *E.g.*, briefs submitted by the Canadian Association of Chiefs of Police and the Canadian Business Equipment Manufacturers Association (CBEMA) to the National Consultation of Computer Crime sponsored by the Dept. of Justice, held in Toronto Mar. 2-3, 1983.

112   1st Sess. 32nd Parl., 29-30-31 Eliz. II, 1980-81-82.

113   *Ibid.*, s. 2(a).

114   *Ibid.*, s. 3.

115   *Ibid.*, s. 5.

posed in Bill C-667.[116] In particular, Bill C-19 contained a general prohibition against dishonestly obtaining a computer service or intercepting any function of a computer system.[117] Moreover, the Bill would have introduced the following wide-ranging classification of data mischief:

> Every one commits mischief who wilfully (a) destroys or alters data; (b) renders data meaningless, useless or ineffective; (c) obstructs, interrupts or interferes with the lawful use of data; or (d) obstructs, interrupts or interferes with any person in the lawful use of data or denies access to data to any person who is entitled to access thereto.[118]

The maximum penalty on conviction for one of these mischief offences or for dishonestly obtaining computer services or intercepting any function of a computer system would have been ten years imprisonment. Unlike the somewhat restrictive definition of "computer" in Bill C-677,[119] such terms as "computer system" and "data" were expansively defined in Bill C-19,[120] and generally the scope of the proposed amendments was comparable to that of some of the American "computer abuse" statutes.[121]

Bill C-19 also progressed no further than a first reading, being cut short by the dissolution of Parliament in July 1984. However, the new Conservative government soon declared its intention to ask Parliament

---

116   Bill C-19, 32-33 Eliz. II, 1983-84. First (and only) reading 7/2/1984.
117   "Every one who, dishonestly and without a claim of right, (a) obtains, directly or indirectly, any computer service, (b) by means of an electromagnetic, acoustic, mechanical or other device, intercepts or causes to be intercepted, directly or indirectly, any function of a computer system, or (c) uses or causes to be used, directly or indirectly, a computer system with intent to commit an offence under paragraph (a) or (b) . . . is guilty of an indictable offence."
118   The Bill would also have made it an offence to attempt to commit one of these mischief offences.
119   " '[C]omputer' means any programmable device or apparatus designed to store or process data or information, but does not include a hand-held calculator or similar device."
120   " '[C]omputer system' means a device that, or a group of interconnected or related devices one or more of which, (a) contains computer programs or other data, and (b) pursuant to computer programs, (i) performs logic and control, and (ii) may perform any other function." The word "function" is defined as including "logic, control, arithmetic, communication, storage and retrieval," and thus the definition of "computer system" would appear to cover digital communication systems. Even a simple telephone with a redial button performs a "function" and does so "pursuant to [a] computer program." The Bill also contained a broad definition of "data" as "representations of information or of concepts that are being prepared or have been prepared in a form suitable for use in a computer system."
121   See section 7.2.3, above.

"to consider amendments to the Criminal Code to deal more effectively with . . . computer crime."[122] It remains to be seen whether the reform proposals will be framed in terms of a specific extension to the theft provisions of the Code, or will be directed more generally to the question of "computer abuse."

7.3.4   Evidentiary Considerations

In the United Kingdom, the admissibility of computer-generated evidence in civil cases has been expressly regulated by statute since 1968.[123] The position in criminal cases, however, has been shrouded by confusion and the mist has only recently begun to clear. The difficulty began when, in 1965, the House of Lords ruled, by a bare majority, that microfilmed records were not admissible as evidence of the serial numbers of components on a vehicle production line.[124] Aware that this decision might provide a *carte blanche* for many engaged in theft and fraud, Parliament rather hastily passed the Criminal Evidence Act in the same year.[125] Under section 1(1) of that Act, a "document"[126] containing a "statement"[127] tending to establish a material fact can be introduced as evidence of that fact provided certain conditions are satisfied. These include a requirement that the documentary record was compiled from information supplied "by persons who have, or may reasonably be supposed to have, personal knowledge of the matters dealt with in the information they supply."[128]

If applied to computer output, this particular admissibility criterion can be problematic, as was demonstrated in 1980 in *R. v. Pettigrew*.[129] In that case, the prosecution sought to introduce in evidence a computer

---

122   Speech from the throne, 1st Sess. 33rd. Parl., 5 Nov. 1984.

123   Civil Evidence Act 1968, s. 64. Section 5 provides that, subject to certain conditions being met, "[i]n any civil proceedings a statement contained in a document produced by a computer shall, subject to rules of court, be admitted as evidence of any fact stated therein of which direct oral evidence would be admissible."

124   *Myers v. D.P.P.*, [1965] A.C. 1001, [1964] 2 All E.R. 881 (H.L.).

125   1965, c. 20.

126   Defined broadly as including "any device by means of which information is recorded or stored." *Ibid.*, s. 1(4).

127   Also broadly defined as including "any representation of fact, whether made in words or otherwise," *ibid.*

128   *Ibid.*, s. 1(1)(a). The other conditions were that the record had been compiled in the course of any trade or business and that the person who supplied the information was unavailable or could not reasonably be expected to remember the matters dealt with in that information." *Ibid.*, s. 1(1)(b).

129   (1980), 71 Cr. App. R. 39.

printout which listed the serial numbers of a bundle of notes sent by the Bank of England to another bank. The Court of Appeal ruled the printout inadmissible on the ground that the information it contained was not supplied by a person who had or could reasonably be supposed to have personal knowledge of that information.[130] Commenting on this decision, Professor J.C. Smith has argued that the attempted reliance on section 1(1) of the Criminal Evidence Act was "based on a misapprehension" and that consequently the case may have been decided *per incuriam.*[131] Rather, the prosecution should have tendered the computer printout not as hearsay to which the Criminal Evidence Act exception applied, but rather as direct evidence supplied by the computer without human intervention.[132] The printout should thus have been admitted by the court as "real evidence."

Such a construction of a computer printout as real evidence rather than hearsay subsequently prevailed in *R. v. Wood.*[133] In support of a charge of handling stolen goods, the prosecution sought to introduce in evidence computer printouts relating to a chemical analysis of processed metals which had been found in Wood's possession. The trial judge admitted the evidence and the accused was convicted. On appeal, Wood's counsel argued that the computer printouts in question were inadmissible at common law as hearsay. Nor, he claimed, were they authorised under the Criminal Evidence Act, 1965 since they failed the personal knowledge test. The Court of Appeal agreed with the latter contention, but found the evidence admissible at common law. The court applied the reasoning of two earlier cases in which data collected by a machine were admitted as real evidence, one relating to a film of radar traces,[134] the other to a tape recording.[135] The records produced by such machines can be admitted as real evidence and need not be considered as hearsay at all.

Moreover, not long after its ruling in *Wood,* the Court of Appeal found a computer printout admissible under section 1 of the Criminal

---

130   It was also argued at trial, though not pursued on appeal, that the Bank of England was not a trade or business as required by the Act.

131   "The Admissibility of Statements by Computer," [1981] Crim. L. Rev. 387-91 at 387.

132   *Ibid.,* at 389-90. Professor Smith argues that to be hearsay, evidence must have passed through a human mind. For other discussions of the *Pettigrew* case see Sizer and Kelman, eds., *Computer Output as Admissible Evidence in Civil and Criminal Cases* (London: Heyden & Son, 1982); Kelman and Sizer, *The Computer in Court* (Aldershot: Gower, 1982).

133   (1983), 76 Cr. App. R. 23.

134   *The Statue of Liberty,* [1968] 2 All E.R. 195, (*sub nom. Sapporo Maru (Owners) v. Statue of Liberty (Owners); The Statue of Liberty*) [1968] 1 W.L.R. 739.

135   *Maqsud Ali v. Ashiq Hussain* (1965), 49 Cr. App. R. 230.

Evidence Act. In *R. v. Ewing,*[136] the prosecution was allowed to introduce a computer-generated bank statement as evidence that the accused had received certain funds. *Pettigrew* was distinguished on the ground that the person who fed in to the computer the information from which the bank statement was prepared had, momentarily at least, the requisite personal knowledge for the purposes of the Act. Taken together, the ratios of *Wood* and *Ewing* suggest that the degree to which data are generated by a computer without human intervention will be determinative of whether a printout is either admissible as real evidence, or alternatively is hearsay which must be brought within a statutory exception to be admissible.

The framework of the 1965 Criminal Evidence Act will soon be superseded by that of the Police and Criminal Evidence Act 1984.[137] Section 68 of that Act will replace the business records exception of the 1965 Act with a provision under which, subject to certain conditions, documentary evidence compiled for any purpose will be admissible. The first condition is that "the document is or forms part of a record compiled by a person acting under a duty from information supplied by a person . . . who had, or may reasonably be supposed to have had, personal knowledge of the matters dealt with in that information."[138] Secondly, the information supplier must be unavailable, unidentifiable or untraceable or it must be unreasonable to expect him to recall the matters dealt with in the information.[139]

The Act contains specific provisions regarding computer output. If a statement is contained in a document produced by a computer, a number of further criteria will have to be satisfied before that statement can be admitted under section 68. Thus section 69 of the Act provides:

> In any proceedings, a statement in a document produced by a computer shall not be admissible as evidence of any fact stated therein unless it is shown - (a) that there are no reasonable grounds for believing that the statement is inaccurate because of improper use of the computer; (b) that at all material times the computer was operating properly, or if not, that any respect in which it was not operating properly or was out of operation was not such as to affect the production of the document or the accuracy of its contents; and (c) that any relevant conditions specified in rules of court under subsection (2) below are satisfied.[140]

---

136   [1983] 2 All E.R. 645.
137   1984, c. 60. Royal Assent October 31, 1984. Commencement expected in early 1986.
138   *Ibid.,* s. 68(1)(a).
139   *Ibid.,* ss. 68(1)(b), (2).
140   Such rules would relate to the manner in which information regarding the computer statement should be provided. At the time of writing no rules had been made. It should be noted that, in addition to the requirements of s. 69(1), s. 72(2) preserves any power which a court may have to exclude evidence at its discretion.

Where a party wishes to introduce a statement in evidence under section 69, information dealing with any of the matters mentioned in section 69(1) together with any relevant technical explanation may be set out in a certificate.[141] Although a court may still require oral evidence of anything which might be set out in a certificate,[142] a certificate "purporting to be signed by a person occupying a responsible position in relation to the operation of the computer . . . shall be evidence of anything stated in it."[143]

The Act also contains guidelines as to how the weight to be attached to a computer statement should be estimated. While "regard shall be had to all the circumstances from which any inference can reasonably be drawn as to the accuracy or otherwise of the statement," particular attention should be given to the following questions. First, whether the relevant information was supplied to the computer contemporaneously, and second whether any person concerned in any way with the production of the statement had "any incentive to conceal or misrepresent the facts."[144] Since the Act allows for the provisions relating to computer evidence to be supplemented by rules of court, it should be relatively easy for any technical flaws in the legislation to be remedied.[145] There is of course a price to be paid for all this detailed statutory guidance. Although undoubtedly intended to clarify the position, it is perhaps ironic that the establishment of special rules for computer evidence means that there will from now on be far more obstacles in the way of admitting computerised records than any other type of documentary record. A characterisation of computer output as real evidence, where such a construction is possible on the facts, is thus likely to be more attractive than ever.[146]

In Canada, arguments as to the admissibility of computer-based evidence have focussed on the interpretation of the statutory exceptions to the hearsay rule contained in sections 29 and 30 of the Canada Evidence Act.[147] The Ontario Court of Appeal has twice held that a

---

141 *Ibid.,* Sch. 3 Part II, para. 8.

142 *Ibid.,* para. 9.

143 *Ibid.,* para. 8. A matter must be "stated to the best of knowledge and belief of the person stating it". Making a false statement in a certificate is an offence carrying a penalty of up to two years imprisonment. *Ibid.,* para. 10.

144 *Ibid.,* para. 11. Para. 12 provides that "For the purposes of paragraph 11 above information shall be taken to be supplied to a computer whether it is supplied directly or (with or without human intervention) by means of any appropriate equipment."

145 *Ibid.,* Sch. 3, Part III, para. 15.

146 *Ibid.,* s. 68(3), provides that "Nothing in this section shall prejudice the admissibility of any evidence that would be admissible apart from this section."

147 R.S.C. 1970, c. E-10.

computer-generated bank statement is admissible under section 29 as a copy of an entry in a book or record kept in a financial institution.[148] Computer output has also been admitted under the general business records exception contained in section 30. The section covers "a record made in the usual and ordinary course of business"[149] and defines "-record" as including "the whole or any part of any book, document, paper, card, tape or other thing on or in which information is written, recorded, stored or reproduced."[150] In 1976, in a case concerning fraudulent telegraphic transfers of funds from various branches of a bank, the British Columbia Court of Appeal ruled that the section "clearly covers mechanical as well as manual bookkeeping records and the . . . printout of [a] bookkeeping system clearly falls within the meaning of 'records' in s. 30."[151]

At present there are no special statutory rules in Canada distinguishing computer records from any other kind of documentary evidence. In its report published in 1982,[152] the Federal/Provincial Task Force on Uniform Rules of Evidence recommended, by a majority, that the requirements for business documents should be supplemented by the following admissibility criteria for computer evidence:

1. proof that the data upon which the print-out is based is of a type regularly supplied to the computer during the regular activities of the organization from which the print-out comes; 2. proof that the entries into the data base from which the print-out originates were made in the regular course of business; and 3. proof that the computer programme used in producing the print-out reliably and accurately processes the data in the data base.[153]

These proposals, together with recommendations for related procedural amendments, were, however, rejected by the Uniform Law Conference of Canada. Bill S-33, based on the Uniform Evidence Act approved by that Conference, similarly contained no special treatment of computer-based evidence.[154]

---

148   *R. v. McMullen* (1979), 25 O.R. (2d) 301, 47 C.C.C. (2d) 499, 100 D.L.R. (3d) 671 (C.A.); *R. v. Bell* (1982), 35 O.R. (2d) 164, 26 C.R. (3d) 336, 65 C.C.C. (2d) 377 (C.A.).
149   Note 147 above, s. 30(1).
150   *Ibid.*, s. 30(12).
151   *R. v. Vanlerberghe* (1978), 6 C.R. (3d) 222 (B.C. C.A.).
152   *Report of the Federal/Provincial Task Force on Uniform Rules of Evidence* (Toronto: Carswell, 1982).
153   *Ibid.*, p. 400.
154   Bill S-33: Canada Evidence Act. First reading November 18, 1982, second reading December 7, 1982. The Bill died on the order paper with the dissolution of Parliament in June, 1984. See "Computer Records as Courtroom Evidence" (1984) 1 Computer Law 57-60, 76-80.

It might be argued that to introduce detailed rules to regulate the admissibility of computer records would be to make the law in relation to computer evidence unnecessarily cumbersome. Conversely, however, it should be remembered that, in the absence of statutory guidelines, it remains open to a court to require comprehensive foundation evidence as to the reliability of any particular computer system before admitting a given printout.[155]

---

155   See *R. v. McMullen,* note 148 above, 47 C.C.C. (2d) at 506.

Chapter 8

Privacy and Data Protection

8.1 Privacy and Computers

8.1.1   The Emergence of Privacy as a Legal Concern

The jurisprudence of "privacy" as a distinct legal concept has its origins in an essay published in the Harvard Law Review in 1890. In "The Right to Privacy,"[1] Samuel Warren and Louis Brandeis reviewed the long history of protection under the English common law for various individual liberties and private property rights and from the ratios of these cases extrapolated a general "right to privacy."[2] Warren and Brandeis considered the absence of formal judicial recognition for this right as a serious anomaly in the development of the common law:

> The common law has always recognized a man's house as his castle, impregnable, often, even to its own officers engaged in the execution of its commands. Shall the courts then close the front entrance to constituted authority, and open wide the back door to idle or prurient curiosity?[3]

Fifteen years after the publication of Warren and Brandeis' essay, the "right to privacy" received its first judicial mandate in the case of *Pavesich v. New England Life Ins. Co.*[4]

In the United States, and to a lesser but growing extent elsewhere, there has since been a steady stream, some would say a plethora, of cases, statutes, articles and books all extolling the virtues of protection for various aspects of privacy for individuals. Much political capital has been made out of the privacy debate. After all, privacy protection is an objective which politicians of all parties can be seen to favour. Not surprisingly, perhaps, much of the literature on the subject is comprised of impressive sounding, but often hollow, rhetoric and the temptation to indulge in sensationalism seems to have seduced many commentators.

---

1   (1890), 4 Harv. L.R. 193-220.
2   *Ibid.*, at 213.
3   *Ibid.*, at 220.
4   50 S.E. 68 (S. Ct. Ga., 1905).

As has so often resulted from sensational crime reporting, the threat of actual victimization, in this case by way of privacy invasion, is now for most citizens probably more perceived than real. Indeed, the stage may have been reached at which reassurance of the public is a more pressing need than the prevention or cure of any actual abuses.

The extent to which fears of privacy invasion are well founded, however, depends to a large extent on the meaning which is ascribed to the word "privacy." If privacy is defined, as it often has been, in very broad terms such as "the right to be left alone,"[5] then the status of private life will only be enjoyed by recluses, if indeed it can be achieved by anyone. Social existence entails a necessary trade-off between exclusive individual autonomy and inclusive social interaction. As Alan Westin has observed:

> Viewed in terms of the relation of the individual to social participation, privacy is the voluntary and temporary withdrawal of a person from the general society through physical or psychological means, either in a state of solitude or small-group intimacy or, when among larger groups, in a condition of anonymity or reserve. The individual's desire for privacy is never absolute, since participation in society is an equally powerful desire.[6]

Characterized in such broad terms, there is no doubt that "privacy," as one of a number of competing goals in social policy formation, is of considerable relevance to many aspects of property law, torts and equity.

However, due to its generality of application, once such a claim to "privacy" is elevated from the level of abstract principle to substantive right, it seems that the boundaries of such a cause of action are limited only by the imagination.[7] Privacy is at the best of times "a large and unwieldly concept,"[8] and a persuasive case can thus be made for eschewing the apparent solution of making it a blanket right. Instead, it may be wiser to seek specific cures to remedy specific ills. It is interesting to note that, in the United States, a very broad common law right to privacy has nevertheless had to be supplemented by specific data protection legislation.

For the purposes of this chapter, the term "privacy" will be used to describe what might more fully be defined as "informational privacy." To adopt Westin's classic formulation of the issue, what is at stake is "the claim of individuals, groups, or institutions to determine for them-

---

5   *Olmstead v. U.S.*, 277 U.S. 438 at 478 (1928). (Brandeis J. dissenting).

6   *Privacy and Freedom* (New York: Atheneum, 1967), p. 7.

7   *E.g.*, the U.S. Supreme Court has ruled that to deny a woman an abortion may constitute an invasion of her privacy: *Roe v. Wade*, 410 U.S. 113 (1973).

8   Wacks, *The Protection of Privacy* (London: Sweet & Maxwell, 1980), p. 21.

selves when, how, and to what extent information about them is communicated to others."[9]

8.1.2   The Implications of Computer Technology

Opinions as to the general social implications of computers vary widely. Some commentators view the very existence of large databanks as an unacceptable threat to civil liberties.[10] Others characterize computer technology as essentially neutral, but as presenting tremendous opportunities for socially beneficial applications, provided the machinery of the information revolution, or "third wave," can be tamed.[11] Some point to the fact that when personal information is processed by computers the result will often be greater anonymity than is possible with manual record systems, and more security and privacy.[12] Indeed, a common complaint about computerised data processing is that the resulting systems are too impersonal and anonymous.

Such complaints should not, however, be allowed to obscure the fact that some computer information systems can, if their operators so desire, be used with great efficiency for surveillance purposes. This concern applies most obviously to the large databanks now maintained in most Western countries by police, welfare services and other public organisations. To the extent that they are allowed to operate without regulation, privately controlled databanks containing credit, employment and other personal information may also give rise to fears for data privacy.

Thus, in the data processing context, the general issue of legal policy is the extent to which the use of computers in the collection, processing, storage and dissemination of personal information should be regulated by law. Such regulation is commonly described, in Europe at least, as "data protection." At stake are conflicting demands for, on the one hand, free circulation of information in society with the attendant benefits this can bring and, on the other hand, restricted access to personal informa-

---

9   Westin, note 6, above, p. 7.

10   *E.g.*, Rule, McAdam, Stevens and Uglow, *The Politics of Privacy* (New York: Mentor, 1980). The book was appropriately dedicated "To the memory of George Orwell."

11   *E.g.*, Toffler, *The Third Wave* (London: Pan, 1981); *Previews and Premises* (London: Pan, 1984); Miller, *The Assault on Privacy* (Ann Arbor: Univ. of Michigan Press, 1971).

12   See the discussion of the security benefits of computer processing in Home Office, *Computers: Safeguards for Privacy* (London: HMSO, Cmnd. 6354, 1975), para. 11.

tion.[13] Even strident critics of the growth of personal databanks have to concede that "few systems of collection and use of detailed personal information ... are foisted on a wholly unwilling public simply for narrow bureaucratic purposes. On the contrary, people often want and even demand the fine-grained decision-making afforded by personal-data systems."[14] "Freedom of Information" statutes and calls for "open government" are also liable to collide with demands for confidentiality and restricted access to public records.[15] The function of data protection measures should thus be to guarantee individuals a degree of control over the use of personal information relating to them, without creating un-necessarily cumbersome obstacles to the free flow of information in society.[16]

It should not be forgotten that the potential for misuse of personal data has long existed in the case of manual processing systems.[17] In an Explanatory Memorandum published in 1981 with its Guidelines on the Protection of Privacy and Transborder Flows of Personal Data, an OECD Expert Group pointed to the "considerable drawbacks" of limit-ing data protection to automatic processing only.[18] While recognizing the "particular dangers to individual privacy raised by automation and computerized data banks,"[19] the Expert Group highlighted two signifi-cant problems with the manual/automatic distinction. The first was the difficulty of defining the distinction between automatic and non-auto-matic data handling systems, for example in the case of computer controlled microfilm readers.[20] The second general concern was that an

---

13   For a fuller discussion of these issues see Feldman, "Commercial Speech, Trans-border Data Flows and the Right to Communicate under International Law" (1983), 17 The Int. Lawyer 87-95; Note (Spear), "Computers in the Private Sector: Right to Informational Privacy for the Consumer" (1983), 22 Washburn L.J. 469-90; Beck, "Control of, and Access to, On-Line Computer Data Bases: Some First Amendment Issues in Videotex and Teletext" (1982), 5 Comm/Ent. 1-19.

14   Rule et al, note 10 above, p. 134.

15   Accordingly, the U.S. Freedom of Information Act (5 U.S.C., s. 552) contains broad exemptions in respect of personal information. See section 8.2.2, below.

16   The difficulty of balancing these objectives is exacerbated when data are to be communicated at an international level. See chapter 9, below.

17   E.g., in World War II the Nazis used Dutch population records as a means of identifying and locating Jews and other enemies of the Third Reich. Hondius, *Emerging Data Protection in Europe* (New York: American Elsevier, 1975).

18   (Paris: OECD, 1981), Memorandum, para. 35. The principle objective of the Guidelines, which became applicable in 1980, is to prevent the development of unnecessary obstacles to transborder data flows. See the discussion in chapter 9, below.

19   *Ibid.,* para. 34.

20   *Ibid.,* para. 35.

exclusive concentration on computers "might lead to inconsistency and lacunae, and opportunities for record-keepers to circumvent rules which implement the Guidelines by using non-automatic means for purposes which may be offensive."[21] Accordingly, the OECD Guidelines are not limited to automatic data systems only.

On the other hand, an argument can be made out for restricting legal safeguards to computer based data systems. For one thing, the speed with which computerised data can be gathered, collated and transmitted and the volumes in which such data can be stored facilitate invasions of privacy on a scale quite impossible with manual records.[22] In short, then, there is a difference in kind between computers and traditional filing systems.[23] A more pragmatic reason for restricting data protection to automatic processing is simply the apparent impracticality of doing otherwise. The characteristics of computers which make the processing and storage of vast amounts of data possible, also greatly facilitate in the searching and monitoring of such data holdings. Very little assistance is available in the case of manual records.

8.1.3   The Essential Principles of Data Protection

What, then, are the essential principles of data protection? In a 1973 Report entitled *Records, Computers and the Rights of Citizens*,[24] an Advisory Committee to the United States Department of Health concluded that the optimal means of protecting an individual data subject was to "assure that individual a right to participate in a meaningful way in decisions about what goes into records about him and how that

---

21   *Ibid.*

22   In a White Paper issued in 1975 the U.K. government highlighted the following practical implications for privacy of computerised information systems: "(1) they facilitate the maintenance of extensive record systems and the retention of data in those systems; (2) they can make data easily and quickly accessible from many distant points; (3) they make it possible for data to be transferred quickly from one information system to another; (4) they make it possible for data to be combined in ways which might not otherwise be practicable; (5) because the data are stored, processed and often transmitted in a form which is not directly intelligible, few people may know what is in the records, or what is happening to them." *Computers and Privacy* (London: HMSO, Cmnd. 6353, 1975), para. 6.

23   As one commentator has put it: "Just as the motor car made highways without white lines, traffic lights and the highway code unsafe for travellers, so the speed, volumes and power of the computer and of modern communications have introduced a new dimension of risk." Chalton, "Data and the Individual" (1983), 11 Int. Bus. L. 41-5 at 42.

24   (Washington: U.S. Govt. Printing Office, 1973).

information shall be used."[25] The Advisory Committee also formulated a set of principles of "fair information practice,"[26] which were substantially implemented in the 1974 Privacy Act.[27]

The OECD Expert Group went somewhat further than this and, in addition to recommending various rights of access and participation, it included in its Guidelines the following principles regarding the extensiveness of data collection and the quality of data holdings:

Collection Limitation Principle

There should be limits to the collection of personal data and any such data should be obtained by lawful and fair means and, where appropriate, with the knowledge or consent of the data subject.

Data Quality Principle

Personal data should be relevant to the purposes for which they are to be used and, to the extent necessary for those purposes, should be accurate, complete and up-to-date.[28]

Other sets of principles have been formulated by the various official groups which have addressed the privacy implications of computerised data handling.[29]

Drawing together the threads from various official reports and existing data protection legislation Mr. Justice Kirby[30] has identified no

---

25   *Ibid.,* p. 41.
26   (1) There must be no personal-data record keeping systems whose very existence is secret. (2) There must be a way for an individual to find out what personal information is in a record and how it is used. (3) There must be a way for an individual to prevent personal information obtained for one purpose from being used or made available for other purposes without his or her consent. (4) There must be a way for an individual to correct or amend a record of his or her own identifiable information. (5) Any organization creating, maintaining, using, or disseminating records of identifiable personal data must assure the reliability of the data for their intended use and must take reasonable precautions to prevent misuse of the data.
27   5 U.S.C., s. 552a. See the discussion in section 8.2.2, below.
28   In all, the Guidelines contain seven principles. The other five have the self-explanatory titles of Purpose Specification, Use Limitation, Openness, Individual Participation and Accountability.
29   *E.g.,* the U.S. Privacy Protection Study Commission identified eight key principles: Openness, Individual Access, Individual Participation, Collection Limitation, Use Limitation, Disclosure Limitation, Information Management and Accountability. *Personal Privacy in an Information Society* (Washington: U.S. Govt. Printing Office, 1977), pp. 501-2; The Council of Europe's *Convention for the Protection of Individuals with Regard to Automatic Processing of Personal Data* (Strasbourg: Council of Europe; 1981) stresses Data Quality, Restrictions on the Processing of Special Categories of Data, Data Security and Individual Participation.
30   Chairman of the OECD Expert Group on Transborder Data Barriers and the Protection of Privacy, and Chairman of the Australian Law Reform Commission.

less than ten "basic rules" of data privacy.[31] With essentially self-explanatory titles, the ten principles are (1) the Social Justification Principle; (2) the Collection Limitation Principle; (3) the Information Quality Principle; (4) the Purpose Specification Principle; (5) the Disclosure Limitation Principle; (6) the Security Safeguards Principle; (7) the Openness Principle; (8) the Time Limitation Principle; (9) the Accountability Principle; and (10) the Individual Participation Principle.[32]

8.2 Data Protection in the United States

8.2.1 Constitutional and Common Law Privacy Rights

There is no express reference to privacy in the United States Constitution. However, in 1958 the Supreme Court held that it was unconstitutional for a state to require a private association to reveal the names of its members before it could be registered as an out-of-state corporation.[33] The Court ruled that, under the First and Fourteenth Amendments, the association members had a right to "pursue their lawful private interests privately."[34] In 1965, the Supreme Court went a step further and held that a general right to privacy was implied by the First, Third, Fourth, Fifth and Fourteenth Amendments.[35]

The question of privacy in relation to a computer data bank was addressed by the Supreme Court in 1977 in *Whalon v. Roe*.[36] The case concerned a constitutional challenge to a requirement under the New York Controlled Substances Act that the identities of patients who had been prescribed certain drugs such as opium and cocaine must be disclosed to the State Department of Health. The practice of the Health Department was to store the names and addresses of the patients concerned in a computer data bank. The plaintiffs argued that the existence of such computer records was likely to discourage potential patients from seeking medical assistance in case their dependence on the drugs in

---

31   "Transborder Data Flows and the 'Basic Rules' of Data Privacy" (1980), 16 Stan. J. of Int. L. 27-66.

32   *Ibid.*, at 46.

33   *N.A.A.C.P. v. Alabama*, 357 U.S. 449 (1958).

34   *Ibid.*, at 466.

35   *Griswold v. Connecticut*, 381 U.S. 479 (1965).

36   429 U.S. 589 (1977). A few years earlier, the Court had dealt inconclusively with data protection in *Laird v. Tatum*, 408 U.S. 1 (1972), ruling that the mere existence of certain government data collection activities could not in itself form the basis of a justiciable claim.

question became known. The court held, however, that there was no invasion of privacy as security at the computer installation was adequate and the information was only revealed to the appropriate officials.[37]

At common law, the right to privacy in the United States is now generally understood in terms of four separate torts.[38] These are appropriation for gain of another's name, picture or likeness; placing another in a false light in the public eye; intrusion into another's physical solitude or seclusion; and public disclosure of aspects of another's private life. The application of these common law torts to the protection of personal data is uncertain. In one of the few reported cases on the point, an Ohio court refused to enjoin American Express and the publishers of a number of magazines from selling personal information about consumers to direct mail advertisers.[39] The court found that the defendants' practice of selling subscription lists did not constitute the tort of appropriation because the plaintiffs' names or likenesses were not displayed to the public as an endorsement of the defendants' product or business.[40] Moreover, the court ruled that "[t]he right of privacy does not extend to the mailbox and therefore it is constitutionally permissible to sell subscription lists to direct mail advertisers."[41] This case is not atypical of the general approach taken by courts to informational privacy claims, and there is some doubt as to whether any of the four privacy related torts are readily applicable to data protection concerns.[42]

8.2.2   Federal Privacy Legislation

The 1967 Freedom of Information Act[43] was intended primarily to provide access to government records. However, there are a number of exceptions to the general obligation which the Act imposes on federal agencies to make information available to the public. In particular, information can be withheld "to the extent required to prevent a clearly unwarranted invasion of personal privacy."[44]

---

37   429 U.S. 589 at 605. Security included a fence and alarm system at the computer installation and off-line access to data only.
38   Prosser, "Privacy" (1960), 48 Calif. L. Rev. 383; *Law of Torts,* 4th ed. (1972).
39   *Shibley v. Time Inc.,* 341 N.E. 2d 337 (Ohio App., 1975).
40   *Ibid.,* at 339.
41   *Ibid.*
42   See Note (Spear), "Computers in the Private Sector: Right to Informational Privacy for the Consumer" (1983), 22 Washburn L.J. 469-90.
43   5 U.S.C., s. 552.
44   *Ibid.,* s. 552(a).

More extensive controls on the disclosure of personal information by federal agencies were introduced in the Privacy Act[45] of 1974. The Act also regulates the collection of personal data and gives data subjects rights of access to information held on them. Agencies which collect data relating to individuals must inform the individuals concerned that such information is being gathered, specify the purposes of the data collection, and inform the individuals of certain procedural rights.[46] Under the Act, individuals are also entitled, on request, to access to any information relating to them and can ask for corrections to be made.[47] If the agency agrees to amend a record, it must notify agencies or individuals to whom the information has previously been disclosed.[48] If the agency refuses to make a requested amendment, the individual concerned has a right to first an administrative review and then a judicial review.[49] Personal data can only be disclosed by an agency in certain circumstances, which include disclosure for specified "routine uses," for certain law enforcement purposes, for internal purposes within the agency and where required under the Freedom of Information Act.[50] Certain agencies, notably law enforcement agencies, can exempt themselves from the collection and subject access provisions of the Act. Such agencies must, however, still comply with the disclosure conditions.[51]

The first major intervention by the federal government in the field of private sector informational privacy was the Fair Credit Reporting Act of 1970.[52] Under that Act, if requested to do so by an individual, a consumer reporting agency must disclose "the nature and substance of all information (except medical information) in its file" relating to that individual.[53] If the individual disputes the accuracy of any information in the file, the agency must reinvestigate and either make any necessary corrections or delete any information which cannot be verified.[54] The Act also imposes a general duty on agencies to take reasonable care to ensure the accuracy and security of any data they hold.[55] An individual

---

45   5 U.S.C., s. 552a (Supp. 1976).
46   *Ibid.*, s. 552a(e).
47   *Ibid.*, s. 552a(d).
48   *Ibid.*
49   *Ibid.*
50   *Ibid.*, s. 552a(b).
51   *Ibid.*, ss. 552a(j) and (k).
52   15 U.S.C., s. 1681.
53   *Ibid.*, s. 1681(g).
54   *Ibid.*, s. 1681(j). If a dispute is unresolved, the individual may file an account with the agency and the account must then be included in all subsequent reports made on that individual.
55   *Ibid.*, s. 1681(e).

who suffers harm due to an agency's negligence can recover damages,[56] and if the agency has acted "wilfully" punitive damages may also be awarded.[57]

Other federal privacy legislation includes the Right to Financial Privacy Act[58] and the Fair Credit Billing Act.[59] The former restricts access to banking, insurance and other financial records, the latter provides protection for debtors who allege inaccuracies in credit billing.[60]

8.2.3   State Privacy Legislation

With certain exceptions,[61] federal privacy legislation is only applicable to the actions of federal government agencies. While the respective jurisdictions of federal and state law in this area are not prescribed constitutionally, the Supreme Court has stated that "protection of a person's *general* right to privacy – his right to be let alone by other people – is, like the protection of his property and his very life, left largely to the law of the individual states."[62]

While a number of states have legislated to protect various aspects of individual privacy,[63] protection of privacy at the state level remains "limited, inconsistent, and fragmented."[64] Many of the state statutes are only applicable to government records, and those which do extend to private sector activities are generally limited to the regulation of financial information.[65]

The state which has come closest to establishing a comprehensive framework of privacy legislation is California.[66] While there is no single

---

56   *Ibid.,* s. 1681(o).
57   *Ibid.,* s. 1681(n).
58   12 U.S.C., s. 340.
59   15 U.S.C., s. 1666.
60   See also the Federal Reports Act, 44 U.S.C., s. 3501, and the Family Educational Rights and Privacy Act, 20 U.S.C., s. 1232g.
61   Notably the Fair Credit Reporting Act and the Fair Credit Billing Act, notes 52 and 58, above.
62   *Katz v. U.S.,* 389 U.S. 347 at 350-1 (1967) (emphasis supplied).
63   For a general review see Lautsch, "Digest and Analysis of State Legislation Relating to Computer Technology" (1980), 20 Jurimetrics J. 201.
64   Soma, *Computer Technology and the Law* (New York: McGraw Hill, 1983), p. 238.
65   See Note (Spear), "Computers in the Private Sector: Right to Informational Privacy for the Consumer" (1983), 22 Washburn L.J. 469-90.
66   See Pilshner, "Its None of Your Business. Or is it? California Addresses the Computer Age" (1982), 8 Rutgers Comp. & Tech. L.J. 235.

statute regulating privacy rights in the state,[67] Californian privacy legislation now covers most major data collection, processing and dissemination activities in both the public and private sectors.[68]

8.3 The United Kingdom Data Protection Act 1984

8.3.1 Background to the Legislation

There is no general constitutional or statutory right to privacy in the United Kingdom, and the courts have been reluctant to develop any such right at common law.[69] Limited data protection provisions are, however, contained in the Consumer Credit Act 1974.[70] Under the Act, which makes no distinction between manual and computerised credit records, a debtor can require a creditor to identify any credit reference agency which has supplied information about him.[71] The debtor is then entitled, on payment of a nominal fee, to a copy of the agency's file relating to him.[72] The debtor can insist that the agency amend or delete any entry in the file considered inaccurate, and can also require the agency to add to the file a notice of correction.[73]

In recent years, Parliament and the courts have been coming under pressure to respond to much broader privacy concerns. The United Kingdom is a signatory to the European Convention for the Protection of Human Rights and Freedoms, section eight of which provides that "Everyone has the right to respect for his private and family life, his home and his correspondence." In one recent decision, the European Court of Human Rights ruled that an incident in which the British police tapped the telephone of a person suspected of handling stolen goods constituted an unwarranted invasion of privacy.[74] The introduction of

---

67   An attempt in 1977 to introduce a general privacy act failed. *Ibid.*

68   See Lautsch, note 63, above.

69   *E.g., D.P.P. v. Withers,* [1975] A.C. 842, [1974] 3 All E.R. 984 (H.L.).

70   1974, c. 39.

71   *Ibid.,* s. 158.

72   *Ibid.*

73   *Ibid.,* s. 159. See generally Dobson, *Sale of Goods and Consumer Credit* (London: Sweet & Maxwell, 1979).

74   "Telephone Tapping Pledge as Court Rules Against Government," Times (3 August 1984), p. 2. Mr. Malone, the plaintiff in the case, had been unsuccessful in suing the Metropolitan Police Commissioner in respect of the same incident five years previously: *Malone v. Metro. Police Commr.,* [1979] Ch. 344, *(sub nom. Malone v. Commr. of Police of the Metropolis (No. 2))* [1979] 2 All E.R. 620. Following the European

piecemeal legislative reforms to deal with such specific concerns will, however, take time and the creation of any general right to privacy remains unlikely.

The Data Protection Act 1984[75] is thus a highly significant landmark in English jurisprudence. Unlike the fragmented assortment of legal controls which have evolved in the United States, the Act establishes a comprehensive regulatory framework to govern the use of computerised data in both public and private sectors. The legislation came about as follows.

During the last two and a half decades, Parliament has been presented with a number of bills, all more or less short lived, which have addressed various privacy and data protection concerns.[76] It was partly in response to one such bill[77] that the Younger Committee on Privacy was appointed in 1970 to consider whether legislation was needed to protect against invasions of privacy in the private sector. The Committee reported in 1972,[78] and by a majority decided against the creation of a general right of privacy.[79] On the specific question of the effect on privacy of private sector computers, the Committee found no present threat but recognised the "possibility of such a threat becoming a reality in the future."[80] The government responded in 1975 with both a White Paper entitled *Computers and Privacy*,[81] and a supplementary report entitled *Computers: Safeguards for Privacy*.[82]

While still of the view that it would be neither "desirable, or practicable, to lay down by law detailed regulations for the operation of all

---

Court's decision, which was its eleventh ruling against the British Government, the Home Office reaffirmed an earlier commitment by the government to introduce legislation to regulate the interception of communications and in February 1985 the government published a White Paper entitled *The Interception of Communications in the United Kingdom* (London: HMSO, Cmnd. 9438, 1985).

75   1984, c. 35. The full title is "An Act to regulate the use of automatically processed information relating to individuals and the provision of services in respect of such information."

76   See Wacks, The Protection of Privacy (London: Sweet & Maxwell, 1980), pp. 5-8; Younger (Chairman), *Report of the Committee on Privacy* (London: HMSO, Cmnd. 5012, 1972), paras. 604-12.

77   Private Members' Bill introduced by Mr. Brian Walden in 1969: 792 *Hansard,* col. 430 (26 Nov. 1969). See Wacks, *ibid.*

78   Younger Committee, note 76, above.

79   *Ibid.,* para. 659.

80   *Ibid.,* para. 619.

81   (London: HMSO, Cmnd. 6353, 1975).

82   (London: HMSO, Cmnd. 6354, 1975). This report contained, *inter alia,* the findings of an interdepartmental committee which had reviewed government computer use in parallel with the Younger Committee's examination of the private sector (paras. 3-4).

computer systems,"[83] the government declared that "the time has come when those who use computers to handle personal information, however responsible they are, can no longer remain the sole judges of whether their own systems adequately safeguard privacy."[84] As a middle road between self-regulation and detailed statutory regulation, the White Paper contained two proposals: first, "the establishment of a set of objectives, to set standards that govern the use of personal information" and, secondly, "the establishment of a permanent statutory agency to oversee the use of computers, in both public and private sectors, to ensure that they are operated with proper regard for privacy and with the necessary safeguards for the personal information which they contain."[85]

Aware that it would take some time to establish a permanent review body, the government announced the immediate appointment of an interim "Data Protection Committee."[86] The Committee, chaired by Sir Norman Lindop, reported in 1978.[87] It proposed the creation by statute of a Data Protection Authority to oversee privacy safeguards and to produce legally binding codes of practice to govern specific types of data processing.[88] The Committee also recommended the establishment of a system of registration of all central and local government systems of computerised personal data processing, together with, where "necessary or helpful," private sector data users grouped according to the codes of practice.[89]

Specific proposals for data protection legislation eventually appeared in a White Paper published in 1982.[90] An admitted motive for proceeding with legislation at that time was the government's wish to ratify the Council of Europe's *Convention for the Protection of Individuals with Regard to Automatic Processing of Personal Data*, which was signed by the U.K. on 14 May 1981.[91] Although it does not stipulate a method for doing so, the Convention requires each signatory state to "take the necessary measures in its domestic law to give effect to the basic principles for data protection."[92] For the United Kingdom, the

---

83   Note 81 above, para. 28.
84   *Ibid.,* para. 30.
85   *Ibid.*
86   *Ibid.,* para. 31.
87   *Report of the Committee on Data Protection* (London: HMSO, Cmnd. 5012, 1978).
88   *Ibid.,* para. 19.24.
89   *Ibid.,* paras. 19.62 and 19.67.
90   *Data Protection: The Government's Proposals for Legislation* (London: HMSO, Cmnd. 8539, 1982).
91   (Strasbourg: Council of Europe, 1981). See White Paper, note 90 above, para. 2.
92   *Convention,* note 91 above, art. 4, para. 1.

obvious step was to introduce the legislation which had been promised since 1975.

Although the idea of data protection legislation met with widespread support, the Data Protection Bill provoked considerable public debate as to both the appropriate scope of and the best means of enforcing statutory safeguards. Some commentators complained that the proposed controls were excessively broad, and warned of severe disruptions to businesses.[93] Others expressed concern at the significant lacunae in the proposed regulatory scheme and, above all, objected to the limitation of controls to computerised records only.[94] The exclusion from the Act of manual files was seen as greatly weakening the protection of the individual. Fears were also expressed that the loophole this created might encourage a significant number of computer users to take the reactionary step of decomputerising their more sensitive records.[95] Other more detailed concerns were also voiced, many of which were dealt with by way of amendments during the prolonged committee and report stages of the Bill.[96]

8.3.2 Structure of the Legislation

The Data Protection Act received Royal Assent on 12 July 1984, although it will probably be mid-1987 before all the provisions of the legislation are in force.[97] The Act is structured around a set of "Data

---

93   *E.g.*, Rumbelow, "Privacy and Data Protection in the UK and Europe," [1984] Int. Bus. L. 153-7; Tettenborn, "The Data Protection Bill: a Summary of the New Controls Proposed" (1983), 4 The Company Lawyer 120-2.

94   A fact which was strongly criticised by a number of lobby groups including the National Council for Civil Liberties and the British Medical Association. See Riley, "Obligations Will be Met Despite a Tricky Passage" 11 Computing (13 Jan. 1983), 22-3.

95   Bell, "Practical Implications of the Data Protection Act" Personnel Management (June 1984), 28-31.

96   *E.g.*, see the Lords' consideration of Commons Amendments in 453 *Hansard,* (29 June 1984) cols. 1155-89.

97   The provisions of the Act take effect in the following four stages: (1) Compensation or erasure orders may be made in respect of damage suffered by a data subject due to loss or unauthorised disclosure of data occurring at any time from 12 September 1984 (Data Protection Act, ss. 42(6), 23, 24(3); see section 8.3.5, below). (2) An Appointed Day Order will specify the date from which application may be made to register as a data user or computer bureau (*Ibid.,* s. 42(1), Pt. II; see section 8.3.3, below). The Appointed Day is expected to be sometime in the autumn of 1985. (3) The following provisions come into effect six months after the Appointed Day: unregistered holding (etc.) of personal data forbidden (*Ibid.,* ss. 42(1), 5; see section 8.3.3, below); computer bureaux must not disclose personal data without the authority of the person for

Protection Principles."[98] Of the eight principles, the first seven relate to "Personal data held by data users," while the eighth applies to such data and in addition to the operations of computer bureaux. The principles are:

Personal data held by data users

1. The information to be contained in personal data shall be obtained, and personal data shall be processed, fairly and lawfully.[99]

2. Personal data shall be held only for one or more specified and lawful purposes.

3. Personal data held for any purpose or purposes shall not be used or disclosed in any manner incompatible with that purpose or purposes.

4. Personal data held for any purpose or purposes shall be adequate, relevant and not excessive in relation to that purpose or those purposes.

5. Personal data shall be accurate and, where necessary, kept up to date.[100]

6. Personal data held for any purpose or purposes shall not be kept for longer than is necessary for that purpose or those purposes.

7. An individual shall be entitled –

(a) at reasonable intervals and without undue delay or expense – (i) to be informed by any data user whether he holds personal data of which that individual is the subject; and (ii) to access to any such data held by a data user; and (b) where appropriate, to have such data corrected or erased.[101]

Personal data held by data users or in respect of which services are provided by persons carrying on computer bureaux

8. Appropriate security measures shall be taken against unauthorised access to, or

---

whom they are holding data (ss. 42(1), 15; see section 8.3.3, below); data users may incur liability for damage caused due to inaccuracy of personal data (ss. 42(5); 22; see section 8.3.5, below); rectification or erasure orders may be made (ss. 42(7), 24(1) and (2); see section 8.3.5, below); Registrar may only refuse applications to register where insufficient particulars supplied (ss. 42(2)(a), 7(2)(a); see section 8.3.3, below). (4) Two years after the Appointed Day, the Registrar may refuse any application to register (*Ibid.*, ss. 42(2)(a), 6; see section 8.3.3, below), and enforcement, de-registration and transfer prohibition notices can take effect (ss. 42(2)(b), 10, 11, 12; see section 8.3.6, below).

98   Data Protection Act, Sch. 1, Pt. I. The principles are closely modelled on the set of principles proposed by the Younger Committee, *Report of the Committee on Privacy* (London: HMSO, Cmnd. 5012, 1972).

99   There is a presumption of fairness where information is supplied by a person who is authorised or required to supply it under any enactment or international convention: *Ibid.*, Sch. 1, Pt. II, para. 1(2). In other cases, in determining fairness "regard shall be had to the method by which it was obtained, including in particular whether any person from whom it was obtained was deceived or misled as to the purpose or purposes for which it was to be held, used or disclosed" (Sch. 1, Pt. II, para. 1(1)).

100   The accuracy requirement is qualified in cases where data are received from the data subject or a third party: *Ibid.*, Sch. 1, Part II, para. 4, and s. 22.

101   The subject access conditions are set out in s. 21. See also section 8.3.5, below.

alteration, disclosure or destruction of, personal data and against accidental loss or destruction of personal data.

These principles may be modified or supplemented by the Secretary of State. Changes can only be made, however, for the purpose of providing additional safeguards relating to information concerning an individual's racial origin, political opinions, religious or other beliefs, physical or mental health, sexual life, or criminal convictions.[102]

In an attempt to exclude manual records, "data" is defined in the Act as "information recorded in a form in which it can be processed by equipment operating automatically in response to instructions given for that purpose."[103] The operation of the Act is further limited to "personal data," defined as data "consisting of information which relates to a living individual who can be identified from the information (or from that and other information in the possession of the data user)."[104] Three points should be noted about this definition. First, "personal data" need not be "personal" in the sense of being private or sensitive but need merely relate to an identifiable person. Secondly, companies and other corporate bodies are not protected by the Act as they are not "living individuals." Thirdly, the phrase "personal data" is further qualified to the extent that it includes expressions of opinion about individuals but not "any indication of the intentions of the data user in respect of that individual."[105] This distinction may prove highly significant in the case of personnel records. For example, in an organisation where personnel records are computerised, an employee will be entitled under the Act to see an assessment of his or her abilities, but such access can be denied if the assessment is phrased in terms of an intention to promote or demote the individual concerned.

A "data subject" is simply an individual to whom personal data relate.[106] Somewhat more complicated is the definition of a "data user" as a person who "holds" data.[107] As a preliminary point, it should be noted that, whereas a data subject must be a living human individual, a

---

102   *Ibid.,* s. 2(3).
103   *Ibid.,* s. 1(2). Some manual records may, however, be covered by the Act. See text accompanying notes 109-11, below.
104   *Ibid.,* s. 1(3). The bracketed part of the definition was added at a late stage in the Bill's passage to make it impossible for "an unscrupulous user to evade the Bill's control by devising a personal code for all data subjects and using manual records as a key to translating the code into names." *Hansard* (29 June 1984) at col. 1156, *per* Lord Elton.
105   Data Protection Act, s. 1(3).
106   *Ibid.,* s. 1(4).
107   *Ibid.,* s. 1(5).

data user may be an individual, a company, a firm, a government department or any other organisation.[108]

Under the Act, a person will be deemed to hold data if (a) the data are processed or intended to be processed by or on behalf of that person, (b) that person controls the contents and use of the data, and (c) the data are in a "form in which they have been or are intended to be processed . . . or in a form into which they have been converted after being so processed and with a view to being further so processed on a subsequent occasion."[109] The first two criteria clearly have the effect of restricting "data user" so as to prevent the term covering a person who is merely in possession of data, such as a postal worker or courier. The significance of the third criterion in the definition of data user is, however, less obvious. How broad is the phrase "in the form in which they have been or are intended to be processed"? In the Act, "processing" data is defined as "amending, augmenting, deleting or rearranging the data or extracting the information constituting the data."[110] There can be no doubt that data stored in computer memory or in peripheral storage media such as disks or tapes will be in the requisite form for processing. In addition, however, information which is printed or typed on paper may also be in the requisite form if the information can be fed into a computer via an optical character reader (OCR). Such information will constitute "data" as it will be "in a form in which it can be processed by equipment operating automatically." However, the data will not be "held" by anyone unless the data have been processed or there is at least an intention to process them.[111]

The Act provides for the appointment of a Data Protection Registrar whose general mandate is "to promote the observance of the data protection principles by data users and persons carrying on computer bureaux."[112] In implementing this objective the Registrar must maintain a register of data users and computer bureaux;[113] he may, and in some

---

108 See definition of "person" in Interpretation Act 1978, Sch. 1.

109 Data Protection Act, s. 1(5).

110 *Ibid.*, s. 1(7).

111 For further discussions of what it means to "hold" data and the boundaries of "automatic processing" see Sterling, *The Data Protection Act 1984* (Bicester, Oxfordshire: CCH, 1984), pp. 45-51; Savage & Edwards, *A Guide to the Data Protection Act 1984* (London: Financial Training, 1984), pp. 24-26; Niblett, *Data Protection Act 1984* (London: Longman, 1984), p. 20.

112 Data Protection Act, s. 36(1). The first Registrar, Mr. Eric Howe, took up the appointment in September 1984. He will be assisted by a staff of 20, operating from headquarters in Manchester and a small London office.

113 *Ibid.*, s. 4. Due to the small size of the Registrar's staff, the operation of the registration data base has been contracted out to a private computer bureau. For an

situations must, consider complaints from data subjects; he must arrange for the public to be given appropriate information about the Act; he may give advice to any person about the Act; and he must, where he considers it appropriate, encourage groups representing data users to introduce codes of practice for their members.[114] The Registrar may also initiate various enforcement procedures to remedy actual or potential breaches of the data protection principles.[115]

Where the Registrar either rejects an application for registration, or makes an order against a data user or computer bureau, the data user or bureau may appeal to the Data Protection Tribunal.[116] The Act does not contain the detailed rules which will govern rights of appeal and the conduct of hearings before the Tribunal. The third schedule, however, empowers the Secretary of State to issue such rules as deemed necessary.[117] The composition of the tribunal is stipulated to the extent that it must have a chairman and deputy chairman, both legally qualified, together with representatives, in equal numbers, of both data users and data subjects.[118]

8.3.3 Responsibilities of Data Users and Computer Bureaux

The Act imposes a general obligation on data users to comply with the data protection principles.[119] In addition, the Act creates a number of specific responsibilities such as the requirement to apply for registration, the duty to ensure the security of data holdings and the obligation to provide access for data subjects.

Unless exempt from the registration provisions, data users and computer bureaux will be required to register as such within six months of an "Appointed Day."[120] Failure to do so may constitute a criminal offence.[121] An applicant for registration must state whether he or she wishes to be registered as a data user, as a person carrying on a computer

---

outline of the registration system see section 8.3.3, below.

114 *Ibid.*, ss. 36(2), (3) and (4). Other duties include reporting to Parliament at least once a year (s. 36(5)) and liaison with other parties to the European Convention (s. 37).

115 See section 8.3.6, below.

116 Data Protection Act, s. 3(1)(b). See section 8.3.6, below.

117 *Ibid.*, Sch. 3. para. 4.

118 *Ibid.*, ss. 3(3), (4) and (5). See also Sch. 2, Pt. II.

119 *Ibid.*, ss. 2(2), 7(2), 10, 11 and 12. The obligation is in fact imposed indirectly by way of sanctions for non-compliance with the Principles.

120 The Appointed Day is expected to be sometime in the autumn of 1985, but at the time of writing no Appointed Day Order had been made. For exemptions see section 8.3.4, below.

121 Data Protection Act, s. 5(5).

bureau, or as both, and must furnish the particulars required to be included in the entry.[122] In the case of a person carrying on a computer bureau who is not also a data user, only the person's name and address will be registered.[123] In the case of all data users, however, the following additional information will be required: a description of the personal data to be held and the purpose(s) for which they are to be held or used; a description of the intended source(s) of the data; a description of any person(s) to whom the data may be disclosed; the names or a description of any foreign countries to which data may be directly or indirectly transferred; and one or more addresses for enquiries from data subjects.[124] Applications for registration must be accompanied by a prescribed fee.[125] The Registrar must notify the refusal or acceptance of an application "as soon as practicable" and in any case within six months.[126]

The Registrar may refuse an application to register either because insufficient particulars have been supplied, or because he is satisfied that the applicant is likely to contravene any of the data protection principles.[127] Where registration is refused, an applicant may appeal to the Data Protection Tribunal.[128] While awaiting the adjudication of an application for registration and pending the outcome of any appeal against a refusal to register, an applicant will normally be treated as though already registered.[129] When an application is accepted, the applicant's particulars will be entered in the register. Initial registration and renewals of registration will normally run for periods of at least three years,[130] but a data user may apply at any time for alteration of the registered particulars, and must make an application whenever necessary to ensure that an entry contains a current address.[131]

Once registered, a data user, or data user who is also a bureau operator, will be limited in the use of personal data to the operations described in the register entry. These will include stipulations as to the

---

122   *Ibid.*, s. 6(1). The Registrar is likely to issue a prescribed form of application.
123   *Ibid.*, s. 4(4).
124   *Ibid.*, s. 4(3).
125   *Ibid.*, s. 6(7).
126   *Ibid.*, s. 7(1).
127   *Ibid.*, s. 7(2).
128   *Ibid.*, s. 13. See section 8.3.6, below.
129   *Ibid.*, s. 7(6). However, if by reason of special circumstances the Registrar wishes a refusal of registration to take effect "as a matter of urgency," the refusal of registration may be made effective in seven days from notification. *Ibid.*, s. 7(7).
130   A longer period may be prescribed (s. 8(2)), or a shorter period of one or more complete years may be requested by an applicant (s. 8(3)).
131   *Ibid.*, ss. 6(3), (5).

types of data which can be held, the purposes for which data can be held or used, the sources from which data can be obtained, the persons to whom data can be disclosed, and the places to which data can be transferred.[132]

The responsibilities of persons carrying on computer bureaux who are not also data users are limited to compliance with the registration provisions, observance of the eighth principle cited above, and compliance with section 15 of the Act. The eighth principle requires bureaux to take "appropriate security measures" to prevent "unauthorised access to, or alteration, disclosure or destruction of, personal data and against accidental loss or destruction of personal data." More specifically, section 15 provides that computer bureaux must not disclose personal data without the prior authority of the person for whom the data are being processed. Appropriate security measures might include restrictions on access to computer installations, the use of hardware and software locks and the use of passwords to restrict access to personal data, the setting up of audit trails to highlight any unauthorised access to and corruption of personal data, and careful screening and education of employees with access to personal data.[133]

8.3.4   Exemptions under the Act

While the general exclusion of manual data systems is undoubtedly the broadest limitation on the scope of the Act, there are several other significant, though more specific, exemptions and exceptions. These will be grouped under four headings: (1) total exemptions from the Act; (2) exemptions from both the registration and subject access provisions; (3) exemptions from the subject access provisions alone; and (4) exemptions from the non-disclosure provisions.

(1)   Total Exemptions from the Act

Three specific types of data are completely outside the scope of the Act: first, data used only for the purpose of preparing the text of documents;[134] secondly, information which is merely an indication of the

---

132   *Ibid.*, s. 5(2). The restrictions on use, sources, disclosure and transfers of data apply equally to a servant or agent of the data user (s. 5(3)).

133   A bureau might also be advised to effect insurance to cover potential liabilities under the Act.

134   Data Protection Act, s. 1(8). This exemption will cover word processing operations, provided the data in question are not used for any other purpose.

intentions of a data user in respect of an individual;[135] and thirdly, data held or processed wholly outside the United Kingdom, provided the data are not used or intended to be used in the United Kingdom.[136] It should be noted, however, that the Act covers foreign-held and processed data if control over the contents and use of the data is exercised in the United Kingdom. Moreover, where a non-United Kingdom resident exercises such control through a servant or agent in the United Kingdom, that servant or agent will be treated as a data user.[137]

(2)   Exemptions from both the Registration and Subject Access Provisions

While not completely outside the scope of the Act, there are seven categories of personal data in respect of which data users need neither register nor provide subject access. Moreover, orders for compensation, rectification and erasure cannot be made in respect of such data.[138] The first category of personal data to which this broad exemption applies is data in respect of which the exemption is required for the purpose of safeguarding national security.[139] The second and third categories relate to personal data held only for certain limited business purposes. These are the assessment or payment of remuneration or pensions relating to any employment or office, and the keeping of accounts and certain other business records.[140] To qualify for an exemption under this category, the data user must not use the data in question for any other purpose, and must only disclose the data in certain specified situations.[141]

The fourth, fifth and sixth categories of personal data within this exemption relate to personal data held for domestic and other limited purposes. The fourth category is data held by an individual concerned

135   *Ibid.*, s. 1(3). See discussion in section 8.3.2, above.
136   *Ibid.*, s. 39(5).
137   *Ibid.*, s. 39(3) and (4).
138   The orders are discussed in section 8.3.5, below.
139   Data Protection Act, s. 27(1). A certificate signed by a Cabinet Minister or the Attorney General (or Lord Advocate) will be conclusive evidence that a national security exemption is required (s. 27(2)).
140   *Ibid.*, s. 32(1)(a) and (b). Disclosure is permitted for auditing purposes and in situations where a general non-disclosure exemption applies. See section 8.3.4(4), below.
141   In the case of payroll and pension data, disclosure is also permitted where the person making the disclosure reasonably believes that it has been requested or authorised by the data subject or his or her agent, and for actuarial and medical research purposes. Where the data user is not personally paying the remuneration or pensions in question, disclosure to the actual payer is also permitted (ss. 32(3) and (4)).

only with the management of personal, family or household affairs, or held only for recreational purposes.[142] The fifth and sixth categories are data held by an unincorporated members' club relating only to its members, and data held only for the purpose of distributing, or recording the distribution of, articles or information to data subjects.[143] In both cases, the data must not be held without the consent of the data subjects concerned, and can only be disclosed in limited circumstances.[144] The seventh category relates to personal data which are required by statute to be made public.[145]

(3)   Exemptions from the Subject Access Provisions

In addition to the categories of data already listed in (1) and (2), there are seven further categories of data in respect of which the subject access provisions do not apply. The first exemption relates to cases where the provision of subject access would be likely to prejudice "the prevention or detection of crime; . . . the apprehension or prosecution of offenders; or . . . the assessment or collection of any tax or duty."[146] The effect of this provision will be that a suspected offender or taxpayer whose affairs are being investigated may be denied access to any relevant files held by the police, the Inland Revenue, the Customs authorities or other investigating authority.[147] The other exempt categories are personal data held by a government department relating to judicial appointments;[148] personal data in respect of which legal professional privilege can be claimed;[149] personal data held only for statistical or research purposes;[150] personal data covered by the access provisions of the Consumer Credit Act 1974;[151] and personal data held only for "back up" purposes.[152]

---

142   *Ibid.*, s. 33(1). Note that this exemption is applicable only to individuals.

143   *Ibid.*, s. 33(2).

144   These are where the person making the disclosure reasonably believes that the data subject or his or her agent has consented, or where a general non-disclosure exemption applies. See section 8.3.4(d), below.

145   *Ibid.*, s. 34(1).

146   *Ibid.*, s. 28(1).

147   It should be noted that the exemption may be invoked in respect of many criminal offences contained in civil statutes such as the Companies Acts, the Trade Descriptions Act, the Consumer Credit Act, the Factories Act, the Copyright Act, etc.

148   Data Protection Act, ss. 31(1).

149   *Ibid.*, s. 31(2).

150   *Ibid.*, s. 33(6). The results of the research must not be "made available in a form which identifies the data subjects or any of them."

151   *Ibid.*, s. 34(3).

152   *Ibid.*, s. 34(4).

This list may be extended by order of the Secretary of State to cover four other types of data. These are personal data relating to the physical or mental health of the data subject;[153] personal data held by designated agencies for social work purposes;[154] personal data held for the purpose of discharging designated "statutory functions";[155] and personal data the disclosure of which is prohibited or restricted under any other enactment.[156]

(4)   Exemptions from the Non-Disclosure Provisions

There are eight situations in which the non-disclosure provisions of the Act do not apply.[157] Despite any general obligations to the contrary, disclosure may be made for the purpose of safeguarding national security;[158] where failure to make the disclosure would be likely to prejudice the prevention or detection of crime etc.;[159] where required by any enactment, rule of law or court order;[160] for the purpose of obtaining legal advice or by a party or witness in legal proceedings;[161] to the data subject or a person acting on his or her behalf;[162] where the data subject has requested or consented to the disclosure;[163] by a data user or person carrying on a computer bureau to a servant or agent;[164] or where urgently required to prevent injury or other damage to the health of any person.[165] In the case of the last four of these categories, the data will also be exempt if the person making the disclosure has reasonable grounds for believing that the disclosure falls within the exemption concerned.[166]

8.3.5   Rights of Data Subjects

The Act creates certain rights for data subjects in terms of access to personal data, compensation for damage caused by data users and computer bureau, and correction or erasure of inaccurate data. As a prerequi-

---

153   *Ibid.*, s. 29(1).
154   *Ibid.*, s. 29(2).
155   *Ibid.*, s. 30.
156   *Ibid.*, s. 34(2).
157   For the general restrictions on disclosure see section 8.3.3, above.
158   Data Protection Act, s. 27(3).
159   *Ibid.*, s. 28(3).
160   *Ibid.*, s. 34(5)(a).
161   *Ibid.*, s. 34(5)(b).
162   *Ibid.*, s. 34(6)(a).
163   *Ibid.*, s. 34(6)(b).
164   *Ibid.*, s. 34(6)(c).
165   *Ibid.*, s. 34(8).
166   *Ibid.*, ss. 34(6)(d) and 36(8).

site to exercising these rights, however, members of the public will need to identify data users and computer bureaux which might hold personal data relating to them. Accordingly, the Act requires the Data Protection Registrar to "provide facilities for making the information contained in the entries in the register available for inspection (in visible and legible form) by members of the public at reasonable hours and free of charge."[167] On payment of a prescribed fee, if one is required, a member of the public will be entitled to a certified copy of the particulars in the register entry.[168] Armed with this information, an individual can request access to personal data files.

Subject to certain exceptions, an individual is entitled both to be informed by any data user whether he or she holds personal data relating to that individual, and also to be supplied with a copy of any such information.[169] Requests for information must be made in writing, and a data user may require payment of a fee not exceeding a prescribed maximum.[170] Separate requests must be made, and separate fees (if required) paid, in respect of data held for different purposes. A data user must comply with any request within forty days, and must also supply an explanation of any unintelligible terms in the data.[171] The requested information must be supplied by reference to the data held at the time of the request, but it may take account of any amendment or deletion made since that time which would have been made regardless of the request.[172] Special rules exist in respect of academic, professional or other examination marks to ensure that access to relevant data need not be given until after results have been announced.[173]

The Act specifies four situations in which a data user may refuse to comply with a request for access. One is that insufficient information has been supplied to identify the applicant and locate the information requested.[174] Another is that the request cannot be complied with without disclosing information relating to another identifiable individual.[175] The

---

167 *Ibid.*, s. 9(1).
168 *Ibid.*, s. 9(2).
169 *Ibid.*, s. 21(1).
170 *Ibid.*, s. 21(2).
171 *Ibid.*, ss. 21(6) and (1). The forty days runs from receipt of the request or from receipt of any additional information or third party consent necessary for complying with the request. *Ibid.*, s. 21(6), (4).
172 *Ibid.*, s. 21(7).
173 *Ibid.*, s. 35.
174 *Ibid.*, s. 21(4)(a).
175 *Ibid.*, s. 21(4)(b). Such information may, however, be disclosed with the consent of the individual concerned. In any event, the data user must supply as much of the information as possible (by deleting names, etc.) (s. 21(5)).

third ground for refusing access is that a request is, in all the circumstances, "unreasonable" due to the frequency of requests or any other reason.[176] Finally, access may be refused where the requested data fall within any of the subject access exemptions.[177]

Where a data subject suffers damage as a result of inaccurate data being held by a data user, the subject will be entitled to compensation for that damage and for any consequential distress.[178] There are, however, two defences available to a data user. One is that the data user can prove that reasonable care was taken to ensure the accuracy of the data.[179] The other is that the data in question accurately record information received from the data subject or a third party, and the data both contain an indication as to their source and a record of any notification by the data subject that the information is incorrect or misleading.[180]

A data subject will also be entitled to compensation from a data user or computer bureau where the subject suffers damage or distress due to the loss or destruction of, or unauthorised access to or disclosure of, personal data.[181] A reasonable care defence is again available, together with a defence that the disclosure was to, or the access was by, a person described in the register.[182]

If a court is satisfied on the application of a data subject that a data user holds inaccurate personal data about that person, the court may order rectification or erasure of both those data and any other data containing an expression of opinion which is apparently based on the inaccurate data.[183] Such an order may be made despite the fact that the data accurately record information supplied by the data subject or a third party. However, provided the data contain an indication of their source together with a record of any complaint made by the data subject that the information is incorrect or misleading, the court may, instead of ordering erasure, order the data to be supplemented by an approved "statement of the true facts."[184] If these requirements have not been com-

---

176   *Ibid.*, s. 21(8). What constitutes a reasonable interval between requests will depend on "the nature of the data, the purpose for which the data are held and the frequency with which the data are altered" (Sch. 1, Pt. II, para. 5(2)).

177   See section 8.3.4(3), above.

178   Data Protection Act, s. 22(1). For compensation purposes "inaccuracy" is defined as "incorrect or misleading as to any matter of fact" (s. 22(4)).

179   *Ibid.*, s. 22(3).

180   *Ibid.*, s. 22(2)(b).

181   *Ibid.*, s. 23.

182   *Ibid.*, ss. 23(2) and (3).

183   *Ibid.*, s. 24(1).

184   *Ibid.*, s. 24(2)(a).

plied with, the court may make "such order as it thinks fit" to secure compliance with the requirements.[185]

Erasure may also be ordered where damage has been suffered due to unauthorised disclosure of or access to personal data, and there is a "substantial risk" of further unauthorised disclosure or access.[186] Where, however, the data in question are held by a computer bureau on behalf of a data user, an erasure order will not be made until a reasonable attempt has been made both to notify and give a right of reply to the data user concerned.[187]

8.3.6   Enforcement Procedures

In addition to the compensation, rectification and erasure provisions, the Act invests a number of other broad enforcement powers in the Registrar and the courts. These range from a simple order requiring a data user to reply to a subject access request,[188] through to the potentially very serious sanction of de-registration of a data user or computer bureau. In fulfilling the general duty of promoting the observance of the data protection principles by data users and computer bureau, the Registrar can issue "enforcement notices," "de-registration notices" and "transfer prohibition notices."

If the Registrar is satisfied that a data user or person carrying on a computer bureau is contravening any of the principles, the Registrar may serve the offender with an "enforcement notice" specifying steps to be taken to comply with the principle or principles in question.[189] In deciding whether to serve a notice, the Registrar must consider whether damage or distress has been or is likely to be caused.[190] Specified steps might include responding to a subject access request, rectifying or erasing data, or supplementing data with a statement of the true facts.[191] A person who fails to comply with an enforcement notice commits a

---

185   *Ibid.*, s. 24(2)(b).

186   *Ibid.*, s. 24(3).

187   *Ibid.*

188   Where a data subject has made a reasonable application in the proper form for information about personal data and the data user has failed to reply within forty days, a court may order the data user to comply with the request. *Ibid.*, s. 21(8). See section 8.3.5 above for a discussion of reasonableness in the context of subject access requests.

189   *Ibid.*, s. 10(1). The notice will also specify a time limit for taking the required steps and will contain information as to appeal rights (ss. 10(1) and (5)).

190   *Ibid.*, s. 10(2).

191   *Ibid.*, ss. 10(3) and (4). There is a considerable overlap between the Registrar's powers and the enforcement jurisdiction of the courts.

criminal offence, but may raise a defence of having "exercised all due diligence to comply with the notice in question."[192]

If the Registrar decides that a contravention of the principles cannot be dealt with adequately by way of an enforcement notice, a "de-registration" notice may be served.[193] Such a notice will state that, at the end of a specified period, the Registrar will remove from the register some or all of the particulars in the entry or entries pertaining to the data user or computer bureau in question.[194] Service of a de-registration notice is a very serious sanction, as the removal of particulars might expose a data user or computer bureau to prosecution for holding or processing data without being registered.

In certain circumstances, the Registrar may serve a "transfer prohibition notice" forbidding a data user from transferring specified data outside the United Kingdom.[195] The prohibition may be absolute or it may remain in force only until the data user has taken steps specified in the notice for protecting the interests of the data subjects in question.[196]

Different grounds exist for the issuing of a transfer prohibition notice, depending on whether the proposed destination of the data is in a state bound by the Council of Europe's Convention.[197] Where data are to be transferred to a country which has not ratified the Convention, the Registrar may serve a transfer prohibition notice if satisfied that the transfer is likely to contravene, or lead to a contravention of, the data protection principles.[198] In the case of a Convention country, the Registrar must be satisfied that a further transfer to a non-Convention country is intended and that the further transfer is likely to contravene, or lead to a contravention of, the principles.[199] In all cases, in determining whether to serve a transfer prohibition notice, the Registrar must balance the need to prevent damage or distress to any person against the general desirability of facilitating the free movement of data between the United Kingdom and other countries.[200]

---

192   *Ibid.*, s. 10(9).
193   *Ibid.*, s. 11(1).
194   The notice must also contain a statement of the alleged contravention of the principles, the Registrar's reasons for concluding that an enforcement notice is insufficient to secure compliance and information as to appeal rights (s. 11(3)).
195   *Ibid.*, s. 12(1).
196   *Ibid.*
197   *Convention for the Protection of Individuals with Regard to Automatic Processing of Personal Data.* (Strasbourg: Council of Europe, 1981).
198   Data Protection Act, s. 12(2).
199   *Ibid.*, s. 12(3).
200   *Ibid.*, s. 12(4). For a discussion of transborder data flows see chapter 9.

A person can appeal to the Data Protection Tribunal against a refusal by the Registrar of an application to register or alter registered particulars, and against enforcement, de-registration and transfer prohibition notices.[201] Appeals may also be made against the inclusion in any of the Registrar's rulings of a statement that the ruling will "take effect as a matter of urgency."[202] Orders containing such a statement take effect in seven days instead of at the expiry of the normal period for lodging appeals.[203]

If the Tribunal finds a refusal or notice to be contrary to law or to have involved an inappropriate exercise of the Registrar's discretion, it must allow the appeal or substitute a different decision or notice.[204] The Tribunal may also review any finding of fact on which the refusal or notice in question was based.[205] The Act empowers the Secretary of State to make rules to govern appeal rights and the conduct of Tribunal hearings.[206] Any party to an appeal to the Tribunal may appeal from the Tribunal's decision to the High Court on a point of law.[207]

The Act also provides for a court to grant the Registrar broad powers "for the detection of offences."[208] If a circuit judge is satisfied that there are reasonable grounds for suspecting either that an offence under the Act has been or is being committed, or that a registered person has been or is contravening any of the principles, the judge may issue a warrant authorising the Registrar to enter and search the premises for evidence of the offence or contravention.[209] Before issuing a warrant, a judge must normally be satisfied that the occupier has refused the Registrar's reasonable requests for access, has been notified of the Registrar's application for a warrant and has had an opportunity to make representations to the court. These further conditions do not apply where the judge is satisfied either that the case is urgent or that compliance with those conditions would defeat the object of the entry.[210]

---

201   *Ibid.*, s. 13(1).
202   *Ibid.*, s. 13(2).
203   See *ibid.*, ss. 7(7), 10(7), 11(5) and 12(7).
204   *Ibid.*, s. 14(1). The Tribunal may substitute any other decision or notice which the Registrar could have made or served, and may cancel any statement of urgency (ss. 14(1), (3), and (4)).
205   *Ibid.*, s. 14(2).
206   *Ibid.*, Sch. 3, paras. 4 and 5. No rules had been made at the time of writing.
207   *Ibid.*, s. 14(5). In Scotland, the appeal lies to the Court of Session and in Northern Ireland to the Northern Ireland High Court.
208   *Ibid.*, s. 16.
209   *Ibid.*, Sch. 4, para. 1.
210   *Ibid.*, Sch. 4, para. 2.

A warrant will authorise the Registrar or any officers or servants of the Registrar to enter and search premises within seven days and to inspect, examine, operate and test any data equipment and to inspect and seize any documents or other material found there which may be relevant as evidence.[211] Reasonable force may be used in the execution of a warrant and, if it seems necessary to the person executing it, a warrant may be executed at any hour of the day or night.[212] There are two categories of data which may not be inspected or seized. These are personal data which are exempt from both the registration and subject access provisions,[213] and communications between a professional legal advisor and his or her client or between either of them and a third party relating to obligations, liabilities, rights or proceedings under or arising out of the Data Protection Act.[214]

The Act has created a number of new criminal offences. Two of these, the holding of personal data by an unregistered person and the failure of a registered person to notify the Registrar of his or her current address, are offences of strict liability.[215] However, many of the offences are only committed by a person who acts "knowingly or recklessly." Most of these offences relate to the obtaining, holding, disclosure or transfer of data by a registered data user in a manner not covered by the entry in the register.[216] Similarly, it is only an offence for a computer bureau to disclose personal data without authority if done knowingly or recklessly.[217] Also in this category is the furnishing by any person, in connection with an application to register or amend registered particulars, of information which is false or misleading in a material respect.[218]

In respect of the offences of failing to comply with an enforcement notice or contravening a transfer prohibition notice, a defence of due care is available.[219] Finally, it is an offence either intentionally to obstruct or fail to give reasonable assistance to a person executing an entry warrant.[220]

---

211   *Ibid.*, Sch. 4, para. 1.
212   *Ibid.*, Sch. 4, paras. 4 and 5.
213   *Ibid.*, Sch. 4, para. 8. For details of such data see section 8.3.4(2), above.
214   *Ibid.*, Sch. 4, para. 9.
215   *Ibid.*, ss. 5(1) and 6(5).
216   *Ibid.*, s. 5(2).
217   *Ibid.*, s. 15(3).
218   *Ibid.*, s. 6(6).
219   *Ibid.*, ss. 10(9) and 12(10).
220   *Ibid.*, Sch. 4, para. 12.

Prosecutions under the Act can only be initiated by the Data Protection Registrar or with the consent of the Director of Public Prosecutions.[221] The following offences can only be tried summarily: failing to notify a current address; furnishing the Registrar with false or misleading information; and obstructing or failing to assist a person executing a warrant.[222] Any other offence under the Act can be tried either on indictment or summarily and, if tried on indictment, there is no limit to the fine which may be imposed on conviction.[223] Where a person is convicted of certain offences under the Act, the court may order any data material apparently connected with the offence to be forfeited, destroyed or erased.[224] Where an offence has been committed by a company or other corporate body with the consent or connivance of any director, manager, secretary or similar officer, that person as well as the body corporate will be liable to prosecution. Such personal liability will also arise if the commission of the offence is attributable to neglect on the part of the individual concerned.[225]

8.4 Data Protection in Canada

8.4.1 General Privacy Rights

Although Canada has privacy legislation both at the federal level and in some of the provinces, the 1982 Canadian Charter of Rights and Freedoms[226] makes no reference to any constitutional right of privacy. An attempt to include such a right in the Charter as a "fundamental

---

221   *Ibid.,* s. 19(1).

222   *Ibid.,* s. 19(3). The penalty on conviction is a fine not exceeding the fifth level on the standard scale (as defined in s. 75 of the Criminal Justice Act 1982). At the date the Data Protection Act came into force the maximum was £2,000.

223   Data Protection Act, s. 19(2). On summary conviction the maximum fine is limited to the statutory maximum as defined in s. 74 of the Criminal Justice Act 1982. In July 1984 this also was £2,000.

224   Data Protection Act, s. 19(4). The relevant offences are unregistered holding, etc., of data (s. 5); non-compliance with an enforcement notice (s. 10) or transfer prohibition notice (s. 12); and unauthorized disclosure of data by a bureau (s. 15). A forfeiture, destruction or erasure order will not be made in such circumstances without giving any person who applies to do so an opportunity to show cause why such order should not be made. *Ibid.,* s. 19(5).

225   *Ibid.,* s. 20(1).

226   The Constitution Act, 1982 (en. by the Canada Act, 1982 (U.K.), c. 11, Sched. B), Pt. 1.

freedom" was defeated while the Constitution Act was in the committee stage.[227]

Some aspects of individual privacy are protected, at least indirectly, under the Criminal Code. For example, it is an offence to loiter or prowl at night near a dwelling house situated on private property.[228] More directly, Part IV of the Code sets out certain offences under the title "Invasion of Privacy."[229] Section 178.11(1) provides:

> Every one who, by means of an electromagnetic, acoustic, mechanical or other device, wilfully intercepts a private communication is guilty of an indictable offence and liable to imprisonment for five years.

This protection against "wiretapping" and "bugging" is significantly diluted, however, by a provision authorizing electronic surveillance by the police in certain cases.[230]

The theft provisions of the Criminal Code may also provide a degree of protection for "private" information. In a controversial decision which may yet be overturned by the Supreme Court of Canada, the Ontario Court of Appeal has held that confidential information is "property" which can be stolen contrary to section 283(1) of the Code.[231] Finally, limited tortious liability for certain specific invasions of privacy can be found in the laws of nuisance and defamation.[232]

8.4.2   Federal Privacy Legislation

Recently enacted federal data protection legislation, although broad in its application to manual as well as computerised records, only covers information held by government institutions. The Privacy Act, 1982,[233]

---

227   A Progressive Conservative motion to include a "freedom from unreasonable interference with privacy, family, home, and correspondence" was defeated by 14 votes to 10. Special Joint Committee of the Senate and the House of Commons on the Constitution of Canada, *Minutes of Proceedings,* Issue 43 (22/1/82). Any preexisting legal rights to privacy are not abrogated by the Charter, however. Article 26 provides that "The guarantee in this Charter of certain rights and freedoms shall not be construed as denying the existence of any other rights or freedoms that exist in Canada."

228   Criminal Code, s. 173.

229   Inserted in the Code by the Protection of Privacy Act, S.C., 1973-74, c. 50.

230   Criminal Code, s. 178.11(b). The surveillance must be authorised by a judge and approved by a Provincial Attorney-General or the Solicitor General of Canada, or a specifically designated agent (s. 178.12-15).

231   *R. v. Stewart* (1983), 42 O.R. (2d) 225, 35 C.R. (3d) 105, 24 B.L.R. 53, 74 C.P.R. (2d) 1, 5 C.C.C. (3d) 481, 149 D.L.R. (3d) 583 (C.A.). See discussion in section 7.3.2, above.

232   See Fleming, *The Law of Torts,* 6th ed. (Toronto, 1983) chapter 25.

233   S.C. 1980-81-82, c. 111, Sch. II.

which was proclaimed in force in July 1983, has superceded earlier federal privacy legislation contained in Part IV of the Canadian Human Rights Act.[234] The Privacy Act complements the Canadian Access to Information Act[235] which, subject to some significant exceptions, provides members of the public with a general right of access to federal government records.[236]

The principal provisions of the Privacy Act 1982 are as follows. The Act restricts the collection of personal information by government institutions to that which is directly necessary to "an operating program or activity of the institution."[237] Such information should "wherever possible" be collected directly from the individual, rather than from a third party, and the individual should be informed of the purpose of the data collection.[238] "All reasonable steps" must be taken to ensure as far as possible the accuracy, timeliness and completeness of personal information, and such information must only be used for limited purposes.[239] Heads of government institutions must ensure that all relevant personal information is included in "personal information banks," an index of which must be published at least once a year.[240]

The Act restricts the disclosure of personal information to a list of specified circumstances. This list includes a blanket authorisation of disclosures:

(m) for any purpose where, in the opinion of the head of the institution,
(i) the public interest in disclosure clearly outweighs any invasion of privacy that could result from the disclosure, or
(ii) disclosure would clearly benefit the individual to which the information relates.[241]

Individuals have rights of access to personal information concerning them which is contained in a public information bank and any other personal information concerning them which is "reasonably retrievable."[242] Following access, an individual may request correction of a record "where the individual believes there is an error or omission therein," and may require a notation to be included of any requested

---

234 S.C. 1976-77, c. 33.
235 Note 233 above, Sch. I.
236 See Janisch, "The Canadian Access to Information Act," [1982] Public Law 534.
237 Note 233 above, Sch. II, s. 4.
238 *Ibid.*, ss. 5(1) and (2). These provisions need not be complied with where to do so "might (a) result in the collection of inaccurate information; or (b) defeat the purpose or prejudice the use for which information is collected." *Ibid.*, s. 5(3).
239 *Ibid.*, s. 7.
240 *Ibid.*, ss. 10 and 11.
241 *Ibid.*, s. 8(2)(m).
242 *Ibid.*, s. 12(1).

correction which is not made.[243] Access may, however, be denied to information contained in "exempt banks."[244] The principal exemptions relate to international affairs and defence,[245] and to law enforcement and investigations.[246] Disclosure may also be refused where the information in question was obtained in confidence from an official source of a specified type,[247] and where disclosure "could reasonably be expected to be injurious to the conduct by the Government of Canada of federal provincial affairs."[248] Other types of information which need not be disclosed include information relating to security clearances,[249] information which relates to another person[250] or is subject to solicitor-client privilege,[251] and medical records.[252]

The Act provides for a Privacy Commissioner to receive and investigate complaints.[253] The Commissioner can investigate files contained in exempt banks,[254] and may also conduct investigations to ensure that government institutions are complying with the restrictions on collection and use of personal information.[255] An individual who has been refused access to information and who has complained to the Commissioner may then, following an investigation by the Commissioner, apply to the Federal Court for review of the matter.[256]

---

243   *Ibid.*, ss. 12(2)(a) and (b). The individual may also require that any person or body who has had access to such information within the previous two years be notified of the correction or notation, and in the case of government institutions, the institution must correct or annotate any copy under its control (s. 12(2)(c)).

244   *Ibid.*, s. 18(1), (2).

245   *Ibid.*, s. 21.

246   *Ibid.*, s. 22.

247   *Ibid.*, s. 19. Disclosure may be made, however, where the government, organisation or institution concerned either consents to the disclosure or makes the information public.

248   *Ibid.*, s. 20.

249   *Ibid.*, s. 23.

250   *Ibid.*, s. 26.

251   *Ibid.*, s. 27.

252   *Ibid.*, s. 28. Other exemptions cover pre-sentence reports on convicted persons (s. 24), and information the disclosure of which "could reasonably be expected to threaten the safety of individuals" (s. 25).

253   *Ibid.*, ss. 29-35; 53-67. Obstruction of the Privacy Commissioner may constitute a criminal offence (s. 68).

254   *Ibid.*, s. 36.

255   *Ibid.*, s. 37. The Commissioner must submit a report to Parliament at least once a year (ss. 38-40).

256   *Ibid.*, s. 41. Various applications to the court may also be made by the Commissioner (ss. 42-3).

8.4.3   Provincial Privacy Legislation

Three Western provinces, British Columbia,[257] Saskatchewan,[258] and Manitoba,[259] have created privacy rights by statute. Typical of the broad scope of these Privacy Acts are the two torts created by the British Columbia legislation, both of which are actionable without proof of damage. First, subject to certain exceptions, it is a tort "for a person, wilfully and without claim of right, to violate the privacy of another."[260] Secondly, it is a tort to use without consent "the name or portrait of another for the purpose of advertising or promoting the sale of, or other trading in, property or services."[261] The Act does not, however, specify any remedies which may be sought against a tortfeasor, unlike the Manitoba Privacy Act which empowers a court to award damages, grant an injunction, order an account of profits or order delivery up of any items obtained as a result of the privacy violation.[262] While none of the three Privacy Acts deals expressly with data protection issues, all are probably sufficiently comprehensive in scope to found an action for abuse of personal data stored in a computer.[263]

Various other provincial statutes deal more directly with the use of personal data.[264] Under the Ontario Consumer Reporting Act, for example, all agencies which supply credit or personal information must apply for registration with the Registrar of Consumer Reporting Agencies.[265] Registrations may be refused or revoked on grounds of financial irresponsibility, or where there is evidence that the credit reporting business will not be carried on "in accordance with law and with integrity and honesty."[266] The Act restricts the types of information which may be

---

257   Privacy Act, R.S.B.C. 1979, c. 336.

258   Privacy Act, R.S.S. 1978, c. P-24.

259   Privacy Act, S.M. 1970, c. 74.

260   Note 257 above, s. 1(1).

261   *Ibid.*, s. 3(1).

262   Note 259 above, s. 4(1). The court may make any one or more of these orders.

263   For an argument, however, that these provincial statutes are of little relevance to informational privacy concerns see Burns, "The Law and Privacy: The Canadian Experience" (1976), 54 Can. Bar Rev. 1-64.

264   *Eg,* Personal Information Reporting Act, S.B.C. 1973, c. 139; Credit Reporting Agencies Act, S.S. 1972, c. 23; Personal Investigations Act, S.M. 1971, c. 23; Consumer Reporting Act, R.S.O. 1980, c. 89; Consumer Reporting Act, S.N.S. 1973, c. 4.

265   R.S.O. 1980, c. 89, s. 3. Section 1(1)(c) of the Act defines a consumer reporting agency as "a person who for gain or profit or on a regular co-operative non-profit basis furnishes consumer reports."

266   *Ibid.*, ss. 4, 5.

reported by agencies,[267] and generally permits disclosure of information only to persons reasonably believed to have "a direct business need for the information."[268] Anyone who intends to obtain a report from a credit reporting agency must first notify in writing the consumer who is to be investigated and, if the consumer so requests, must supply the name and address of the agency which will be used.[269] Following a written request, a consumer is entitled to be informed, free of charge, of the nature and substance of all information in his or her file, the sources of credit information, and the names of people to whom consumer reports have been supplied.[270] Copies of recent reports can also be obtained.[271]

Where a consumer disputes the accuracy or completeness of any of the information in his or her file, the agency must "use its best endeavours to confirm or complete the information and shall correct, supplement or delete the information in accordance with good practice."[272] To secure compliance with these obligations the Registrar may order an agency to "amend or delete any information," or may by order "restrict or prohibit the use of any information."[273] A detailed investigation into the affairs of an agency may also be conducted by the Registrar or other authorised person.[274] Entry and search powers may be exercised under a magistrate's warrant and any relevant "books, papers, documents or things" may be removed for copying or examination by an expert.[275] The word "thing" in this context would presumably cover computer data storage media, especially since "file" is defined in the Act as "all of the information pertaining to a consumer . . . regardless of the manner or form in which the information is stored."[276] The Act has created a number of criminal offences, including the furnishing of false information, failure to comply with any orders made under the Act and contravention of any provision of the Act.[277] Corporations may be fined up to $25,000, and directors or other officers may be personally liable and incur a fine of up to $2,000 or imprisonment for up to a year, or both.[278]

---

267   *Ibid.*, s. 9.
268   *Ibid.*, s. 8(1).
269   *Ibid.*, s. 10.
270   *Ibid.*, ss. 11(1)(a), (b) and (c). Certain medical information must not, however, be disclosed (s. 11(2)).
271   *Ibid.*, s. 11(1)(d).
272   *Ibid.*, s. 12.
273   *Ibid.*, s. 13.
274   *Ibid.*, ss. 15, 16 and 17.
275   *Ibid.*, ss. 17(4), (5) and (7).
276   *Ibid.*, s. 1(g).
277   *Ibid.*, s. 22(1).
278   *Ibid.*, ss. 22(1) and (2).

This statute, together with similar legislation in other provisions, provides quite detailed data protection safeguards in the specific context of private sector consumer reporting. At the same time, the Privacy Act 1982 provides members of the public with quite broad rights of access to federal government records. However, due to the constitutional division of powers between Ottawa and the provinces, it is most unlikely that Canada will ever have a comprehensive system of data protection regulation covering both public and private sectors.

Chapter 9

Transborder Data Flows

9.1 The Nature of Transborder Data Flows

9.1.1 The Growth of Telematics

A recurrent theme of this book has been that the legal systems of the United States, England and Canada are hard pressed to cope with technological change. As has been seen, attempts to apply traditional legal concepts to specific aspects of computer technology, and in particular to the protection of software and data, have produced at best an uneasy fit. Similarly in the communications field, regulators have repeatedly found themselves to be at least one step behind the current technology. The focus of this last chapter is on some of the international law implications of "telematics" and "transborder data flows," phenomena produced by the union of the until recently separate technologies of data processing and communications.

The word "telematics"[1] has two components, "informatics" and communications. The former has been defined by the Intergovernmental Bureau for Informatics as "the rational application of information to economic, social and political development."[2] The last few decades have been marked by a rapid growth in the significance of information, a growth which may prove to be as historically significant as the Industrial Revolution. In 1977, a report prepared for the American government estimated that over forty percent of the U.S. workforce was already employed in the sector of information, computer and telecommunications technology.[3] From the start, computers have fulfilled both a catalytic and a sustaining role in what might reasonably be called the

---

1   The term was first coined in French as "télématique" by Nora and Minc, *Rapport sur l'Informatisation de la Société* (Inspection Générale des Finances, 1978). Some writers prefer the term "teleinformatics," *e.g.*, Eger, "The Global Phenomenon of Teleinformatics: An Introduction" (1981), 14 Cornell Int. L.J. 203-34.

2   "Informatics: Its Political Impact" (1980) IBI Doc. D.G. 1-04 at 2.

3   Porat, *The Information Economy* (U.S. Dept. of Commerce, Office of Telecommunications, 1977). The proportion has undoubtedly grown since 1977.

"information revolution," a revolution which has crept in largely unheralded. As microchip technology advances, ever greater quantities of data are being processed at ever increasing speeds, and more and more applications for automatic data processing are being devised.

The other half of "telematics" is the increasing use of telecommunications to facilitate rapid exchanges of data. The present world growth in telecommunication services is estimated to be twenty to twenty-five percent *per annum* and, in Europe alone, a twelvefold increase in data traffic was predicted for the decade ending in 1985.[4] The combination of telecommunications with computers is already producing a burgeoning international trade in information and data processing services. One commentator has given the following examples:

> News, health services, education, agriculture, manufacturing, transportation, marketing, credit, banking and finance, accounting, insurance, law enforcement, and every government function from security and national defence to weather prediction and disaster relief are increasingly dependent on computer and telecommunications technology.[5]

Exchanges of data commonly take place in the following manner. Information is transferred from one computer location to another by landline, microwave or satellite. At the remote, or "host," computer it is stored or processed and may then be returned to the originating computer or redistributed to other locations for further processing or storage. Data traffic knows no natural boundaries, and such transfers frequently occur across national borders and thus constitute "transborder data flows."

In one sense, any form of international communication involves some kind of transborder data flow. Business uses of telephone and telex across borders are commonplace and may already give rise to legal problems, such as choice of law in international contracts. Even the routine sending of a letter by air mail initiates an international transfer of information. However, in international law, a more specialized meaning is usually given to the phrase "transborder data flow." For the present discussion, to qualify as a transborder data flow data must not merely have been transmitted across a national border but must also have been stored or processed outside of the originating jurisdiction.[6]

---

4   Bigelow, "Transborder Data Flow Barriers" (1979), 20 Jurimetrics 8-17.
5   Eger, "Alliance for World Communications" in Online Conferences, *Transnational Data Regulations: The Realities* (Wellesly, Mass.: QED Information Services, 1979) at 27-3.
6   One commentator has suggested that both storage and computation must occur for there to be a transborder data flow: Novotny, "Transborder Data Flow Regulation: Technical Issues of Legal Concern" (1981), III Computer/Law J. 105-24. This definition seems too narrow, however, as much of the concern about transborder data flow

Within this definition it is useful to distinguish various types of data and various types of flow.

9.1.2   Types of Data

Data transmitted across national boundaries can be loosely divided into four types: personal, business, technical and organizational. These groupings are by no means discrete. Personal data, for example, may be a component in any of the other three. The distinctions are useful, however, as a means of clarifying the issues involved in the regulation of transborder flows of different kinds of data.

From a privacy perspective, the most obviously sensitive type of data is personal information. Such data may simply relate to an airline reservation or credit card billing, or it may concern a more delicate matter such as a person's criminal or medical history. At the domestic level, an increasing number of countries are recognizing the need to provide some form of protection against unauthorized processing of sensitive personal data. As has been seen, the United States, England and Canada have all legislated to some extent in the area of data protection.[7] Unless there are controls on transborder flows of such data, such domestic privacy protections can easily be eroded. Sensitive data can simply be transferred abroad for processing.

A second broad category of data pertains to financial and business transactions whereby, for example, money is transferred, or contracts are executed, by means of transborder computer links. In the banking sector in particular, the volume of data of this kind is growing rapidly. The Society for Worldwide Interbank Financial Telecommunications (SWIFT) provides electronic funds transfer (EFT) services through a steadily expanding network of systems.[8] Apart from privacy considerations, governments may wish to regulate the movement of such data for economic or political reasons.

---

arises where data is simply stored in a foreign jurisdiction, out of reach of an interested individual, corporation or government. See text accompanying notes 13 to 18, below.

7   See chapter 8, above.

8   Zaki, "Regulation of Electronic Funds Transfer: Impact and Legal Issues" (1983), 26 Communications of the ACM 112-118. At the present time, SWIFT is especially concentrating on the development of networks in South East Asia and the Pacific region. By 1980, SWIFT facilities were being used by over 600 banks. Gassman, "Privacy Implications of Transborder Data Flows: Outlook for the 1980s" in Hoffman, ed., *Computers and Privacy in the Next Decade* (New York: Academic Press, 1980), at 114.

A third type of data is information of a technical or scientific nature. This category includes, for example, data relating to weather forecasting, geological exploration, market research and experimental results of many kinds. Such information can be of considerable strategic and economic importance, and is usually a central component in transfer of technology arrangements.

Fourthly, an increasing quantity of organizational data is crossing national boundaries. Such information, sometimes described as "operational data,"[9] relates to the administrative functions or decisions of an organization. Most commonly, such data flow between a company and its foreign distributors or licencees, or between the headquarters and the various subsidiaries of a multinational corporation. Apart from possible privacy considerations as, for example, where information concerning employees is transferred, the primary motivation for regulating the movement of such data will be to exercise political or economic control over the organization in question.

9.1.3   Types of Flow

(1)   *One-way Flows*

The simplest type of data traffic is "data throughflow,"[10] which occurs where data from one country (A) is transported through a second country (B) without any use or processing occurring en route. This type of flow will only fall within the definition of transborder data flow if, as is often the case, it is temporarily stored in country B awaiting retransmission.

Most other one-way flows occur where data are collected abroad for use by an organization in a home country. Examples would be sales reporting by a foreign subsidiary to its parent company and the billing of a foreign credit card transaction. Also, data gathered in one country may be distributed to many different countries, as is the case, for example, with meteorological reports.

(2)   *Two-way and Multiple Direction Flows*

Computerized data often flow in more than one direction. Two scenarios are common. First, data may be transmitted from country A

---

9   Novotny, "Transborder Data Flow and International Law: A Framework for Policy Oriented Inquiry" (1980), 16 Stan. J. of Int. L. 141-80 at 156.

10   Bing, "Transborder Data Flow: Some Legal Issues and Possible Effects on Business Practices" in Online Conferences, note 5 above, at 26-3.

for processing by a service bureau located in country B. After processing, and perhaps also storage, the data are returned to the originating computer. Such transnational data processing is commonly used by organizations lacking the resources necessary to establish and maintain computer systems and data bases adequate to their needs.[11]

Secondly, data flow in more than one direction where data banks are shared internationally. An example would be a credit reporting agency which gives a subscriber access to its credit reference files and in return receives information relating to the subscriber's own clients. Where exchanges are complex it may be more appropriate to speak in terms of a "multinational data network" in which "[d]ata flows are characterized by multiple-user, multiple-host interactions, where information and processing can be centralized, distributed or both."[12] In some cases, a multinational corporation could itself support such a system, but often unrelated organizations obtain mutual benefits by subscribing to outside networks such as the SWIFT banking system referred to earlier.

9.1.4   Consequences of Unregulated Flows

As the volume and diversity of transnational data traffic rapidly increases, concerns are being voiced about possible adverse side effects of this quiet information revolution. In particular, restrictions on transborder data flows have been proposed by some governments as being necessary to reinforce domestic privacy legislation or to secure national sovereignty. However, these are not the only reasons why a state might wish to regulate the movement of data. As information becomes an increasingly valuable commodity and pressures to compete in the international data processing market intensify, there will be a growing temptation for states to use data flow restrictions to advance protectionist economic policies.

In an attempt to reconcile these conflicting priorities, a number of schemes have been proposed for harmonizing national data protection policies. The discussion has centred mainly in Europe, with the United States observing, somewhat anxiously it seems, from the sidelines. American service bureaux have much to lose if "data curtains" are erected in Europe. Before outlining the initiatives of the OECD, the

---

11   Katzen, *Multinational Computer Systems* (New York: Van Nostrand Reinhold Company, 1980), chapter 6. The availability of specialist software may also be a relevant factor.

12   Novotny, note 6 above at 112.

Council of Europe and the EEC Commission, an attempt will be made to identify the motivations of the various interested parties.

9.2 Grounds For Regulation

9.2.1 Privacy and Data Security

A number of countries have already established statutory schemes regulating the storage and use of personal information in data banks, and many more are actively considering some form of data protection legislation. Apart from any domestic enforcement problems, there are fears that such protective provisions will be undermined if there are no restrictions on the removal of data to other jurisdictions for processing or storage. Just as money tends to gravitate towards tax havens, so sensitive personal data will be transferred to countries with the most lax, or no, data protection standards. There is thus a possibility that some jurisdictions will become "data havens" or "data sanctuaries" for the processing or "data vaults" for the storage of sensitive information.[13] Indeed, to extend the tax analogy a little further, it is quite possible that skilful "data protection avoidance" schemes will be devised.[14]

At present, the above scenario is largely speculative, since most countries have no restrictions on data processing at all.[15] However, as more data protection laws are enacted, the existence of differential standards will become increasingly important. Some countries are already taking precautions to preempt the bypassing of domestic privacy legislation. Sweden, for example, which introduced the world's first data protection legislation a decade ago,[16] does not permit the transborder flow of personal information unless expressly authorized by the country's Data Inspection Board. Kerstin Amer, an Under Secretary of State in the Swedish Government, has explained the rationale for such restrictions:

---

13   Katzen, note 11 above, pp. 6-7.

14   On the other hand, governmental supervision of data banks may not always be perceived as benign. In some situations, data might be stored in a foreign jurisdiction with the purpose of achieving a greater, rather than a lesser, degree of protection for personal information.

15   Hondius, "Data Law in Europe" (1980), 16 Stan. J. of Int. L. 87-111 at 103.

16   Data Act 1973, as amended in 1977, reprinted in OECD Expert Group on Transborder Data Barriers and the Protection of Privacy, *Compilation of Privacy Legislation in OECD Member Countries* (ICCP/77.46).

> [W]e do not really trust the Data Acts in other countries or . . . we understand that there are none at all. So we feel unprotected in those countries with our data – walking down Fifth Avenue in our underwear.[17]

Similarly, restrictions on the export of data already exist under Austrian, Danish, French and Norwegian privacy legislation.[18] In the absence of any internationally agreed minimum standards of data security and privacy, other countries will most likely follow suit.

Thus, on an *ad hoc* basis, privacy conscious countries are effectively censoring the data processing regulations of other, less protective states. On a global scale this practice could produce some very unsatisfactory consequences. In a paper urging the international community to reach agreement soon regarding the "basic rules" of privacy protection, Mr. Justice Kirby, Chairman of the Organization for Economic Cooperation and Development (OECD) Expert Group on Transborder Data Barriers and the Protection of Privacy, has warned that "[t]he bureaucratic nightmare, impossibly cumbersome, ineffective, and expensive impediments to international data traffic could still develop."[19] Certainly much more is at stake than simply guaranteeing respect for personal privacy rights. Indeed, were privacy the only consideration, harmonizing national data protection laws would probably be a very low priority on most governments' agendas.

Thus, although there is still much talk of privacy as a major motivation for regulating transborder data flows, other considerations are gradually coming to the fore. Personal information is only one of the four broad categories of data identified earlier. The other three – business, technical and organizational data – place transborder data flow regulation in a far wider context in which information is viewed as an important resource to be controlled for political and economic ends. As a member of the French judiciary has forcefully stated:

> Information is power, and economic information is economic power. Information has an economic value and the ability to store and process certain types of data may well give one country political and technological advantage over other countries. This in turn may lead to a loss of national sovereignty through supranational data flow.[20]

---

17   Amer, "The New Swedish Data Act" in Online Conferences, note 5 above, at 43-9.
18   Turn, ed., *Transborder Data Flows: Concerns in Privacy Protection and Free Flow of Information* (Washington: Amer. Fed. of Information Processing Societies, 1979). See section 8.3.6, above, for a discussion of restrictions which may be imposed under the U.K. *Data Protection Act.*
19   "Data Flows and the Basic Rules of Data Privacy" (1980), 16 Stan J. of Int. L. 27-66 at 29.
20   Statement of Louis Joinet, French Magistrate of Justice, at the OECD Symposium on Transborder Data Flows and the Protection of Privacy (Vienna, 1977).

In a country's telematics policy, such political and economic concerns will often overlap. At a theoretical level, however, a distinction can be drawn between considerations of national sovereignty and security, on the one hand, and the pursuit of economic advantage on the other.

9.2.2   National Sovereignty

"Sovereignty," like privacy, is a somewhat nebulous concept. In essence, however, it seems to concern a country's ability to preserve its political autonomy and cultural integrity. A good definitional starting point is the one adopted by the Consultative Committee on the Implications of Telecommunications for Canadian Sovereignty (Clyne Committee).[21] The Committee felt that sovereignty in the Canadian context meant: "the ability of Canadians (both in government and in the private sector) to exercise control over the ... direction of economic, social, cultural and political change."[22] Despite its vast territory and wealth of natural resources, Canada is in general heavily dependent on the American economy, and the specific field of informatics is no exception.[23] Many Canadians seem acutely sensitive to the attendant risks of political and cultural domination. Hence it is not difficult to understand the genesis of the Federal Government's "fear of being swamped with foreign broadcasting programming"[24] and its strong emphasis on fostering, even mandating, higher levels of "Canadian content" in both business and cultural affairs. In 1972, a federal government report on *Computers and Privacy* noted that "as a sovereign state, Canada feels some national embarrassment and resentment over increasing quantities of often sensitive data about Canadians being stored in a foreign country."[25] More recently, the Clyne Committee, concerned at the increasing volume of data flowing from Canada to the United States for processing and storage, concluded that governmental intervention was necessary to reassert Canadian national interests.[26]

---

21   *Telecommunications and Canada* (Ottawa: Minister of Supply and Services, 1979).
22   *Ibid.,* p. 1.
23   Gotlieb, Dalfen and Katz, "The International Transfer of Information by Communications and Computer Systems" (1974), 68 Am. J. of Int. L. 227-257.
24   See note 21 above, p. 5.
25   Canada, Combined Task Force of the Department of Communications/Department of Justice, *Privacy and Computers* (Ottawa: Information Canada, 1972).
26   Recommendation 24 of the Committee's Report reads: "The Government should act immediately to regulate transborder data flows to ensure that we do not lose control of information vital to the maintenance of national sovereignty." See note 21 above, p. 64.

In Europe, threats to sovereignty have generally been preceived more in terms of political autonomy and national security. An OECD report on *The Usage of International Data Networks in Europe* has noted that:

> Fears have been expressed that as national interdependence increases the activity of a country to control its own affairs will be reduced, thereby infringing on its sovereignty. Certainly the increasing influence of multinational companies in the trade and industry of many different countries has resulted in data relevant to the day to day functioning of a country being held outside its borders. If that data is withheld for hostile or other reasons then the industry of a country may be put at risk. Furthermore, if the multinationals hold vital data relating to the operations of the company in distant computers then the ability of a Government to direct the operations of that multinational in its area of authority is reduced.[27]

A specific concern in Europe is that eavesdropping of strategically sensitive data communications may easily occur, and this fear of interception may motivate a government to regulate the outward flow of such data across its borders. Such intervention is already sanctioned under the International Telecommunications Convention of Malaga Torremolinos (ITU).[28] The ITU gives signatory nations broad rights to intercept, monitor, and stop international communications in the name of national security. As a result, the international law principle of free flow of information is severely curtailed,[29] and interests of national security can easily be invoked to justify restrictions on transborder data flows.

Third World countries are also becoming aware that a heavy dependence on foreign data processing services may constitute a threat to national sovereignty.[30] Matters of specific concern include the control of natural resources, security considerations and fears of cultural erosion.[31] Particularly active in developing a national informatics policy which includes restrictions on transborder data flows, the Brazilian Government has declared its commitment to the following objectives:

> To maximise the information resources located in Brazil, both imported and locally produced;

---

27   ICCP 2 (Paris: OECD, 1977), at 34.
28   28 UST 2510, TIAS No. 8572.
29   Novotny, "Transborder Data Flows and International Law: A Framework for Policy Oriented Inquiry" (1980), 16 Stan. J. of Int. L. 141-80.
30   For an account of Third World concerns as perceived by the American Government, see: U.S. Congress, House, Committee on Governmental Operations, *International Information Flow: Forging a New Framework* (1980) 96th Cong., 2d Sess., H. Rep. 1535.
31   Bortnick, "International Information Flow: The Developing World Perspective" (1981), 14 Cornell Int. L.J. 333-53.

To acquire and maintain national control over the decisions and technologies related
to the Brazilian data industries;
To enable Brazilian society to have universal access to information; and
To administrate information resources in such a manner that they contribute to the
enhancement of Brazil's cultural and political environment.[32]

Although there is no express mention of economic interests in this list,
other statements of Brazilian policy make it quite clear that the regulation of transborder data flows is seen as essential for protecting Brazilian
interests in the world data market.[33] Indeed, in most discussions of the
impact of data flows on national sovereignty, the question of economic
control is an explicit consideration.

9.2.3   Economic Considerations

Telematics does not fit easily within the conventional classification
of trade in either "goods" or "services." The economic significance of
transborder data flows, however, may be considerable. To return to
Canada as an example, it has been estimated that by 1985 Canada will be
importing $1.5 billion worth of computer services *per annum,* and that
the country will have lost some 23,000 directly related jobs.[34] In response
to this gloomy prediction, the Clyne Committee recommended that the
Canadian government "[r]equire that data processing related to Canadian business operations be performed in Canada except when otherwise
authorized."[35]

Similarly, for Brazil the regulation of transborder data flows is just
one means by which the country is pursuing its wider objective of
"maximising the amount of information resources in the country, while
at the same time increasing universal access to the international data
market."[36] Accordingly, the government's policy regarding foreign service bureaux is that "teleprocessing services provided by means of computers located abroad are not, in principle, used by Brazil."[37]

In the final analysis, rather than concerns of privacy or sovereignty,
the pursuit of economic advantages will probably be the driving force in
the erection of barriers to transborder data flows. The United States,
whose multinational corporations rely heavily on free information flows
around the world, is already complaining that other countries are using

---

32   Brizida, "Transborder Data Flows in Brazil" (1982), 13 CTC Reporter (U.N. Centre
      on Transnational Corporations) 11-12, 38-40 at 11.
33   *Ibid.,* at 38.
34   Clyne Committee, note 21 above, p. 63.
35   *Ibid.,* p. 38.
36   Brizidia, note 32 above, at 38.
37   *Ibid.*

privacy concerns as a smokescreen for what are essentially protectionist economic policies. As a spokesman for the American government has put it:

> One way to "attack" a nation such as the United States which depends heavily on information and communications is to restrain the flow of information – cutting off control between the headquarters and the overseas branches of a multinational firm; taxing telecommunications crossing borders; building information walls around a nation.[38]

Whatever may motivate states in regulating transborder data flows, it seems desirable that there be some rationalization of such regulations on a global scale. Certainly, the use of "hidden" barriers to the information trade should be discouraged.

Concerns about privacy and sovereignty may be well founded and arguably should take precedence over dictates of economic efficiency. Nevertheless, there is no reason why the establishment of international standards of data protection should necessarily stifle the legitimate flow of information. A nation which cuts itself off from foreign data traffic, perhaps in an attempt to preserve its cultural identity or national security, is likely to become a cultural and economic backwater. In terms of macro-economics, under a global system of complex and contradictory tariff and non-tariff barriers to the free flow of information, both "information rich" and "information poor" countries will be losers.[39]

Against this background of general concerns there have recently been several proposals for the harmonization of national data protection laws, including transborder data flow regulations. Significant initiatives have come from the OECD and the Council of Europe. Meanwhile, the European communities are endeavouring to develop a coherent telematics policy which will recognize privacy and sovereignty concerns but primarily aim to promote the economic interests of member states.

9.3 International Initiatives to Harmonize Transborder Data Flow Regulations

9.3.1 The OECD Guidelines

In 1974, the OECD established an Expert Group, the Data Bank Panel, to study various aspects of computers and privacy. In 1977, the

---

38   McGovern (Chairman of the Subcommittee on International Operations of the Senate Committee on Foreign Relations), *New York Times,* June 7, 1977.

39   Eger, "Emerging Restrictions on Transnational Data Flow: Privacy Protection or Non-Tariff Barriers?" (1978), 10 Law & Policy in Int. Bus. 1055-103.

Panel organized a symposium in Vienna to develop a general framework for international action regarding transborder data flows and the protection of privacy. A number of guiding principles were outlined as a basis for reconciling the following potentially conflicting priorities: facilitating the free movement of data between countries and providing for fair competition in the international data processing and distribution markets and at the same time protecting individual liberties by ensuring the security and confidentiality of data.[40]

A new Expert Group was established in 1978. Under the chairmanship of Mr. Justice Kirby, Chairman of the Australian Law Reform Commission, the Group worked to develop guidelines on basic rules to govern transborder data flows so as to facilitate the harmonization of national data protection laws.[41] Draft Guidelines were presented to the Council of the OECD in 1979 in the form of a Recommendation of the Council. The Recommendation was adopted by the Council[42] and became applicable on 23rd September, 1980. It reads as follows:

THE COUNCIL, . . .

RECOGNISING:

that, although national laws and policies may differ, Member countries have a common interest in protecting privacy and individual liberties, and in reconciling fundamental but competing values such as privacy and the free flow of information;

that automatic processing and transborder flows of personal data create new forms of relationships among countries and require the development of compatible rules and practices;

that transborder flows of personal data contribute to economic and social development;

that domestic legislation concerning privacy protection and transborder flows of personal data may hinder such transborder flows;

Determined to advance the free flow of information between Member countries and to avoid the creation of unjustified obstacles to the development of economic and social relations among Member countries;

RECOMMENDS

1. That Member countries take into account in their domestic legislation the principles concerning the protection of privacy and individual liberties set forth in the

---

40   OECD, 1 *Transborder Data Flows and the Protection of Privacy* (Paris: OECD, 1979). The Principles are set out at pp. 17-19.

41   OECD, *Guidelines of the Protection of Privacy and Transborder Flows of Personal Data* (Paris: OECD, 1981), Memorandum, para. 18.

42   Australia, Canada, Iceland, Ireland, Turkey and the U.K. have abstained.

Guidelines contained in the Annex to this Recommendation which is an integral part thereof;

2. That Member countries endeavour to remove or avoid creating, in the name of privacy protection, unjustified obstacles to transborder flows of personal data;

3. That Member countries co-operate in the implementation of the Guidelines set forth in the Annex;

4. That Member countries agree as soon as possible on specific procedures of consultation and co-operation for the application of these Guidelines.

The Guidelines, which are themselves accompanied by an Explanatory Memorandum,[43] are divided into five parts. Part Three deals specifically with transborder data flows under the heading "Basic Principles of International Application: Free Flow and Legitimate Restrictions":

15. Member countries should take into consideration the implications for other Member countries of domestic processing and re-export of personal data.

16. Member countries should take all reasonable and appropriate steps to ensure that transborder flows of personal data, including transit through a Member country, are uninterrupted and secure.

17. A Member country should refrain from restricting transborder flows of personal data between itself and another Member country except where the latter does not yet substantially observe these Guidelines or where the re-export of such data would circumvent its domestic privacy legislation. A Member country may also impose restrictions in respect of certain categories of personal data for which its domestic privacy legislation includes specific regulations in view of the nature of those data and for which the other Member country provides no equivalent protection.

18. Member countries should avoid developing laws, policies and practices in the name of the protection of privacy and individual liberties, which would create obstacles to transborder flows of personal data that would exceed requirements for such protection.

These paragraphs represent an attempt to balance the conflicting priorities of data protection and the free flow of information. The general rationale is that, while "the encouragement of international flows of personal data is not an undisputed goal in itself . . . [t]o the extent that such flows take place they should, however, be uninterrupted and secure."[44] More specifically, the reference in paragraph 15 to the "re-export" of data is directed to the problem of data havens and to the need for co-operation between member states in preventing the flow of personal information to "territories and facilities for the processing of data where control is slack or non-existent."[45]

---

43   The Memorandum is an "information document" and is subordinate to the Guidelines, "but is supplied to help in their interpretation and application." See note 41 above. Introduction to Memorandum. Due to the open texture of the *Guidelines*, the extra explanatory material is essential.

44   *Ibid.*, Memorandum, para. 66.

45   *Ibid.*, para. 64.

The most fundamental limitation of the Guidelines is that they have no legal force. They are not embodied in any convention. On the other hand, supporters of the Guidelines argue that they represent a broad and significant consensus on the transborder data flow question.[46] At a time when many countries have not yet developed domestic data protection schemes, "guidelines might positively influence the direction of domestic lawmaking."[47] The global distribution of the OECD's twenty-four member countries adds force to this harmonization argument.[48] However, the open textured nature of the Guidelines means that they can only serve as a loose framework for the harmonizing of national data laws. Even the Memorandum leaves a great deal unspecified and serves more to highlight the unresolved issues of principle than to flesh out the Guidelines. For example, paragraph 18 (quoted above) points out the likely adverse repercussions of data flow restrictions for "free trade, tariffs, employment and related economic conditions for internal data traffic."[49] These matters were nevertheless beyond the mandate of the Expert Group.[50] Similarly, the difficult issues of conflicts of laws in terms of jurisdiction and choice of law are identified in the Memorandum but are not analyzed.[51] Finally, although there is a statement in Part I of the Guidelines that exceptions to the principle of free information flow "should be (a) as few as possible and (b) made known to the public,"[52] in practice there will be almost unlimited scope for the imposition of restrictions in the name of national sovereignty, security or public policy.

9.3.2   The Council of Europe Convention

Unlike the OECD, which is essentially concerned with the economic development of its member states, the Council of Europe has a broader political mandate. Created after World War II, the Council's original membership of ten countries has since more than doubled to twenty-one.

---

46   Fishman, "Introduction to Transborder Data Flows" (1980), 16 Stanford J. of Int. L. 1-26.

47   Kirby, "Data Flows and the Basic Rules of Data Privacy" (1980), 16 Stan. J. of Int. L. 27-66 at 45.

48   Although European nations dominate in terms of numbers, several non-European countries which are influential in the international data processing field are also members, notably the United States and Japan.

49   Note 41 above, Memorandum, para. 68.

50   *Ibid.*.

51   *Ibid.*, paras., 74-6.

52   OECD, *Guidelines,* note 41 above, para. 4.

In 1968, the Parliamentary Assembly of the Council of Europe expressed concern over the adequacy of the European Convention on Human Rights in securing personal privacy protections in the context of information technology. As a response, the Committee of Ministers conducted a study and subsequently passed two resolutions establishing data protection principles, one for the private sector[53] and another for the public sector.[54] The Committee of Experts which prepared the resolutions called for the development of an international data protection agreement. After many stages of drafting and redrafting, the final text of the *Convention for the protection of individuals with regard to automatic processing of personal data*[55] was adopted by the Committee of Ministers and was opened for signature on 28 January 1981.

The Convention is divided into seven chapters. Chapter III deals with transborder data flows as follows:

Article 12
Transborder flows of personal data and domestic law

1. The following provisions shall apply to the transfer across national borders, by whatever medium, of personal data undergoing automatic processing or collected with a view to their being automatically processed.

2. A Party shall not, for the sole purpose of the protection of privacy, prohibit or subject to special authorisation transborder flows of personal data going to the territory of another Party.

3. Nevertheless, each Party shall be entitled to derogate from the provisions of paragraph 2:

(a) insofar as its legislation includes specific regulations for certain categories of personal data or of automated personal data files, because of the nature of those files, except where the regulations of the other Party provide an equivalent protection;

(b) when the transfer is made from its territory to the territory of a non-Contracting State through the intermediary of the territory of another Party, in order to avoid such transfers resulting in circumvention of the legislation of the Party referred to at the beginning of this paragraph.

The Explanatory Report which accompanies the text of the Convention states that Chapter III "aims at reconciling the simultaneous and sometimes competing requirements of free flow of information and data protection, the main rule being that transborder data flows between Contracting States should not be subject to any special controls."[56]

While these words may have some merit as a statement of principle, the text of Chapter III is so vague as to offer even less assistance on

---

53   Resolution (73) 22.
54   Resolution (74) 29.
55   European Treaty Series, No. 108.
56   Council of Europe, *Explanatory Report on the Convention for the Protection of Individuals with regard to the Cutomatic Processing of Personal Data* (Strasbourg: Council of Europe, 1981), para. 21.

reconciling conflicting priorities than the OECD Guidelines. Moreover, in the second paragraph of Article 12, the expression "for the sole purpose of the protection of privacy" indicates that the Convention makes no provision for restricting data flows on grounds of national sovereignty, security or economic policy.[57] This seems unrealistic, and it is surprising that the derogations from domestic data protection principles, which are expressly permitted in Chapter II of the Convention,[58] are not also allowed in the case of data exports.

Nevertheless, the Council of Europe Convention has one obvious advantage over the OECD Guidelines. Once ratified, the Convention will be legally binding as an international treaty, and a procedure for interpretation and enforcement can be developed accordingly.[59] The Convention is not, however, self-executing and it will only come into force when five states have ratified it. So far, of the dozen or so states which have signed the Convention, only Sweden, Norway, France and Spain have ratified it. Before they will be in a position to ratify, many of the other signatories will need to modify their existing data protection statutes or introduce such legislation for the first time. Given the politically sensitive nature of privacy legislation, these will undoubtedly be long processes for some states.[60]

In the meantime, the European Economic Community (EEC) is in the process of developing a coherent telematics policy for adoption by its ten member countries.

9.3.3 The Telematics Policy of the EEC

At this stage in its development the EEC is essentially an economic and not a political union. However, in many of the fields which fall

---

57   As the Explanatory Report puts it, "a Contracting State may not invoke this Convention to justify interference with transborder data flows for reasons which have nothing to do with the protection of privacy (for example, hidden trade barriers)." *Supra,* note 56, para. 67.

58   Article 9 provides that: "2. Derogation from the provisions of Articles 5, 6 and 8 of this Convention shall be allowed when such derogation is provided for by the law of the Party and constitutes a necessary measure in a democratic society in the interests of: (a) protecting State security, public safety, the monetary interests of the State or the suppression of criminal offences."

59   As a preliminary measure, Chapter IV of the Convention provides for "Co-operation between Parties" and the rendering of "mutual assistance" in the implementation of the Convention. Note 55, above, Art. 13.

60   In the United Kingdom, for example, it took two and a half decades of public discussion and draft legislation before the Data Protection Act reached the statute book in July 1984. The purpose of the Act, *inter alia,* is to enable the U.K. to ratify the Council of Europe convention. See section 8.3, above.

within the Community's jurisdiction, economic matters become unavoidably intertwined with considerations of domestic politics and public policy. The regulation of transborder data flows is one such problem area.

For some time the EEC Commission has been working on a Community Data-Processing Policy which includes the development of a new data network called EURONET. To this end, studies have been undertaken on such matters as software portability (including the development of a standard European programming language), programming techniques, data security, data base management, and high-speed data transmission techniques.[61] The aims of the Community Data-Processing Policy seem to be twofold. First, the Commission is anxious to develop an efficient and homogenous market for data processing within the EEC. It is seeking to minimize the practical barriers to the free flow of data between member countries. Secondly, the Commission wishes to strengthen the EEC's position in international data processing and has proposed that member states secure one-third of the world market by the late 1980s.[62] Thus, the Commission's general policy in this area is to facilitate exchanges of data between member states and at the same time regulate the import of data processing services and equipment from outside the EEC.

However, the implications of transborder data flows for data security and individual liberties have complicated this telematics strategy. On a number of occasions, both the EEC Commission and Parliament have been forced to consider the non-economic aspects of international data traffic. In 1975, the European Parliament resolved that a directive be prepared requiring member countries to provide adequate protections for individual liberties, while at the same time endeavouring to harmonize their national data protection laws. After public hearings in 1978, the "Bayerl Report" appeared in 1979,[63] and this in turn was followed by a further resolution of the European Parliament.[64] The latter contained

61   Commission of the ECs, Communication from the Commission to the Council, *Community Data-processing Policy: Report on the status of Community programmes at 31 May 1982.* Doc. COM (82) 452 final.

62   Commission of the ECs, *European Society Faced With the Challenge of New Information Technologies,* (1979 Doc. COM (79) 650 final [The Dublin Report]. For an analysis of this report and the EEC's telematics policy in general see Ramsey, "Europe responds to the Challenge of the New Information Technologies: A Teleinformatics Strategy for the 1980's" (1981), 14 Cornell Int. L.J. 237-85.

63   European Parliament, *Report Drawn up on Behalf of the Legal Affairs Committee on the Protection of the Rights of the Individual in the Face of Technical Developments in Data Processing* (1979) Eur. Parl. Doc. No. 100/79 PE 56.386/final.

64   European Parliament, *Resolution on the Rights of the Individual in the Face of*

a statement of the principles which were to form the basis of future Community policy and a recommendation that the Council and Commission issue a directive concerning data protection harmonization.

Concerned whether the EEC has competence under the Treaty of Rome to deal with data protection and wishing to avoid duplication of or conflict with other schemes for harmonizing national data controls, the Commission moved cautiously in further developing its own policies.[65] Thus, although it actively participated in the work of both the OECD and the Council of Europe, the Commission refrained from formulating a definite EEC strategy until both the Guidelines and the Convention had been finalized.

However, soon after the Council of Europe Convention had been opened for signature, the EEC Commission recommended that the member states which had not already signed should sign the Convention and seek to ratify it before the end of 1982.[66] The wording of the Recommendation suggests that earlier doubts as to the Community's competence to involve itself with data protection matters have faded:

> Data-protection is a necessary part of the protection of the individual. It is quite fundamental. In the Member States of the European Community it is desirable that an approximated level of data-protection be achieved. This will be an important contribution to the effective establishment of citizen's rights at European level.[67]

Nevertheless, the Recommendation proceeds to relate, and to a degree subjugate, the issue of individual liberties to the need to rationalize transborder data flow regulations for economic reasons:

> Divergent data-protection law in the EC Member States creates disparate conditions for data processing. The establishment and functioning of the common market in data processing calls for extensive standardization of the conditions obtaining in relation to data processing and, therefore, to data-protection at European level. Approximation of data-protection is desirable so that there can be free movement of data across frontiers and in order to prevent unequal conditions of competition and the consequent distortion of competition in the common market.[68]

Should this Recommendation fail to achieve the desired effect, the Commission has declared that it may engage in a compulsory harmonization programme.[69]

Technical Developments in Data Processing (1979), 22 O.J. Eur. Com. (No. C 140) 34.

65   Hondius, "Data Law in Europe" (1980), 16 Stan. J. of Int. L. 87-111 at 109.

66   Recommendation of the Commission No. 81/679. A goal which was certainly not achieved.

67   Ibid., Part 1, para. 2.

68   Ibid., para. 3.

69   Ibid., para. 5.

The EEC's view on transborder data flows, and in particular its economic concerns, has been outlined in more detail in a Note from the Commission.[70] In part, the Note was a response to American allegations that the development of EURONET is essentially an exercise in protectionism.[71] In its defence, the Commission argued that EURONET represents a positive first step towards a rational system of regulating transborder data flows on a global scale, and that in any event there are no special restrictions on the use in Europe of American data bases.[72] The Note added that, in the Commission's view, the gradual increase in the use of European data facilities is not due to artificially imposed restrictions. Rather, it is a reflection of the greater efficiency which can be achieved when trans-Atlantic telecommunication costs are eliminated and computers attached to the EURONET system are used as a substitute.[73]

However, despite these arguments of justification, there can be little doubt that, in pursuit of its goal of securing a one-third share of the world data processing market, the EEC would be prepared to utilize both tariff and non-tariff barriers to regulate transborder data flows.[74] In doing so it would not be alone. On a global level, the countries which favour free data flow and those which favour regulation are gradually polarizing into two fairly distinct camps. On the one side, the more service intensive countries, in particular the United States, are calling for a liberalization of international data flows. On the other side, countries which have lagged behind in the development of data processing industries wish to erect barriers. Some are even calling for a New International Information Order to be established, somewhat along the lines of the New International Economic Order.

---

70   EC Commission, Direction Generale des Relations Exterieures, *Elements de concertation pour les Etats membres CEE au sujet des problemes concenatn [sic] les flux transfrontiere de donnees et la Declaration sur les flux de donnees (proposition USA)* 26 Mar. 1982 (AC/gh).

71   *Ibid.*, para. 5.

72   *Ibid.*, para. 5(b).

73   *Ibid.* In its further defence, the Commission pointed out that approximately 70% of the information circulated on EURONET is of American origin, while the U.S. imports less than 20% of its data from Europe. Moreover, European tariff levels are comparable to those in North America. *Ibid.*, para. 5(c).

74   The EEC's protracted and acrimonious antitrust dispute with IBM was an indication of the Commission's willingness to agressively pursue the goals of its telematics policy.

9.4 Outlook For The Future

9.4.1   A New International Information Order?

Over the past two decades the fastest growing component in international trade has been the service sector. It now accounts for roughly one-third of total world trade, and the proportion is growing steadily.[75] The United States, which is the most service intensive nation, now depends on services for an estimated two-thirds of its GNP and seventy percent of its jobs.[76] By 1980, more than half of those employed in the service sector were already working in the field of information technology.[77]

Thus it is hardly surprising that as data protection laws have gradually emerged in Europe, and as the EEC and countries such as Brazil have begun to develop a calculated telematics strategy, Americans have watched from the sidelines with both anxiety and annoyance. They have a great deal to lose. As one commentator has put it:

> The United States is highly vulnerable to emerging tariff and nontariff trade barriers in the data processing and service industries. . . . [M]any nations are already intent on inhibiting U.S. "data trade" by some degree of blocking or taxing the flow of information and information products crossing their borders. . . . [T]hose countries constraining the transnational flow of information may be constructing a whole body of contradictory international law that will cause worldwide confusion in communications, perhaps ultimately blocking information flow altogether.[78]

As was noted earlier,[79] Americans perceive this threat to their data processing industry as coming not only from Europe but also from the Third World.

Certainly the force of the maxim that "information is power" is not lost on nations like Brazil. A growing number of other Less Developed Countries (LDCs) are realizing that control of telematics will be a crucial

---

75   Winham, "GATT and the New Trade World" (1983), 4 Int. Perspectives 3-5.
76   *Ibid.*
77   "Informatics: Its Political Impact" (1980) IBI Doc. D.G. 1-04 at 2.
78   Eger, "Emerging Restrictions on Transnational Data Flow: Privacy Protection or Non-Tariff Barriers?" (1978), 10 Law & Policy in Int. Business 1055-103 at 1062-6. See also Olen, "Transnational Data Flow: Data Protection or Economic Protectionism?" in Communications Media Centre, New York Law School, *The New World Information Order: Issues in the World Administrative Radio Conference and Transborder Data Flow* (1979).
79   See text accompanying notes 30-37 above.

factor in their future economic development.[80] For some such countries, fears of political or cultural domination will continue to be strong additional motivation for the regulation of transborder data flows. However, there are signs that not all LDCs will follow Brazil's approach of imposing strict controls on data traffic. The developing countries of Africa, for example, have tended to be more in favour of free flow. This is perhaps because, unlike Brazil, such countries are at present so far behind in developing information technology as to have little or no data processing industry to protect. Since for development purposes they are thus dependent on access to foreign service bureaux, they also have potentially much to lose from restrictions on the international free flow of data.[81]

Meanwhile, the United States has indicated that it would like to use the General Agreement on Tariffs and Trade (GATT) as a forum for promoting its free flow policies. So far, however, American proposals for an extension of the GATT to cover not merely trade in goods but also trade in services have met with a cool reception.[82] Perhaps a more promising forum for debate of the transborder data flow question is the Intergovernmental Bureau for Informatics (IBI), which is at present studying possible compromises between the extremes of heavy regulation and total deregulation.

Common ground is unlikely to be found overnight, however, especially since on a state by state basis even internal policy positions can be slow in crystallizing. Indicative of the complex and controversial nature of the issues in this area was the fate of the Canadian government's Interdepartmental Task Force on Transborder Data Flow. Set up in 1981, the Task Force comprised twenty federal agencies and an industrial advisory group. It amassed nine hundred pages of discussion papers and industry submissions but was dissolved in August 1983 without having produced any kind of final report.[83]

For Canada, a sensible first step would perhaps be to concentrate on reaching agreement with the United States regarding the treatment of data flows across their shared border so as to avoid inefficient and obstructive controls on data traffic. To this end the Royal Bank of

80   Bortnick, "International Information Flow: The Developing World Perspective" (1981), 14 Cornell Int. L.J. 333-53. For some of the criticisms which have been levelled at the LDCs position see Kroloff, "The New World Information Order" in Online Conferences, *Transnational Data Regulations: The Realities,* 18/1-10.

81   For a fuller discussion of the African position see Ennison, "Legal Aspects of TDF in Developing Countries: Sovereignty Considerations," [1984] Int. Bus. L. 163-170.

82   Winham, note 75, above.

83   See "Papers on the flow of transborder data lack clear directives" *Globe and Mail,* 16 Dec. 1983, B.13.

Canada has proposed an open-ended bilateral arrangement, with membership being offered to other states in the future. The general aim of such an agreement would be to establish a free trade in computer and information services between the parties, while at the same time ensuring compliance with some minimum standards of privacy protection and data security.[84]

9.4.2   Concluding Remarks: Can the Technology Be Regulated?

Just as an assertion of proprietary interests in software and program-related inventions is necessitating a reappraisal of the conceptual and practical limits of copyright, patent, trade secret and criminal laws, so transborder data flows are posing a major challenge to established frameworks of international legal relations. Moreover, even if an acceptable compromise can be struck in theory between the competing goals of privacy, security, and economic control on the one hand and free flow on the other, the regulation of international data flows will not cease to be a contentious issue.

Indeed, the establishment of ground rules for data flow regulation may represent only the tip of the iceberg of the problem of regulation. Enforcing any agreed standards may prove to be the far more difficult task. This is due mainly to the intangibility of data. Once reduced to digital form, data are simply electronic pulses which can be transmitted at great speeds and through many different media. In addition to any special land, radio, microwave or satellite data links, data may easily be transmitted through conventional communication links, including telephone systems.

Transborder data flows are already so ubiquitous, rapid and invisible that for a regulatory body to monitor even a modest sample of data traffic would be an enormous task. This logistical problem has significant implications for the policing of all rights and duties relating to the communication of information, not least in relation to intellectual property and data protection. As Pool and Solomon have observed:

> In the technology of the 1990s there will be no practical way to control who transmits what text to whom anywhere in the world. Just as xerographic copying has made it practically impossible to control who reproduces what text in a particular location, the introduction of high capacity telecommunications networks, especially those using computer switching and encrypted data, will make it practically impossible to control

---

84   See Burnett "A Common market in Traded Computer Services?" (1984), 1 Computer/Law 72-74.

who transmits what text to another person. It will become just as impossible to control data flows as it now is to control who says what to another person over the telephone.[85]

Given the existence of such practical constraints, the legal net should not be cast unnecessarily wide. While they may have been useful for identifying the underlying issues of principle which are at stake in the transborder data flow debate, the proposals raised so far by such bodies as the OECD and the Council of Europe may prove to be of limited practical utility. For example, the definitions of "personal data" in the OECD Guidelines and the Council of Europe Convention are broad enough to encompass almost all data traffic.[86]

Undoubtedly, the prospect of a comprehensive international scheme to deal with all conflicts in this area will continue to be attractive. In terms of workable solutions, however, it may be more realistic at this stage for interested parties to seek to develop specific remedies to deal with specific problems, rather than waiting for an omnibus convention covering all aspects of data traffic. Thus, procedures might usefully be developed for dealing with international computer frauds or for regulating data processing contracts.[87] This is not to say that one or more broad-based international conventions will not eventually be needed. Indeed, once procedures become established for securing specific remedies, some common standards will become essential if unnecessarily complex and conflicting regulatory schemes are to be avoided. Nevertheless, in view of the rapid pace at which the field of computer communications is currently evolving, schemes which paint with too broad a brush are likely soon to be overtaken by the technology they purport to control.[88]

---

85   "Intellectual Property and Transborder Data Flows" (1980), 16 Stan. J. Int. L. 113-39 at 114.
86   For a discussion of the broad application of the term in the United Kingdom's Data Protection Act, see section 8.3.2, above.
87   Pool and Solomon give as other examples of possible areas of concern, data sanctuaries and the setting up of quack medical treatment by telecommunications. Note 85, above.
88   See Janisch and Irwin, "Information Technology and Public Policy: Regulatory Implications for Canada" (1982), 20 Osgoode Hall L.J. 610-41.

Index

Note: This index contains references to substantial material derived both from the text and from the footnotes. Purely bibliographical footnotes are not indexed. Cases and legislation discussed specifically in the text or footnotes, or both, are listed in the tables of cases and statutes on pages xi and xix. References to the footnotes are set in italic type.